Our Muslim Neighbors

Achieving the American Dream,
An Immigrant's Memoir

Victor Begg

Read the Spirit

For more information and further discussion, visit

OurMuslimNeighbors.com

Published by
Read the Spirit Books, an imprint of
Front Edge Publishing, LLC
42015 Ford Road, Suite 234
Canton, Michigan

Cover design by Brad Schreiber
By Design Graphic Arts

English translations of the Quran vary widely. No one translation can hope to capture all nuances of the original Arabic. The author used the Islamicity website (http://www.islamicity.org/) for selecting the transliteration from multiple respected sources. In addition, he used a recent all American translation and commentary *The Study Quran* (https://www.harpercollins.com/9780062227621/the-study-quran/). Sayings of Prophet Muhammad are from the authentic collections of Bukhari. Out of respect for the Prophet Muhammad and other Biblical prophets, Noah, Abraham, Joseph, Moses, Jesus and others, it is an Islamic tradition to say: peace be upon him. Due to frequency and repetition, the honorifics in the book are omitted.

Front Edge Publishing specializes in speed and flexibility in adapting and updating our books. We can include links to video and other online media. We offer discounts on bulk purchases for special events, corporate training, and small groups. We are able to customize bulk orders by adding corporate or event logos on the cover and we can include additional pages inside describing your event or corporation. For more information about our flexible publishing or permission to use our materials, please contact Front Edge Publishing at info@FrontEdgePublishing.com.

To Shahina—my wife; my life partner

Her unwavering support enabled me to pursue the American Dream
and
to serve our community together

Contents

Praise for
Our Muslim Neighbors

Victor Begg's new book comes at a perfect time. *Our Muslim Neighbors* offers a window to the daily life and beliefs of those few million ordinary Muslims living as citizens in America today. In fact, it removes the window altogether. Victor's clear, colloquial voice gives its target audience, his American neighbors, an unimpeded view. Only one in three Americans have ever met a Muslim. For the other two out of three—here is your chance. A lot of foggy information clouds the American brain concerning Muslims, put there by a variety of sources ranging from terrorist cults to supremacist hate groups to myopic media pundits. Victor's representative story, his steady, 40-year love affair with America, blows much of it away. *Our Muslim Neighbors* is a fascinating family story, coupled with the defense of a vulnerable minority. Do yourself a favor: Read this book.

Michael Wolfe, author of *One Thousand Roads to Mecca.*

Our Muslim Neighbors is a book that Americans certainly will enjoy. It's a heroic story of a young man who comes to the U.S., embraces the American Dream and then achieves a great deal for his family and his community. However, this book's importance really is global, considering how often migrants, refugees and Muslims in particular are demonized by extremists around the world. Victor Begg backs up his argument that Muslim migrants benefit American communities with examples from history as well as solid research data. Then, what makes his book most convincing to readers is the simple narrative of his own life as a community builder. As a Muslim journalist based in Algeria, I found myself fascinated by Victor's detailed narration of how he lived through 9/11 and the years after that as a Muslim living among non-Muslims. One of the biggest challenges for Muslims who have never visited the U.S. is getting a clear sense of how Muslims live there in these turbulent times. There are so many conflicting claims and stories about life in the U.S. Through reading Victor's true stories, I was able to experience American life for Muslims—without ever leaving my home. The lasting impression I am left with, after reading Victor's memoir, is that anyone would be lucky to have a Muslim neighbor like this living next door.

Larbi Mageri is a scholar and journalist who lives in Algeria and serves as the Co-managing Director of the International Association of Religion Journalists. He has helped to organize conferences around the world for journalists seeking to follow best practices in their profession.

~

Our God seems to have placed Victor Begg at just the right places—at just the right times—where and when he is needed. As Victor writes about these many fascinating experiences, he shows us the commonality in our values and our lives. Along the way, he shatters stereotypes about Muslims, always writing a style that is perfect in delivery and tone.

Gregg Krupa, a 40-year veteran of journalism at newspapers including *The Boston Globe* and *The Providence Journal*. Since 2009, he has covered sports for *The Detroit News*.

~

Our Muslim Neighbors is an outstanding and compelling journey of hope, struggle, perseverance and finding meaning among the chaos of life. Victor Begg shares his incredible journey of learning and his growing faith using heartfelt stories from his struggle to find and live the American Dream. His voice will transport every reader back to the roots that made America the land of opportunity while recognizing that there are still many bridges that need to be built between people of all faiths and ethnicities.

S.E. Smith, *The New York Times* and *USA TODAY* best-selling author.

What a wonderful read! At times, moving. At times, informative. And, still at other times, inspirational. Victor's honest, and sometimes vulnerable, story is personal account of a lifelong journey in Islam. It is a 21st-century memoir that reveals his part of an interfaith movement in the United States—an undertaking that is trying to mend a broken world with compassion and justice; by concrete action, or as Victor says, "Person by person, friend by friend, good-hearted people change the world." I write this in the days immediately after the anti-Semitic murder of 11 Jews in their Squirrel Hill synagogue. I feel, once again, a sense of urgency for building bonds between people of different faiths (including those with no faith, at all). I've known Victor for over 20 years, and, I hope you will read this book and get to know him, too. For in doing so, you may catch a glimpse of hope of a mended world.

The Rev. Daniel Appleyard, retired Episcopal priest who served parishes in Dearborn, St. Louis and Kansas City.

Foreword

By Rabbi Bruce Benson

On occasion, prayers are answered.

Since 9/11, many Americans have been on a journey to encounter a member of the Muslim community, both physically and spiritually. For many Americans, our first encounter with Muslims was in the news coverage of that fateful day, which clearly was not a moment of understanding. All of us had so many questions!

My own efforts to reach out personally began shortly after 9/11—in a supermarket check-out line. In front of me was a husband and wife, both young and unremarkable except for the hijab the woman was wearing, the only sign that they were Muslim. I assumed this was a perfect time to begin my education regarding the Muslim community.

Of course, I was anxious. I assumed they would be anxious, too. I summoned my courage and decided to start a conversation. All I had to guide me were my general assumptions from the media, so I thought I was being respectful by greeting the man and asking if I could speak with the woman. He politely said, "Of course."

I could tell right away that my first question had been awkward. They were wary of what I would say next. She was particularly ill at ease. As I turned toward her, she stepped back several steps to put more distance between us. The fear in her eyes made me regret how I was handling this conversation. I was horrified that I could instill such anxiety in a young woman by simply wanting to ask about her culture.

But, at that point, I had to forge ahead. "I can see from your head covering that you are a Muslim woman and I have a question. I know this is Ramadan and I don't know the proper way to acknowledge Ramadan to a Muslim."

Her eyes did not meet mine. She said softly, "Happy Ramadan."

That surprised me and, without thinking further, I said quite honestly, "You're kidding! I'm Jewish and we know all about fasting. Nothing to eat! Not a drop to drink! What's to be happy about?"

Silence. Had I offended them?

Then, she took two steps toward me—and laughed. I thought: Oh, thanks be! Sometimes, stupid makes you smarter. I had said the right thing, after all. As she laughed, and welcomed my attempt to express friendly interest, my prayers for the healing of our broken world were answered in a small way that day in a supermarket checkout line.

Hajj Victor Begg's book, *Our Muslim Neighbors*, is truly another answer to the prayers of a seeker. In this book, Victor answers so many of our questions in good faith with facts, humor, irony—and challenges, too. In one book, I have come to understand much more about Islam, its followers and its teachings. I've come to realize that the challenges Muslim immigrants have faced are similar to what Jews and many other immigrant groups have experienced as they tried to settle in America. By the end of this book, I hurt with Victor and I laugh with him, because—as Americans—we share so much. We **are** him. His journey is our journey. This is our story.

Reading about Victor's parents, I see my parents. His experiences trying to start a business—and all the challenges he faced—were no different than what many of my friends have encountered. I found myself laughing with Victor as his recollections merged with mine through so many strands of his narrative.

If you are a person of faith—or simply a sojourner looking for truth on our shared journey through life—you will find a friend in the pages of this book. You will gain an understanding of our Muslim neighbors that is unapologetic, funny at moments, and a story we can all relate to having walked those steps on almost every page.

There are few words that can properly express my honor at being asked to offer this Foreword to Victor's life story, except to say: I cannot recommend this book with more vigor. After you read it, commend this book to others—as I have done here.

Victor and I agree: Go looking; God is good; you'll likely find what you seek.

Thanks to our shared God that my life's path crossed with Hajj Victor Begg's journey. I found a wonderful companion. Imagine what you will find.

Shalom Aleichem.

As-salmu alaykum.

Rabbi and Cantor Bruce Benson leads Temple Beth El Israel in St. Lucie, Florida. Ordained in 1978, he has served congregations in five states. An author and musician, he has created many works for Jewish and interfaith settings, which have been used nationwide. His community outreach has included visits to houses of worship, hospitals, jails and even to San Quentin Prison.

Preface

By the Rev. Daniel L. Buttry

You could call Victor Begg my neighbor, at least if you use a broad geo-graphic definition as we shared metro-Detroit. We met at an interfaith meeting at a Dearborn mosque shortly after the 9/11 terrorist attacks. Both of us spoke out challenging our interfaith friends and colleagues to do, as Victor said, "more than pray and hold hands."

In the next day or two, Victor invited me to his yacht at a Detroit river-front marina. I'd never been on a yacht before! He invited others who had the same activist passion to take interfaith relationships to the next level. If the terrorists were going to hijack our faiths for violence, we would do the hard organizing and community building to turn people back to our faiths' deeper roots of love, mercy, justice and peace. You can read about what flowed from that meeting on the yacht in the pages of this book.

Many of us started by simply getting to know each other. There was a lot of first-date carefulness, not wanting to insult anyone even with our good intentions. Victor brought serious commitment to our work, but he also brought a playfulness to our interactions with his humor, such as nicknaming us the "Ramada Ramblers," when we moved from the yacht to later meetings in a conference room in a Ramada hotel. That playful-ness invited us not only to interfaith relationships but interfaith friendship and comradeship.

Before too long we realized it wasn't just Victor and me in the friend-ship, but Victor and Shahina and Sharon and me. Our wives also were interested in interfaith work. Victor shares in his book about Shahina's companionship and labors. My wife Sharon, an ordained American Baptist clergyperson and urban missionary, became the first staff person for Interfaith Partners when we got a grant from the Andrus Foundation.

Later Shahina and Sharon would work with others in the formation and growth of WISDOM, an interfaith women's network. Along the way, we became friends, couple to couple. We ate many meals together at the Beggs' home or at one of the excellent local South Asian restaurants in Hamtramck where Sharon and I live. Victor and I even became prayer partners, praying for our sons in the challenges they faced.

A few years ago, a conservative Protestant pastor wrote in a Christian online magazine that all Muslims want to kill us Christians and should be driven from our country. I wrote that magazine and pastor (I never heard back from him) that he was bearing false witness about a neighbor, thus breaking one of the Ten Commandments. I knew his statement was a lie, whether from ignorance or deliberate deception, because I know Victor and so many other dear Muslim friends. Not only does Victor not want to kill me—I know, if worse came to worst, Victor would be among those willing to lay down his life for me. The sentiments of that pastor are sadly too often found in our diverse but divided society.

We need stories of our Muslim neighbors like Victor to break down the walls that separate us and to educate us about those who might seem so strange at first but might become heart friends if given the chance. Along the way, we might discover not only some new neighbors but also some true American heroes. Victor Begg is just such a hero, self-less, ordinary, but willing to risk to make our nation and our world a better place. I'm honored to be counted as his friend.

The Rev. Daniel L. Buttry is the Global Consultant for Peace and Justice for International Ministries of the American Baptist Churches. He was a co-founder with Victor Begg of first the Interfaith Partners, then the InterFaith Leadership Council of Metro Detroit. Dan and his wife Sharon Buttry live in Hamtramck, Michigan.

In The Name of God, The All Merciful, Redeemer of Mercy

From the Author

*And be good to the neighbor who is your relative
and to the neighbor who is not a relative.*

Quran 4:36

Said Jesus, "Love your neighbor as yourself."

Mark 12:31

"You shall love your neighbor as yourself."

Leviticus 19:18

*Prophet Muhammad said, "The Angel Gabriel kept on recommending
that I treat the neighbors in a kind and polite manner, so much so
that I thought that he would order me to make them my heirs."*

In Sahih Bukhari, arguably the most influential compilation of his sayings

You're holding in your hands a summary of my journey to build a better future for my family and our community. Along the way, I found America's promise is true for those who believe in it.

Everything in this book really happened. No names have been changed.

This is a true-blue American story in which I hope you may find your own family mirrored. We share so much as Americans.

CHAPTER I

An Accidental Activist

Nothing will transpire except what God has prescribed for us.
Quran 9:51

I am an accidental activist.

I arrived in America at Kennedy Airport in 1970 as a student en route to the University of Detroit Mercy—barely noticing the Twin Towers rising against Manhattan's skyline. The North Tower wouldn't be completed until that December; the South Tower took another year. The American Dream was calling me as it had called millions of immigrants before me. I could see the path so clearly: become a citizen, raise a family, lead a good life and help my neighbors build a healthy community for all of us. As I carried my luggage and my hopes toward Detroit, I knew that I was right on track. The next decade strengthened that confidence: I met my wife in graduate school, we started a business upon graduation, we raised children. I was able to give back to our community.

My story might have started and ended much like the stories of your ancestors—fondly remembered by family and friends but unremarkable to most readers. Then, just as the new millennium was dawning, a man who claimed to profess my faith sent his followers to attack American landmarks, including those iconic Twin Towers. Suddenly, my faith was part of horrific headlines on a daily basis, thousands of Muslim neighbors coast to coast instantly were regarded with suspicion—and I became a voice of America's real Muslim community.

September 11, 2001, was the first day of a new calendar for all American families, including those like my own, who truly follow the faith of Islam. Soon, our nation would engage in a series of overseas wars. Muslim Americans would be viewed as a suspect community, our constitutional rights violated with impunity in far too many cases. Like most Americans, I had always contributed to community institutions. As a successful businessman, I had even more opportunities to serve during the booming era of the 1980s and 1990s. I became active in the Republican Party, was appointed by the governor to Michigan's Community Service Commission and, like many Americans in the 1990s, I helped to build a new suburban congregation—in our case, a mosque.

After what became known simply as "9/11," Muslims like me were catapulted into the role of defending our cherished American values of freedom and equality—on a national stage with extremely high stakes. That certainly wasn't part of my American Dream when I first set foot on these shores, but life in this turbulent era led me step by step, from one moment to the next, until … until … well, until one day I woke up staring at an entirely new landscape for Muslim-American relations and I found myself accidentally in a very public arena. I am proud of how I responded, but this was not the trajectory I had envisioned half a century ago.

There was no way to see those explosive events on 9/11 coming. Even our government's intelligence experts did not take the threat seriously, much to our regret in the investigations that unfolded after the attacks. And that, too, is part of this story. I understand why our leaders couldn't fully envision what happened that day. There is nothing inherent in Islam that produces violence—just as there is nothing at the core of Christianity that inevitably produced the Inquisition or the Crusades or the KKK or the Christian churches in Germany that backed Hitler's regime. Quite the opposite! There is a strong tradition in both of our faiths that sees America as an ideal land that embodies our core spiritual values and gives our families the freedom to pursue happiness even in the midst of our diversity.

I may be preaching here, unintentionally. I wrote this book to provide a window into the family, community and spiritual values of ordinary Muslim families. I don't expect everyone to love Muslims, but research shows that men and women who don't know a Muslim are more likely to express hostility toward us. One Pew study showed that only about one-third of Americans have had meaningful contacts with Muslims. That leaves a majority of Americans more prone to adopting without question the myths and biases so prominent in contemporary media. Rather than fading in the years since 9/11, 2018 ushered in a new era of demonizing our neighbors with efforts to establish a Muslim travel ban or add other restrictions based on one's faith or country of origin. I hope that as you read this heartfelt story, you will discover how much we share.

It's hard to recall, today, America's high hopes in the 1990s for world peace, democracy, freedom and cultural diversity. Here's a reminder: I appeared in a 1994 cover story in *U.S. News & World Report* about how much all Americans share in their deepest spiritual desires. In that story, seven years before 9/11, I told the magazine's millions of readers: "It's very easy to be a Muslim in the United States." I had no reason to question that assertion.

We need to reclaim that earlier optimism and that focus on our shared values. In these pages, I hope you will feel right at home. As a Muslim, I am happy to tell people about achieving the American Dream—and I frequently do so when I am invited to speak to groups. Now, as a senior citizen, I enjoy living in a beach condo in Florida. But my retirement plans are on hold because of the renewed prejudice stoked by the toxic attitudes so publicly proclaimed these days toward people perceived as foreigners. So, I continue to claim my status as a proud American—and my obligation as an accidental activist. For my part, I am sharing this story with readers in the hope that one day we all will see our grandchildren living in peace, free from any guilt by association.

The most important truth about Muslims is that—just like the American population as a whole—we are not a monolith as a people of faith. The truth is, we come in all skin colors, ethnicities, nationalities and linguistic roots. Like Christians, with many denominations and a range of theological perspectives, we have various branches of Islamic thought and practice. In fact, the Pew Research Center recently reported: "American Muslims openly acknowledge that there is room for multiple interpretations of the teachings of Islam. A majority (64 percent) say there is more than one true way to interpret the faith's teachings." That's very similar to Christian attitudes, Pew reports: "Among U.S. Christians, there is a

similar balance: 60 percent say there is more than one true way to interpret the teachings of their religion."

One of the most visible symbols of Muslim identity is the hijab, or
headscarf, worn by many Muslim women whatever their particular perspective on Islam might be. My wife Shahina chooses to wear hijab as
a proud sign of her identity, but the headscarf has nothing to do with
extremism. Shahina serves on our condo association's welcoming committee. We enjoy making friends with our non-Muslim neighbors. We have
developed many close relationships across all cultural, racial and religious
lines. Shahina's engaging smile helps—and her love of inviting people to
visit for a meal, often to share dishes with us from their tradition and our
own. In writing this book, I'm hoping to expand that diverse reach, opening the doors of our family life to the world.

Shahina and I can vividly tell our immigrant story, because it happened
within our adult lives. But a large number of Muslims are not newcomers. Many Muslim families—just like other American families—can
barely remember their own immigrant roots because they unfolded so
many generations ago. Most American-Muslim communities today are
mixed: Some families are recent arrivals, like us; some have been here
for a century or more. Our collective roots on this continent stretch back
more than 500 years. Some historians say that Muslims likely reached the
New World long before Columbus, as ocean currents pushed boats from
West African shores across the Atlantic. Others accompanied Spanish
and Portuguese explorers in the 1500s. Any child in school today knows
that slave labor in the South built up our national economy in our first
century as a nation. Many of those enslaved men, women and children
were taken from Muslim villages in Africa. Muslims also migrated will-
ingly, to ply their trades and professions in the promising New World.
Some Muslims came to these shores from the Middle East as traders and
farmers; craftsmen came from Eastern Europe; and agricultural workers
journeyed halfway around the world from Punjab, India. The Hart-Cellar
Immigration and Nationality Act of 1965 lifted earlier race-based restrictions, allowing Asian and African emigration to the U.S. As a result, I am
part of that post-1965 wave.

As Muslim immigrants, we tend to share these values: a desire for
higher education, the pursuit of professional careers and opportunities to

set up our own businesses—so that we can contribute in helpful ways to our new homeland. The latest Pew report on Muslim Americans shows that I am among 58 percent of U.S. Muslim adults who were born in another country. About 18 percent of U.S. Muslims are "second generation," born in this country with at least one parent who was an immigrant. That means that one-quarter of all American Muslim families have been living here for at least three generations.

That same 2017 Pew report says, "No racial or ethnic group makes up a majority of Muslim-American adults." That busts the common myths that Muslims are all Arabs, which could not be further from the truth. Pew reports, "No single country accounts for more than 15 percent of adult Muslim immigrants to the United States." That 15 percent is from Pakistan. My own country of origin, India, accounts for 7 percent of Muslim immigrants. "Among U.S. Muslim adults who were born abroad, more come from South Asia (35 percent) than any other region," Pew reports. In other words, as an Indian immigrant, I'm not a rare exception. I'm in the largest ethnic group among Muslim Americans today.

The other fundamental value that unites us as Muslims in this country is that we recognize America as our homeland and we want to contribute to a healthy, successful future for our nation. Pew researchers found that "the vast majority of Muslims living in the U.S. (82 percent) are American citizens."

What all of this demographic data means is that, like other groups who have migrated to these shores from around the world, Muslims arrived in fragmented communities separated by cultural roots. So then, as the American story has always been told—our nation's founding values have the potential to unite us. A century ago, American Protestants from northern Europe and newly arrived Catholics from southern Europe violently feuded. Today, these distinctions are barely noted in neighborhoods or workplaces. The same is true for Muslims. Today, despite our original diversity, American Muslims are organically coalescing. Time is pulling us together, as it always has worked on newcomers. And, today, anti-Muslim bigotry is pushing us together, much as anti-Semitism pressed Jewish Americans to establish consolidated institutions.

I grew up in India as a cultural Muslim. Islam was a central part of my family identity, but on a daily basis I was disengaged from the heart of the faith. In the early 1980s, living in southeast Michigan with a young family, I wanted to instill more of that Islamic identity in my family life, so I decided to attend a mosque in Troy, just north of Detroit. It was primarily an Indo-Pakistani congregation, and really was more of a social gathering place, revolving around the subcontinent's Muslim culture. It was a place to share old stories and enjoy spicy cuisine. The observance of religious rituals was incidental. My mother, who had come to live with me upon my father's passing, found company from the old country. She made new friends with whom she could speak Urdu. Few Arabs came to pray with us, and whites or blacks didn't frequent our mosque at the time. That's how it was for many years in Muslim communities across the U.S. Mosques had their official names, but most Muslims referred to them in ethnic shorthand: "Oh, that's the Yemeni mosque." Or, "That's an African-American mosque." That's the same way urban Catholics used to identify immigrant parishes: "That's the German parish." Or, "That's the Polish parish."

The congregation attending our Indo-Pakistani mosque grew and we hired a scholarly imam. Emphasizing Islamic values, he taught us that practicing our faith went far beyond the rituals we perform. I began discovering the depth of my own religion. Back home in India, Muslim education typically focused on reading and memorization of the Quran. Pious but uneducated mullahs tended to focus more on God's wrath and less on God's compassionate attributes. In my region of India, as in most Muslim lands around the world, only men went to pray at mosques. But in the U.S., families are encouraged to attend together. Programs at Muslim centers across the U.S. welcome women and children as well as men. Friday sermons gather us under one roof. In my family, all of us were going through this religious awakening. My wife, being a convert, was happy that our children were learning religious values at the Sunday school. The sermons were in English and mosque services included regular religious programming, lectures, summer camps for the youth and weekend social events for all. Young and old alike participated.

As my awareness of Islam grew, I learned more about Muslim spirituality, the Muslim sense of fairness and justice and the role of Prophet Muhammad as a "Mercy to the world, Quran 21:107." I learned that the Prophet's mosque in Medina was inclusive, socially engaging and offered community services. In my experience, I believe America is guiding many Muslims back to their spiritual roots.

I was born a Muslim in India, but I also can say that I truly found Islam in all its breadth and depth on American shores. Early in my life, for example, I attended services twice a year, on the two main religious holidays. That's just like many Christians who jokingly call themselves "Chreasters," attending only on Christmas and Easter. Now, I rarely miss Friday prayers, never miss daily prayers and always fast in the holy month of Ramadan.

This is true coast to coast. Faithful Muslim observance and public service is growing along with our communities. When I arrived at the University of Detroit in 1970, there were only a few mosques in the entire metropolitan area. Today, the university now has its own campus mosque and there are more than 50 mosques in metro Detroit. A growing number of Islamic schools operate in the region, like Jewish and Catholic parochial schools. There are several Muslim cemeteries; my parents are buried alongside generations of Muslims in the Roseland Park Cemetery in Berkley, Michigan, where a dedicated area is reserved for Muslim graves. I've purchased two sites next to theirs.

To experience our unity in diversity, visit a Friday congregational prayer. I've often invited non-Muslim friends to participate in one of our weekly events. When they do, people often tell me that, if America needs a lesson in race relations, they should turn to Muslims. Dr. Martin Luther King Jr. famously called Sunday morning the most racially segregated hour of the week. This growing experience of Muslim unity for Friday afternoon prayers represents the most racially and ethnically united hour of the week.

That diversity is especially visible in southeast Michigan, because metro Detroit is now internationally known as a mecca for immigrants of all colors, creeds and cultures. Journalists from around the world report that Dearborn has the largest Arab-Muslim population of any city outside of the Middle East. The story of the birth and growth of the auto industry is told in countless books—especially the role played by the controversial visionary Henry Ford, whose home was in Dearborn. Today, we know a lot about Ford's personal bigotry, but he committed his company a century ago to hiring workers of all races and ethnicities. It was no accident that the nation's first purpose-built mosque was a short distance from Ford's first major factory in the city of Highland Park, now an enclave within Detroit. Lebanese, Yemeni, Iraqi, Syrian, Palestinian and Egyptian immigrants settled here for work in Ford plants. In Henry Ford's once-segregated hometown, Muslims now serve on the city council and the police chief is an Arab Christian. Dearborn's Warren Avenue is now a tourist destination due to the many Middle Eastern businesses and eateries serving halal food, businesses that contribute in a major way to reviving the local economy. Nearby is Hamtramck, a former Polish enclave that now is a tiny diverse city within the city of Detroit. That community fell on hard times in recent decades, but is being revitalized now by newcomers, primarily Bangladeshi, Yemeni and Bosnian. The rest of the tri-county area has large populations of Indo-Pakistani Muslims, as well as other ethnicities. Detroit is also the birthplace of the Nation of Islam—originally an African-American separatist movement. Through its evolution half a century ago, the Nation became an important stepping stone toward orthodox Islam, made famous by Malcolm X. So, we have a vibrant African-American Muslim community around us, as well.

The beauty of the area's diverse Muslim population inspired me to lead the effort of establishing a mosque in Detroit's upscale suburb of Bloomfield Hills. That's why we chose the name "Unity Center." We hoped this would become a place where diverse cultures would forge a new Islamic-American identity.

It has been my privilege to actively participate in the growth of southeastern Michigan's Muslim community, building coalitions along the way. I also led in the formation of the Council of Islamic Organizations of Michigan (now called the Michigan Muslim Community Council). Its mission is to:

- Promote unity and cooperation among the diverse Muslim communities, cultures, ethnic backgrounds and races
- Promote American and Islamic values through advocacy, organizing service, education and partnerships and coalitions with ethnic, racial, religious, educational, government, media and civic organizations
- Pursue social justice, improve human relations and uphold human rights in America

Collectively, the story of our acceptance as Muslim neighbors nation-wide is very similar to the stories of overcoming bigotry told in Catholic and Jewish immigrant families. While the tragedies faced by our Jewish friends are well known, we may forget that Catholic families had to overcome centuries of bigotry, legal barriers and physical violence. The historian John Tracy Ellis wrote that a "universal anti-Catholic bias was brought to Jamestown in 1607 and vigorously cultivated in all the 13 colonies from Massachusetts to Georgia." Mob violence against Catholics broke out in the mid-1800s in a number of cities. In that same era, the Know Nothing political party supported Millard Filmore for president and ran on an anti-Catholic platform, like Donald Trump's politically charged campaign in 2016. In the 1920s, however, the Ku Klux Klan staged brutal anti-Catholic attacks. Today, many Americans recall that John Kennedy broke the bar of bigotry for Catholic political candidates. But most Catholic families remember little about the 200 years of hostility before Kennedy's election.

For Muslim families, the threats are recent memories. On November 4, 1979, Iranian students took 52 Americans hostage at the U.S. Embassy in Tehran, touching off the longest hostage crisis in American history. For 444 days, Americans were aware of the hostages' plight and demonized Imam Khomeini's support for this politically motivated revolution in Iran. I describe it this way because American anger about the hostage crisis and Khomeini's later fatwa against author Salman Rushdie was centered more on Khomeini and Iranian politics than on Islam per se. Nevertheless, I was involved in that era as a guest on radio talk shows, articulating perspectives many Americans were not hearing. In that era, not many journalists recognized the importance of including the voices of Muslim community leaders in their news reports. I remember editors rejecting my submissions for op-ed-page essays. Frustrated, I asked whether *The Detroit News* and *Detroit Free Press* would let me purchase an advertisement to publish a statement by a nonprofit group focused on cultural understanding. This turned into a frustrating and humiliating experience. Our shared frustration within the Muslim community, over these refusals to even include our viewpoints, became a springboard for my actions. Americans want to hear from Muslim leaders who condemn violence in the name of our faith—and the vast majority of American Muslims do condemn

such acts in very public ways! Simply visit websites for major Muslim-
American groups today and you will find these public condemnations. But
for many years, our strong protestations against violence were hard to find
in American news media. I learned that developing relationships with
media professionals is essential if we are to have our voices heard. As I
recount such memories, I pray you'll find in the twists and turns of my life
that these stories represent decades of struggles in America, suspenseful
at times, funny at other times, heartbreaking occasionally, often intriguing,
a little exotic, quite fascinating, illuminating and revealing, but hopefully
compelling enough for you to turn the pages—to know your neighbor a
little better.

We have come a long way. Today, the same newspapers that once rejected
my submissions out of hand now regularly seek my input. Together, we all
have weathered so many crises since the hostages were taken four decades
ago. The attacks on September 11, 2001, were the watershed. But in recent
years, the barbaric ISIS group rose its ugly head. Living along Florida's
Treasure Coast today, I began contributing regularly to local newspapers
and eventually became a regular guest writer on Muslim issues. I joined
the local association of religious leaders. The charged election primaries in
2015 began with the demonization of Muslims and Islam. ISIS-inspired
attacks continued. Once again, I have become as busy as I ever was in
Michigan in my work with media and interfaith networks, promoting
both peace and accuracy in reporting on Islam.

I cannot retire as an activist. Ominous headlines never seem to stop. In
the early hours of June 12, 2016, I woke up to the news of the Orlando
nightclub shooting that killed 49 people and wounded 58 others. Hearing
the awful news, I prayed: "Lord, let it not be a Muslim!" Eventually, reporters revealed that the shooter was Omar Mateen—a man from our local
community. My heart sank!

I asked my wife, "Shahina, what is Brother Siddique Mateen's son's
name?" She thought it was Omar. We knew his relatives well, although
we did not know Omar. I did not want to believe these reports about
him! His father, an Afghan immigrant, had been heavily traumatized
by the war there. Now, his whole family was in deep shock over Omar's
horrifying crime. National media descended upon our small town. Our
mosque leadership, afraid all Muslims would be forced to account for this

young man's rampage, was unprepared to deal with this awful situation and asked me to be their spokesperson. I was caught in a hurricane, once again. Events beyond our control were suddenly affecting all Muslims by association, especially those who live in Florida.

I helped organize an interfaith memorial service at the Community Church of Vero Beach and a candlelight vigil at the riverside park. These were planned jointly with the LGBTQ community and deeply appreciated by all. A thousand mourners congregated! I wrote a guest column in the Treasure Coast Palm newspapers that week, denouncing the crime. The Fort Pierce Police Department asked for my help in holding cultural competency training for its officers. The goal was to promote an understanding of Islam and the local Muslim community.

Working with colleagues across this region, my wife and I were able to make a positive difference. Unlike decades ago, news media professionals, political leaders, law enforcement officers and other community leaders have warmly welcomed our efforts. This tells me that Americans are open-minded and accepting of diversity—if only they can get to know their Muslim neighbors.

We need to reach out to one another. That's why I wrote this memoir. I'm not arguing that we deserve more sympathy than any other group of Americans. On the contrary, I advise Muslims to step up to the challenges and work to lift up our entire country. I am encouraged to see so many people of good will coming forward to support us in the effort. When extremists publicly attack us for our faith, other Americans stand shoulder to shoulder with their Muslim sisters and brothers against bigotry.

This book is the story of my family and the American Dream we share with millions of other families nationwide. I also draw on research data, historical sources and quotations from the Quran, but I am not claiming that every point I make in this book should be accepted without discussion. I am a typical American in 2019. I follow tweets, check Facebook postings, encourage friends and often argue with them as well. We live in a world of daily engagement. We know that friendly engagement with our Muslim neighbors breaks down the barriers of bigotry. This book is an invitation to conversation. In fact, I'm providing a free discussion guide with this book to actively encourage a national conversation.

I am not alone in this. In the summer of 2015, my wife and I set out on an 11,000-mile, 29-state journey around this country in our SUV, stopping along the way at mosques from Florida to California. We travelled the fabled Route 66 westward from Chicago, driving through the flyover states on our way back to Florida. We spent time in colorful Muslim communities from coast to coast. My immediate family members are now spread out across that entire map, wherever economic opportunities have taken them. Geography isn't a factor for Muslims, but urban areas have become hubs, as they have for American Jews and other minorities. In our travels we found that, yes, there is a lingering fear due to the toxic rise of anti-Muslim voices. However, we also found that Muslims generally are going about their daily lives, believing in the American Dream, relying on protections guaranteed under our constitutional democracy. Muslims are ordinary people with ordinary problems, no different from other Americans.

Islam is an Abrahamic faith comprising one-fourth of all humanity on this planet—including more than 3 million followers in America. We reside in every part of the North American continent. Thousands of us serve in the U.S. armed forces. We are part of every segment of American society. We are represented in all branches of government, Fortune 500 companies, schools and public service agencies from hospitals to senior-citizen centers. The person caring for your elderly mother in an assisted living center may very well be a Muslim. The person who supervised construction of your office complex, the engineer who designed a component in your car, the developer who set up your company's website, the Uber driver who took you home, the doctor who replaced your bad knee with a titanium joint—all may have been Muslims.

As I advance in age, I want the next generation of Muslim Americans to join me in working for a better America and a peaceful world, shunning radical influences as well as destructive bigotry. We want to confront these challenges with our neighbors. That's how the healthiest American communities always have worked. Cooperation, understanding and goodwill are essential values.

There are many ways that my life is vastly different than that of J.D. Vance, who grew up in a poor Rust Belt community and wrote the best-selling *Hillbilly Elegy: A Memoir of a Family and Culture in Crisis*. But there is a fundamental truth we share. Why did he write down his family's "quite ordinary" story? Because "we're more socially isolated than ever, and we pass that isolation down to our children." What's the solution? Learning about each other beyond the vicious stereotypes. Vance writes, "I want people to understand the American Dream as my family and I encountered it."

In that pledge, we are brothers.

You can see why I'm calling on you, as you read this book, to help us get to know each other as neighbors. That is an important calling for all of our families today—and for all of our children who will one day claim their roles in this great country.

CHAPTER 2

Lady Liberty Beckons

*God created the heavens and the earth … God knows all that enters the
earth and all that emerges from it—and all that comes down from the
sky, and all that ascends therein. And God is with you, wherever you are.*

Quran 57:4

*"The bosom of America is open to receive not only the opulent and respected
stranger, but the oppressed and persecuted of all nations and religions; whom
we shall welcome to a participation of all our rights and privileges."*

George Washington

On a late August morning in 1970, as my flight from London's Heathrow
Airport began its descent to Kennedy Airport under a clear blue sky, my
eyes were searching for that welcoming figure: the Statue of Liberty. She
stands for freedom, democracy and the Declaration of Independence. The
signers in Philadelphia, including George Washington himself, welcomed
immigrants a century before Lady Liberty became the official beacon in
New York Harbor in 1886. In 1903, Emma Lazarus's lines were added,
calling her Mother of Exiles and inviting all of us to find shelter here: "I
lift my lamp beside the golden door!" There are so many symbols associated with the statue that you may not immediately recall the broken
chain at Lady Liberty's feet. Those shattered links are a powerful symbol
of immigrants' hopes as they settle in the United States. On my own first
day in America, I did not understand the break I was making with the
land of my birth and my past. Now, of course, I can see how my outlook,
character and vocation all were transformed by my new homeland. Even
my faith underwent a rebirth and reformation.

My concerns on that first day were much more immediate as my plane
landed and I disembarked. I had arrived in New York City via Beirut
and London, after spending a year working in Saudi Arabia. My heart
was fluttering with uncertainty and excitement combined with awe. I had

never experienced such feelings—even though I knew they were the emotions of millions of men and women before me.

"We are a nation of immigrants." Americans have been proclaiming those words to the rest of the world from the political activist Thomas Paine more than 200 years ago to a host of our leaders in business, politics and the arts today. From Mitt Romney to Barack Obama, our leading lights repeat those six words: "We are a nation of immigrants." Of course, we all know the stories of our Native American and African-American neighbors are different, but the vast majority of Americans today do, indeed, spring from immigrant roots. That's why President Reagan and Chrysler chairman Lee Iacocca were able to raise more than $350 million in donations from American families to restore the Statue of Liberty for its centennial in 1986. For years to come, Lady Liberty will continue calling out to the world as the embodiment of the American Dream.

So, what does that life-changing encounter feel like? What stirs in the hearts of immigrants, giving up their place of birth to circle the globe and claim this new homeland? What unites us in our response? Well, the first sensation is that overwhelming churn of emotion I experienced as I landed in New York. For me, coming to America was such an enormous risk that I had been warned to expect only a "dark future." That's how my late father vehemently tried to discourage me from moving to the U.S. He wrote long letters, putting it in blunt terms: "Don't go to America!"

At the time we were corresponding, I was working in Saudi Arabia, where I had found a job through a family connection. "Stick to it!" my father would write. "You're doing fine financially. Stay!" In letter after letter he argued that America offers too many risks. He would repeat stories of Indians who lost their jobs and status in America and were deported. He had no confidence in my future—and certainly not in America. I recall him chiding me repeatedly: "Your intention is just to fool around by going to America."

Certainly, the charms of America, from Lady Liberty to Hollywood, attracted me, but my immediate intention was quite serious: higher education. Even though my family prized education, my plan did not sway my father. Many of my relatives had gone abroad to complete their education, but their preferred destination was England. My father proudly displayed the letters—M.A., Cantab—after his name to show that he had graduated from Cambridge University. He was not impressed that I would seek a degree from an American school. His perspective was quite different. For generations, Europe had been the center of higher learning for aspiring young colonial-age Indian students, who then returned home and settled into careers in civil service or management. That was the highest aspiration in elite Indian families. My generation was a stark contrast in our eagerness to break those old chains—so the conflict with my father was to be expected. We both knew that my journey to America would be life-changing. After all, almost all of the immigrating students I knew wound up becoming American citizens. The traditional chains were shattering all across Indian society. We clashed because he regarded these sweeping changes as an ominous foreshadowing of tragedy. For me, this was a dream.

My father did have a point. While my family shared the value of higher education, one major difference was that my grandfather had paid for my father's education. I would be paying for mine, with the grace of the Almighty. My decision was risky because I wasn't only cutting ties with generations of vocational expectations for promising young men born in India—I was intentionally cutting the family purse strings, too. My mantra was: "I want to make my own fortune." America was the land of entrepreneurs and I dreamed of joining their ranks.

My aversion to inheritance was colored by the many conflicts I had witnessed among siblings who would squabble over property or, worse yet, wound up fighting over the estates of parents who died without a will. I was so determined to avoid that kind of conflict that I wrote to my father, urging him to pass any inheritance to my brother—or to anyone else he pleased. I looked at inheritance as a crutch, rather than a blessing. Those were shocking statements for a young man from an upper-class family in Hyderabad. It wasn't a surprise that my father thought I was doomed.

Nothing could change my resolve. I knew that my father wasn't a risk taker. He had always lived a quiet life, partly because he was secure with inherited wealth. A family connection had helped my father find a job with the Provincial Legislative Assembly and he stuck to the civil service all his life. An uncle in Saudi Arabia helped me find a job in the Kingdom, so my father thought I should follow in his footsteps. He tried to convince me that I should regard this job offer as a blessing from God. I should grab it, hang onto it and never leave. This was my security. That's how he had lived his life. But my family was large and other voices encouraged my restless desire to keep moving around the world. My grandfather frowned on nepotism and his values fueled my own desire to stand on my feet through my own efforts. I didn't want to live my life with the obligation of my uncle's patronage. He was helping me to get a first foothold in adult life, which I appreciated. However, as soon as I had saved enough money and secured a student visa to the U.S., I was ready to abandon security and ignore my father's stern warnings.

Leaving Saudi Arabia, my first stop was Lebanon. There was no U.S. consulate in Jeddah, so I had to get my F-1 International Student Visa from the U.S. Embassy in Beirut, which was widely regarded as the Paris of the Middle East. It was a friendly and cosmopolitan Muslim city in that era, with exciting entertainment, great food and captivating vistas along the blue waters of the Mediterranean. What a welcoming transition after Saudi Arabia! I was on my way to the Promised Land!

At that time, airline tickets were bought through travel agents, and a friend suggested a good agent in Lebanon. I told him that I needed to save every nickel I could for my new life in the U.S.—and I paid him in cash. To get the cheapest flight for me, the agent bought me a ticket on a charter flight and told me to tell anyone who asked: "I'm on the rugby team."

The problem was: I'd never heard of the sport. This arrangement might have been a bit shady, but it wasn't illegal. Lots of people filled out extra seats in charters in that era. But I was apprehensive about that particular flight. What if someone asked me to describe my role with the team?

"I'm not sure about lying to officials at the airport," I told the agent.

"You're not lying," he said. "Just say you play rugby." And he indicated that that was the end of the conversation.

Thankfully, no one tested my knowledge of my newfound sport before, during or after my flight. Perhaps the officials didn't know the game; perhaps they didn't care. As I looked around, I saw lots of American students on tight budgets heading back home from a summer in Europe. That plane ride was noisy! Once again, I thought of my father's warnings, because these kids clearly were fooling around! At one point, someone tossed a ball that missed its target and hit me. While that might seem annoying, this actually was an exciting, new experience for me: boys and girls having fun together in public. I remembered *Summer Holiday*, the 1963 teen musical starring Cliff Richards that I had seen in a movie theater in India with songs like *Let Us Take You for a Ride, Bachelor Boy* and *A Swingin' Affair*. The love-starved emotions in that film were right in line with the passion-flushed Bollywood movies that were all the rage in India. A whole new world was opening up around me on that flight. Sitting next to me was a girl who offered to give me her phone number. Sheltered by my family's social customs and a year in Saudi Arabia, I had never met a girl who would offer such personal contact information.

All around me were high-energy young men and women, many of them couples showing obvious affection. So, what did I do? Mostly, I was silent on that flight—staring at everything around me. I was flying into a new life by the seat of my pants. I shut my eyes, but could not sleep. Even the time zones conspired to disorient me—flying eight hours in the air, minus multiple time zones, meant I was reaching America in a flash. By the clock, just two hours passed in our trans-Atlantic flight.

When we landed, I was exhausted but soaking in every detail with an incredibly heightened state of awareness and making indelible memories. In one journey, life in India was rapidly receding like a fading dream— that is, until my line of passengers reached the customs and immigration desk. This is an intimidating experience for any young foreigner arriving in the U.S., but especially for students from developing countries, where we grow up with a fear of authorities. Standing in that line, all of my father's warnings came rushing back. I had quit my secure job. I had spent too much on this journey.

If these U.S. agents turned me back, I would be ashamed. Crushed. Defeated.

"Next!" Suddenly, it was my turn.

I stepped forward and handed over my passport. The man looked up, stared at me, then looked down and scrutinized the papers. I didn't know what to expect. Then, the man simply stamped the passport and handed it back. My second stop, Customs, was also a breeze.

I was so relieved; I strolled along happily toward the exit. Then, a burly immigration officer, twice my size, snatched the papers from my hands. A fresh wave of anxiety jolted me. This was it! My worst fears resurfaced.

I simply stared up at the man.

Then, after studying my papers, he handed them back. "You're good," he said, so casually that he did not even look at me as he turned and disappeared.

I thanked God: *"Alhamdulillah!"* There are certain incidents in life, no matter how trivial, that are impossible to forget. Such are the times when even a nonbeliever thinks of a higher power.

Finally, I made it to the main terminal, carrying a beat-up suitcase without wheels. Three days earlier, I had left the 1950s-style airport in Jeddah. Now, I was surrounded by modern design and all the colors and claims of American culture. I stared at everything. I was aware of everyone.

No one paid any attention to me. I felt invisible.

When I landed that day, now nearly half a century ago, international travel was not as common as it is today. The digital devices that stream the whole world into our hands 24/7 were pure science fiction. My culture shock was a lightning bolt. My hometown in India was slow and leisurely. In Hyderabad, a former princely state, I grew up sheltered in an aristocratic family where everyone was comfortable with the limitations of small-town life.

My next goal in the airport was to telephone a friend, but I had little idea how to use American payphones. At that time, payphones were not common in India or Saudi Arabia. Of course, I had seen them in magazines and movies, but how did they operate? I said to myself: "What kind of coins do I need? How many?" I had some paper U.S. currency in my pocket, but no change.

Finally, I asked for help and to my surprise, I was given a crash course in this new technology. As the man made change for me, he described the process: "Pick up the receiver, then drop coins in the slot. Listen for the tone. Dial the number. Wait for the ring. Talk."

Sound simple? It was head-spinning for me. On my first day in America, I was dependent on strangers. I felt insignificant. In the social order of India and Saudi Arabia, I could lean on extended family for support—but none of that was available to me in this new land. No one was waiting to receive me, and my family name didn't mean a damn thing here. I was just one among millions. God had helped to get me here, and from now on I could only depend on God's grace. That was a powerful spiritual reminder for a fairly secular young man like me.

Trying to conserve my funds, I spent the night at a YMCA, where I was warned: "Watch your luggage." I checked in for the night and made a supper of some dates I had brought with me. Fortunately, a good night's sleep began to free me from the jet lag. Eager to start the next day of my trip, I headed to the showers, which no one had warned me were communal at a YMCA. This was one more cultural jolt for me, given my background. I was so unsettled at this prospect that I skipped the badly needed shower and set out to catch a bus to Detroit.

I quickly discovered that my more expansive Indian manner of conversing with people was a handicap. When I wanted help locating the bus station, I found a passerby willing to make eye contact and began, "Sir, I'm going to Detroit."

"Great! Have a safe trip." And he was gone. This confirmed my impression of New York: all business and impersonal.

Something else was at work as well. I was a skinny Indian kid dragging along a crappy old suitcase. People assumed I was a homeless panhandler, asking for bus fare. The prevalence of homeless people on New York streets shocked me. America seemed to be the world's richest country, the most advanced in the world. The U.S. had planted its flag on the moon! I didn't simply appear stupid to these New Yorkers; I seemed to be an outcast.

The next time I managed to catch someone's eye, I was polite but got straight to the point: "Sir, where is the Greyhound bus depot?"

That worked! As it turned out, the station was a short walk. I arrived early for my bus, bought my tickets, checked my suitcase and was able to get a window seat. As my bus finally pulled out of the station, I thought: I feel like such an idiot in this strange new land. The sun set. New York's bright lights surrounded me as we crawled out of the city and accelerated toward the interstate.

Over the next 12 hours, I couldn't sleep. I was heading to Detroit, a place that I could not even begin to envision as a place I would call home. Today, after nearly half a century of life in the Detroit area, I know how groundless my fears were on that red-eye bus trip. But back then? What did I know about Detroit? It was the Motor City, the fifth largest metropolis in the U.S. at the time. I had heard its crime rate was astronomical. People called it the Murder Capital.

Of course, adapting to Saudi Arabia also had been a challenge and, even after a year, I never felt fully welcomed in the Kingdom. I was always a foreigner in that inhospitable terrain and inaccessible Saudi society. It didn't help that I hated the idea of a family ruling a so-called Islamic nation with an iron fist. Never mind their claim to be Guardians of the Holy Sites. I saw the royal family's tribal practices tarnishing my faith in the eyes of the world. Their harsh punishments and misogyny were not true Islamic values. Their excesses only fueled the bigotry of Islamophobes. During my year, I had no chance to interact with Saudis in any meaningful way. The one memory I truly cherish from my days in the Kingdom was the opportunity to perform the pilgrimage, the Hajj. I also enjoyed time with my uncle's family. But the vast majority of that year was marked by hard, sweaty work and boredom. I was allowed to spend time in the Kingdom as part of a highway construction project, keeping track of supply and demand for machinery parts and construction material. When I wasn't working in the warehouse, there was little for me to do. The Arabic term for my work permit was *iqama*, which means "residence" but also can mean "overstay." Whenever I looked at my permit, it was a signal saying: "Time to go!"

As I rolled through the night toward Detroit, I thought: In the Kingdom, we built highways, but those were nothing compared to the vast sweep of these American freeways. Mile by mile, hour by hour, I watched the headlights and taillights of countless other vehicles, occasional billboards and flashes of towns we sped past. We switched buses somewhere in Ohio. As vivid as these memories remain today, I was so exhausted that I cannot recall the name of the town where I changed coaches.

I did remember my lesson from New York: When asking for help, be simple and direct. But I wasn't brave enough to ask for an explanation of the fast-food menu in the station. I had heard of hamburgers, but thought that meant they were made with ham, so I avoided that as a Muslim. Instead, I settled on a mysterious dish: French fries. Every choice I made carried a surprise.

After 614 miles, just as dawn was breaking, my bus pulled into the station and the front door hissed open. I stumbled down the steps into

Detroit so sleepless that I wasn't surprised to find that my first greeting was a badge thrust in my direction by some kind of plain-clothes officer. I was an obvious target: Grey pants made in India and a pink-and-white polka-dot shirt with a trendy long-lapel collar, purchased at a department store in London. My hair was overgrown with extra-long sideburns—going for a Carlos Santana look.

I knew that I was facing some kind of cop. I had read the Perry Mason novels and knew all about that classic move—flashing a badge. This wiry officer looked at me with cool, piercing eyes. He demanded my passport, which he checked without a word, nor a smile. Then, he simply nodded at me and went after his next quarry. This time, I wasn't as scared as I had been when challenged at Kennedy. I was already adjusting to this strange new land—now, a little less alien than 48 hours ago.

Then, my old friend Mujahid greeted me: "Good to see you again, man!"

I was so glad to see a friendly face—to hug and peck each other's cheeks in the way we would greet back in India—that I didn't ask him why he had called me "man." He knew my name. I was clueless about the trendy lingo in America. We crawled into the borrowed VW Bug he was driving that day. At that time, downtown Detroit was still open for business with its traditional retailers, including the vast Hudson's department store, now long gone. As we turned from Woodward Avenue onto Jefferson Avenue, Mujahid pointed out Canada on the other side of the Detroit River—another nation, and yet so close we could see people walking along the Canadian shore. I saw African American neighborhoods for the first time as we drove through Detroit.

On that day, as I settled into my new hometown, I was overwhelmed by the vast sweep of this nation and the international mix of its cultures. Memories of my arrival in America will remain fresh forever. That was the moment I began to realize the true potential of my new homeland. I became convinced that the Motor City—in the industrial heart of America—was my kismet. The University of Detroit Mercy would equip me with an MBA. I would meet my wife here. The metro-Detroit community would help me to build a home and a prosperous life as a successful entrepreneur. Not far from the bus stop where I first set foot in Detroit was the spot where I would eventually take the oath of U.S. citizenship in a public ceremony.

My father was wrong.

The irony was that, two decades after my arrival, he passed away during a family visit. America became his final resting place. He's buried in the Roseland Park Cemetery in Royal Oak, just north of Detroit and not far from a commercial property I owned. My mother was buried next to him, 12 years later. I ask God's blessing on their souls.

CHAPTER 3

My Namesake

If your Lord had willed, He could have made mankind one community.
And, they will not cease to differ.
Quran 111:118

The prison of life and the bondage of grief are one and the same.
Before the onset of death, why should we expect to be free of grief?
Mughal poet Ghalib

I was born in turbulent times. My journey as an activist for peace and interfaith understanding spans my entire life, starting with my birth in the midst of a conflict that nearly led to my death before my first birthday.

I came into the world in November 1947, when the monsoons were giving way to winter in the Princely State of Hyderabad. Relatives tell me that my patriarchal grandfather picked up a Quran, opened a page and placed his finger on a random Arabic word, *ghalib*. That may be all there is to the story. But, perhaps a greater Spirit was moving grandfather's finger that day, because my given name "Ghalib" means "victorious" in English. Choosing that particular name in that deeply troubled era was auspicious, indeed.

I was born at a historic crossroad—between the collapse of the British Raj and India's march toward establishing a new national government, with all of the tragedies that accompanied that grand effort. To rule the vast subcontinent with a relatively small number of bureaucrats and soldiers, the British strategy had been to divide and conquer. With a ruthless disdain for Indians themselves, the British cunningly played one princely state against another and, for the most part, those princes and maharajahs accommodated the British game. That's why, in the wake of independence and the British departure after World War II, political leaders within India were able to manipulate centuries of injustices and stroking of communal disharmony under colonial rule. Those lingering wounds bleed to this day.

Within the colorful map of princely states, my family was part of an especially magnificent kingdom. Today, telling Americans about Hyderabad and the rule of the Nizams sounds like a fairy tale. To begin with, most Americans living today have never heard of Hyderabad. That was different during the year of my birth, because the Princely State of Hyderabad was frequently on the front page of newspapers around the world. In those news reports, readers were reminded of the Mughals, my family's ancestors. Those longtime Muslim rulers contributed immensely to Indian civilization, history, culture, language, art and diversity. The Mughals' rise began humbly enough, as some of the soldiers who had swept across Asia and Persia with Genghis Khan settled into Turkish territories. Many married and converted to Islam. Later, these Mughals consolidated their power, moved into the heart of what is India today and defeated the sultan of Delhi. India became the heart of the Mughal Empire in the early 1500s. A century later, at the zenith of Mughal art and architecture, a global symbol of immutable love was built: the Taj Mahal. My own ancestors moved to Samarkand (modern-day Uzbekistan) before migrating to India in the 1700s. When the Mughal Empire eventually crumbled, Hyderabad remained a semi-independent vestige of their culture. The Hyderabadi elite prized the Mughals' patronage of the arts, literature, architecture and the finest in cuisine and jewelry. They spoke in a colorful dialect of the Urdu language. At the summit of aristocracy in Hyderabad was a prince called the Nizam—a lineage that began with a Mughal imperial appointee with that title in the early 1600s and evolved into a royal line of succession in Hyderabad. Seven Nizams ruled for 224 years.

By the early 20th century, Hyderabad seemed like a fantasyland to Americans. The last of the ruling Nizams was featured on the cover of *Time* in 1937 as "The Richest Man in the World." The magazine reported, "India has no native state as rich, potent and extensive as Hyderabad, about the size of the United Kingdom." After the independence of India in 1947, the Nizam announced to other world leaders that he was refusing to join with the emerging Muslim nation of Pakistan or the Hindu-majority India. He would maintain Hyderabad's independence. The vast majority of Hyderabad's population was Hindu, but the Muslim minority had dominated ever since the Mughal era, and the Nizam assumed this could last. He was still in touch with his former imperial friends. British officials publicly described the Nizam as an important ally—even after they were forced to retreat from India back to the U.K.

In the months just before my birth, Gandhi himself set the stage for what was about to unfold in Hyderabad—as if delivering a prologue in a Shakespearean tragedy. While he certainly would have condemned the violence that followed, Gandhi told the whole world that the Nizam was wrong to call for the independence of his state. "Such a thing is inconceivable, especially when the particular prince has no backing from his people," Gandhi said. "Such a declaration was possible when the princes had the backing of British power." In his wry way, Gandhi then added: "If I am not mistaken, things are changed now." Then, Gandhi himself fell to a Hindu extremist in early 1948 and had no role to play in what happened next.

Throughout 1948, newspaper correspondents forecast the religious bloodshed that was expected in Hyderabad if world leaders did not intervene to enforce a peaceful resolution. In addition to the Nizam's own military, a force of extremists took up arms to try to prop up his regime and reports emerged of those extremists' Muslim-on-Hindu intimidation and violence. Hyderabad was rapidly reaching a boiling point.

By mid-September, when I was 10 months old, Hyderabad leaped onto the front page of *The New York Times* and stayed there for more than a week. The *Times'* leading correspondents—including Abe Rosenthal, who later became the paper's executive editor—were dispatched to London, Paris and New Delhi, and their typewriters never stopped rattling as they filed breathless front-line dispatches. The former British overlords of India, frustrated and largely powerless in London, wanted to save the Nizam and tried a desperate end-run. They summoned diplomats to a hastily called United Nations session in Paris to hear the Nizam's pleas for independence. Chronicling the day-by-day movements of ambassadors and armies, the *Times* published maps and even a big photo of the Nizam's grim-faced delegates lining up in Paris. But, the Indian army efficiently surrounded Hyderabad, invaded from four directions and within a matter of days overwhelmed the Nizam's poorly trained force, as well as the extremist militias.

As in earlier surrenders in that era of global conflict, Hyderabad's hereditary ruler broadcast via radio. The first time many of the Nizam's subjects ever heard his voice, he was announcing surrender. "I am opening a new chapter of friendliness with India," he said. In a longer radio message, later, he blamed that entire year of conflict on armed extremists who had manipulated Islam for political gain. The Nizam said that their only goal was to "spread terror," and compared their leaders to Adolf Hitler. At that point, of course, his protestations were moot. The Nizam retired with his wealth and lived comfortably until his death in 1967.

What the world did not know—and would not learn for 65 years—is that the invading Indian army was focused on disarming Muslims and set the stage for a horrific final act in this drama. Hindu-on-Muslim reprisals and mob violence broke out across much of Hyderabad, claiming victims mainly among poorer Muslim families who could not lock themselves away behind the gates of their homes. In some cases, Hindu mobs spontaneously overwhelmed their Muslim neighbors. In others, Hindu militias carefully planned and carried out deadly attacks. Businesses and homes were looted. Men, women and children were killed. When the evidence of this rampage finally came to light in 2013, the BBC called it "India's Hidden Massacre" and estimated that tens of thousands of Muslims lost their lives in the weeks after India invaded. The documentation comes from a report by a blue-ribbon, mixed-faith trio of emissaries sent by Prime Minister Jawaharlal Nehru to travel throughout Hyderabad and report on the aftermath of the invasion. However, Nehru's close advisors were horrified when they read this team's estimate of as many as 40,000 deaths—and the team's passionate plea for the Indian government to make restitution to the devastated families. The report was classified in the interest of maintaining a positive worldview of the emerging Nehru regime. The text only came to light many decades later.

At the time of the invasion, my own family was relatively safe, staying inside our home. But my relatives were terrified by the unfolding violence. I caused them even more anxiety, because I had developed a serious illness and was running a perilously high fever. My family wanted to call our doctor, but that was impossible, given the invasion. Although our home was not attacked, we were isolated. My older sister remembers that the whole family was frantic, crying and praying. In the midst of this, my sister recalls, "We were running around fetching cold wet cloths to place on your forehead, desperately trying to lower your body temperature."

Hour after hour, fear spiraled. Yet, with my family's careful attention, my fever eventually broke. I survived the illness and my family survived the invasion and the reprisals.

Whether the story about my grandpa's selection of my name from the Quran is true or not, I've always been aware that I also have a spiritual namesake within my family. As my grandpa intended, my name, Ghalib, will always remind me of its literal meaning—"victor," in English translation. But I feel a much deeper link to the man I consider my true namesake: an ancestor who was the last of the great Mughal poets, Mirza Asadullah Baig Khan. He has always been better known by a simple pen-name: Ghalib. I am no poet, but I share with my ancestor the skill of writing honestly about the cost of the many conflicts that seem to constantly enflame our world.

He was born in 1797, just after the American Revolution, and died in 1869, just after the American Civil War and the declaration of the British Raj in India. He died an entire century before that all-powerful Raj would collapse—but Ghalib was astonishingly prescient about the future. Even in 1827, Ghalib could see what was coming in India over the next century. He wrote:

> Sir you well perceive,
>
> That goodness and faith,
>
> Fidelity and love
>
> Have all departed from this sorry land.
>
> Father and son are at each other's throat;
>
> Brother fights brother.
>
> Unity and Federation are undermined.

I wish that more Americans had access to Ghalib's poetry in new translations. His artistry in the original Urdu is hard to convey in English—but sharing his work could be helpful today. His heart certainly was attuned to the themes of our era. Ghalib wrote about the search for love in troubled times and he called for a spiritual awareness that was broader than literal readings of our scriptures. He was a devout Muslim throughout his life, but he saw a depth to spirituality that could transcend the divisions and flash points among factions who want to split hairs. If we seek the true essence of faith, he believed, then we must reach beyond what we can hope to know for sure. He would have little patience for today's fundamentalists. One famous Ghalib line was:

The object of my worship lies beyond perception's reach.

As Muslims, we should not fear the world's ever-growing diversity, even though we know that sometimes tragedies result from cultural clashes. We should fix our eyes, as Ghalib did, beyond the dangers and onto the new wonders awaiting us just beyond our old assumptions. That's what Ghalib was reaching for in his verses. We should welcome movement around this miraculous planet we have been given. Migration is ingrained in our faith (Quran, 4:97). The Islamic calendar is called *hijri*, meaning pertaining to *hijr*, or migration, which started with the first date of the Prophet Muhammad's migration from Mecca to Medina. He was forced to leave home, escaping persecution and imminent assassination. As Muslims, we see the potential of the whole world as an entire community—so we can make our home wherever we travel.

Movement is in my DNA as well. In Hyderabad, my surname was Beg, a Turkish title and a link with my family's long-ago sojourn in that part of the world. When I came to America, I added another "g," making my last name Begg, which seemed to be a more common form of the name for my new country. In Hyderabad, Mirza also was added to male names, denoting our descent from Persian nobles. My early school certificates list me as Mirza Ghalib Beg. Today, my business cards say: Victor Ghalib Begg.

One of the poet's direct descendants was Mirza Agha Beg, my own great-grandfather. He arrived in Hyderabad in the mid-1800s from Delhi. That was the era of the Indian Rebellion against the rule of the British East India Company, when Indians rose up and tried to elevate the remaining Mughal King Bahadur Shah Zafar to become their new emperor. Instead of independence, however, the rebellion led to Zafar's exile and the dawn of the British Raj, also known as direct Crown rule. As a Moghul, my great-grandfather was targeted by the British. Our family still tells the dramatic story of his escape along primitive pathways, walking for months with his family through forested and mountainous terrain. Much like American pioneers heading West in the 1800s, my great-grandfather had a humble cart—in his case, a very slow two-wheeled cart pulled by two buffalo bulls. When they finally reached the relative safety of Hyderabad, he was rewarded with a royal title and became a teacher to the crown prince. His Oxford- and Cambridge-educated children went on to acquire their own high statuses, including his oldest son: my mother's father.

On my father's side, my grandfather was the Chief Justice of the Hyderabad High Court, recruited by the Nizam from Lucknow, another princely state and an important Muslim cultural center in northern India. That scenario eventually brought my parents together, as the privileged class preferred to intermarry.

We spoke a regional version of the language of the Muslims of India. Urdu is a rich mixture of Persian, Arabic, Turkish and Sanskrit. I loved Urdu then and still do. It's the medium of Bollywood songs, poetic and sweet. Hindi is the Sanskritized version of Urdu, pushed as the national language of India. Telugu was spoken in villages—among Hindus and Muslims—and is a regional language today. English is the bridge among India's 14 official languages. During a conversation, switching between an Indian language and English is common among the educated.

The great tragedy of the massacre that followed India's invasion of Hyderabad is that Hindus and Muslims had lived and worked together there for many generations. Christian missionaries were allowed to build their churches and schools, because a solid education was prized. I was enrolled in one: St. George's Grammar School. Upper-class families wanted the quality of their children's education to reflect European standards. Our high school papers were sent back to London, where they were evaluated at Cambridge and graduates received "Senior Cambridge" certificates.

We got along at school, despite our varied backgrounds. Our mornings started with the Christian Lord's Prayer in the school gym—and the Muslims didn't mind. The words weren't that different than the opening prayer in the Quran, the al-Fatiha. Our school curriculum included studies of the Gospels and the book of Acts. As Muslims, we were familiar with many of the biblical stories we were taught—because many of the great figures of the Christian Bible are in the Quran as well. And, Hindus didn't mind. They had grown up with their own fantastic stories of gods and men. Our Christian educators—in our school, they were Australian evangelicals—made no overt attempts to convert us. This was another reflection of the caste system at that time. The evangelicals reserved their public campaigns for lower-caste Hindus. They knew the rulers of Hyderabad wouldn't mind. I am not praising this antiquated system, I am merely describing it. The system held many fatal flaws. The main temptation among the elite families of Hyderabad was to become so focused on emulating the values of European society that we began to underrate our own Islamic and Hindu cultures. We shared a creeping secularism.

As a boy, I had little exposure to the breadth and depth of Islam. The extent of my religious education was a bearded mullah coming to our house, pushing us to study the Arabic alphabet and to memorize and then recite passages from the Quran. Those lessons were a dreaded hour, forced upon us primarily by my mother. The mullah got a free meal and a few rupees. The irony was that, other than memorizing lines from the Quran by rote, the mullah was not fluent in Arabic. He only understood the text through some rough translations in Urdu. Our Quran lessons had little chance of conveying to us the true meaning of Islam.

Here is what I learned about being a good Muslim: You pray when you can, especially on the main holidays, dress in cultural garb on special occasions and remain proud of your ancestral faith. Islam pretty much rested at that. To the adults in my family, Islamic values seemed to be: refrain from alcohol and cigarettes, wear modest clothes and generally follow upright conduct. My father and his generation lived accordingly.

Special occasions were rich glimpses that there might be something larger in Islam, even if I could not fully guess the scope of our faith at the time. The fasting month of Ramadan arrived with much hoopla—like celebrating the Twelve Days of Christmas, but our festival lasted for 30 days! Each day began very early with men singing—more like screaming—to wake us up for a pre-dawn meal. At a young age, I wanted to imitate some of the elders, but my mother would not allow me to fast as a little boy. My diabetic father also skipped that pillar of Islam, along with daily prayers. But, he happily joined us in the evening repast. A cannon shot marked the end of each daylong fast. Hyderabad had a tradition of firing a cannon from a hill, Naubat Pahad. It was a spectacular limestone rock formation and, at other times, men pounding huge drums with enormous drumsticks heralded events from that hill.

Whether we had fasted or not during the day, we all anxiously waited to hear the boom at sunset. Appetizers, before the evening meal, had been prepared, along with sweet juices. The scent of food mingled with a rising aroma from the freshly sprinkled red soil unique to Hyderabad, doused with water to contain the dust clouds that breezes could stir in our yard. Each night was a feast for all of the senses.

At the end of Ramadan, I always accompanied my father and my brother to Eid prayers. There are two major Eids, or celebrations, in Islam, and those were the only times we went to pray together. Much fanfare was involved! We rode in our canvas-top Fiat in new clothes. The Nizam, along with his royal entourage, joined the congregational service at the main mosque in a park setting, known as Public Gardens. The women stayed home.

Early on Eid, my mother would start yelling at the servants to prepare for the reception of visitors after the prayers. Neighbors and friends showed up unannounced throughout the day, offering greetings. Special Eid dishes were ready for them. My focus stayed on the rupees my father would hand out after the Eid prayers. That was the only day we found him to be generous—perhaps like gifts at Christmas in Christian families.

Beyond the holiday fanfare, however, I saw little understanding of Islamic concepts such as social justice, charitable projects or community service. Those were duties for the government to manage. We didn't identify with the poor. Hindus had their caste system. We had our own division of classes. Contrary to the humble character of the Holy Prophet of Islam, upper-class Muslims had abandoned humility. Even middle-class families had servants. A part-time chauffeur drove our car, a rickshaw puller took us to school, a cook prepared our meals, a gardener tended the grounds and other servants maintained our house. As a boy, I assumed that each had been born to perform these inherited tasks. The system was not far from slavery, and mistreatment of servants was common. Inside our house, servants slept on the floor, along with the dog. Our gardener slept in a hovel without electricity or running water. I now feel sorry for those who labored in our household. At one time, the great appeal of Islam among the poor was that the Prophet called for a classless society—but I had no concept of that as a boy.

Of course, India was changing more dramatically than almost any other nation in the post-World War II era. Hyderabad could not hope to escape that turbulence, but my parents did their best to shelter us. As a child in our Australian-run private school, I felt few of the changes sweeping across the subcontinent. Toward the end of my high school years, my older sister got married in Lucknow, located in a northern province. On that occasion, cousins encouraged me to enroll at Aligarh Muslim University, simply known as Aligarh, about 75 miles southeast of Delhi. Rajdhani Express, the fast train heading north from Hyderabad, took 22 hours to reach Aligarh in 1963.

Once again, I was sheltered in a school under vestiges of the old regime. Sir Syed Ahmad Khan, a Muslim scholar, jurist, reformer and social activist, established Aligarh in 1875, modeling it after Cambridge and Oxford. His goal was to train students in the British model of English in order to maintain Muslim political influence in India. Graduates were ready for advanced training in the U.K. with the goal of joining government service. Aligarh was run by the central government; India's president appointed the head of our school. As a result, students flocked to Aligarh from all corners of the country, as well as from Africa, West and Southeast Asia. In 2015, *U.S. News and World Report* ranked it sixth in India. Among its alumni was the nonviolent freedom fighter Khan Abdul Ghaffar Khan, who influenced Mahatma Gandhi's own approach to nonviolence. Our alumni also included India's third president, Zakir Hussain, and Pakistan's second president, General Ayub Khan.

Aligarh was an exciting, all-consuming culture with its own distinctive lore, ethics, rituals, humor and jargon, which we liked to call Aligarian. At that time, the dress code was suit-and-tie—certainly no blue jeans, shorts or casual shirts. Black sherwani, the traditional Indian long coat, had to be worn at graduation and other official events. Students paid respect to seniors, a status that wasn't entirely defined by grade level. Since I had cousins at the school, I was able to move into higher social circles than most incoming students.

Our university anthem, composed in poetic Urdu by the cherished Aligarian poet Majaz, was sung on important occasions. Flowery words summoned mythical imagery of romantic evenings by the Nile, intoxicating Persian nights, battles engaged and wine spilled. The student body joined hearts and voices in the chorus, promising to shower the earth with our talents.

My family had set my course toward medicine, so I enrolled in science classes. Every aspiring Indian family hoped that a son would become a physician. I liked sports, but I was a skinny kid, so the coach at the school gym recommended weight training. Eventually, I made the varsity lifting team, competing in inter-varsity meets. In my second year, I was vying for a national title in my weight class. My most valuable prize was a university blazer with a sports emblem, plus a special ration of a bottle of milk and two eggs each day as an athlete—a real bonus, because the university kitchen normally served a poor regimen of basic curries and bread. In high school, I had been a short, skinny, unhealthy kid prone to infections. My appearance had turned me into an introvert. Moving north and joining Aligarh had transformed me into an energetic, brash fellow.

For a time, my family's desire to see me become a doctor led to an ill-fated transfer to a school in Kashmir, where I enjoyed meeting more of my extended family—but then ran into the political disturbances of that era. Just as I arrived in Kashmir, my school was closed for an indefinite time. In truth, I wasn't crushed. I never saw myself as a physician—that was a dream of my parents. So I headed back to Aligarh, where I enrolled in the business school and earned a one-year diploma in business administration.

Upon graduation, I wasn't sure what to do. In Hyderabad, everything was changing. Father retired. He decided to sell our house and use the proceeds for a business venture. The opulent, imported European furnishings my ancestors proudly brought into our family home had vanished. Gone was the gorgeous Queen Anne dining set that could seat 24 for dinner. Gone were the matching china cabinets filled with fine English china and accompanying silver. Gone was an ornate wall-to-wall carpet imported from Persia. Gone was the oil painting of Rabindranath Tagore, the first non-European to have won the Nobel Prize for Literature. Gone was a collection of books in our library that, today, would be worth a small fortune. And gone was the magnificent roll-top desk that dominated the library with its secret compartments, where I used to hide my meager savings as a little boy. To me, this was nothing short of sacrilege. The trinkets that my younger sisters managed to save became priceless to me: a walnut cigar box with my grandfather's name carved on it and two large pictures of my grandparents that, to this day, hang in our home.

What did my father do with the proceeds from the auctioneer? He invested in an enterprise that, given his lack of business expertise, was doomed to fail. He should have known what would happen, but he was blind to the dangers of the financial swamp into which he waded. I offered to help him develop a business plan to get out of his mess—but, in our tradition, that idea was not even considered. A kid fixing a father's problems? Not a chance! For centuries, our family had lived with inherited wealth. In a matter of years, I watched it evaporate.

Today, Hyderabad is India's Silicon Valley. Presidents Bill Clinton and George Bush both visited to witness the progress. But, at that time, the old regime was still in the midst of its long, slow decline, and I could not find work. Tea estates in the mountainous regions of India employed English-speaking young men from well-to-do families in managerial roles. So, I applied for that kind of work—but didn't get lucky. Some of my other contemporaries joined the armed forces. Not for me. Next, the obvious solution was to move to the Middle East, where booming economies were fueled with oil wealth and guest workers were needed.

I chose Saudi Arabia, where a family connection came in handy. My mother's youngest sister was married to a naturalized Saudi citizen originally from Hyderabad. The easiest way to enter the Kingdom was on a visa for the Hajj, issued through a lottery system because of strict quotas set by the Saudis. I got lucky and won a spot. My mother convinced my father to scrape up the train fare to the coast, where I caught my Hajj charter flight to Jeddah—my first air travel and the best investment my father ever made.

Saudi regulations require that foreign pilgrims must stay with their *wakil*, or authorized guide, through the course of their pilgrimage. My uncle, Khwaja Hassan, and his older son, Mahmood, technically were not allowed to pick me up at the airport. The fact that they did, and then took me home with them, was a sign of their influence. I admit that this pilgrimage was not the result of a deep desire to fulfill the fifth pillar of Islam. It was my means to finding a job. I did successfully finish the rituals of the Hajj, but I did not fly back to India.

My uncle helped me to obtain a work permit and I wound up staying for more than a year. I helped to manage a warehouse for an Italian construction company building a new highway connecting the port city of Jeddah with Medina, the holy city where the Prophet is buried. Although I was ostensibly living near the global heart of Islam, I was part of a decidedly un-Islamic community of workers. Alcohol was freely available in the construction camp—and liberally consumed when the work was done. On days off, porn movies were shown—even though they officially were taboo in the Kingdom. Also forbidden by Saudi authorities were those wonderfully lovesick Bollywood musicals. We watched them on makeshift outdoor screens, despite the rules. But, we always set up the screen in the desert, so that the movies were not visible from the highway.

I longed to go to America, if only I could save up enough Saudi riyals to finance my escape. There was no other option. My father wasn't going to pay for me to study in the U.S. There was no scholarship awaiting me at an American university. So, I scrimped and saved and counted the days until I had enough in the bank for travel costs, living expenses and a year's tuition. A close friend was enrolled at the University of Detroit. He helped me initiate the admission process to secure my I-9 student visa. Finally, I had saved enough and passed the required TOEFL (Test of English as a Foreign Language). The results on my certificate said: "Speaks in a distinctly foreign accent." I departed Jeddah for Detroit, via Beirut and London.

If this story of my life with my family in Hyderabad sounds like a fairy tale—then, you are not alone. A recent travel section in *The New York Times* compared today's "congested urban abyss" of Hyderabad with the graceful architecture, estates and gardens prior to 1948. Today, the *Times* correspondent wrote, those memories of elegance seem as implausible as legends of Atlantis. To this day, some Hyderabadi expatriates like to celebrate under the banner, "Glory of Hyderabad"—even among immigrants in major U.S. urban areas who left our princely state behind many decades ago.

I agree that there are moments of greatness in Hyderabad's history that we all should remember. Back in 1948, in that typewritten report to Nehru by the mixed-faith delegation about the atrocities during the invasion of Hyderabad, the litany of violence is heartbreaking. But, toward the end of their report, the authors included a brief account of Hyderabadis at their best. The example they chose was the courage of humble weavers. In that era, these craftsmen certainly were not aristocrats. They lived their lives far from the world of my family's enlightened European education. Yet, when the Hindu-on-Muslim violence began, the Hindu weavers of Hyderabad risked their lives to reach out and protect Muslim weavers. Despite the danger and their long-standing cultural differences, these Hindu weavers protected their fellow craftsmen. In the quaint style of the day, the report's authors called this "a silver lining to the dark clouds of communal strife."

I am not one to glorify the past, but I am always touched by stories of those who transcend the temptations of division—by people who simply act as good human beings in showing compassion to others. If I learned anything in my years in India, it was that there is no easy pathway to a good life. The fabled glories of Hyderabad included riches and elite culture as well as depths of poverty and a blindness toward the injustice of the class system. Yet, even in this land of obvious disparities, there were bonds that transcended class and faith and valued each human life. The weavers certainly showed that in the worst of times.

Ghalib would understand. He saw the potential as well as the looming dangers. In the sub-continent, his truths have not been forgotten. He has been the subject of popular movies and TV series over the years, and in December 2017—to mark his 220th birthday—Google India redesigned its home page with a tribute to Ghalib.

I like to think that if I somehow met my namesake, today, we would share kindred hearts. As he wrote in one of his most famous couplets:

Even a task that looks easy can prove to be a difficult thing!

Indeed, it's hard for any man to be a simple human being!

CHAPTER 4

All-American Pioneers

God is kind unto His servants; He provides for whomsoever He wills.
Quran 42:19

When I arrived in 1970, the Motor City had been a global destination for workers since Henry Ford announced in 1914 that he would pay an astonishing $5 for a day's work at his factory in Highland Park, now an enclave within Detroit. Three years later, just west of Detroit in Dearborn, Ford began building the River Rouge Complex, which would become the largest integrated factory in the world. Huge ships navigated the Great Lakes waterways to reach the Rouge plant, where all of the raw materials were processed to build Ford's sturdy, affordable vehicles. Ford was savvy enough to price his autos so that his own workers could afford to buy the cars they were assembling. What a deal! And—the essence of the American Dream.

Newspapers around the world heralded that $5-a-day offer. Muslims soon were among the immigrants of all races and nationalities flocking to this land of opportunity. Of course, a small number of Muslim families had moved to Michigan long before that. Syrian merchants had been settling in Detroit since the late 1800s. While most of them were Christian, some Muslim Syrians arrived as well. After Ford's offer, a new wave of Middle Eastern laborers joined them. In 1916, the automaker noted that there were more than 500 Syrians among the company's employees. The first wave clustered around Ford's Highland Park plant. Historian Sally Howell, head of the Center for Arab American Studies at the University of Michigan-Dearborn, has been documenting those early arrivals. These immigrants were intent on supporting their growing communities. Howell points out that, in 1914, Turkish immigrants already had organized a housing cooperative. The first purpose-built community mosque in the U.S. opened in Highland Park in 1921 to serve all Muslims, whatever their branch of Islam might have been back home. When Ford moved his center of operations to Dearborn, Muslim immigration followed. For decades, segregationists ruled Dearborn with an iron fist, but these Muslim immigrants from the Middle East were regarded as white. They were able to cluster in the far eastern tip of Dearborn as well as in the adjacent section of Detroit—within walking distance of the Rouge. Of course, Muslims of color also were arriving in Detroit. The city was a major destination in the Great Migration of 6 million African Americans from the South seeking new opportunities across the North. The vast majority of those black families were Christian. But among them was Elijah Poole and his family, who left their Georgia home for the promise of good jobs in Detroit. Poole settled in Hamtramck, the little city next to Highland Park that now is also an enclave within Detroit. That's why southeast Michigan became the birthplace of his Nation of Islam in the 1930s, as he became Minister Elijah Muhammad.

Despite Henry Ford's role in igniting this vast movement of migrants, he remained an outspoken bigot. Why did he hire so many minorities? Ford was such an astute industrialist that he saw the value of a diverse workforce. At first, Ford assumed he could tightly control his workers' lives. The $5 workday came with a requirement that each worker allow the company's sociological department to evaluate their living conditions, thrift and modesty. Ford also was betting that diversity would be a hedge against unions. History proved Ford wrong in both cases. The sociologists' reign didn't last long—and workers of all races and creeds learned to cooperate in a powerful union movement.

That did not mean these families lived next to each other. Despite all of the sprawling development by Ford, General Motors, Chrysler and other manufacturing companies, deep racial and ethnic divisions were enforced both legally and illegally in neighborhoods across the metropolitan area. Even though Henry Ford died in 1947, the city of Dearborn remained segregated through the 1950s and '60s. Systemic injustice was the powder keg always threatening to explode in southeast Michigan. Just three years before I started my management courses at the University of Detroit, Detroit was the battleground for one of the deadliest and most destructive civil conflicts in American history.

In 1970, as I looked across this diverse and troubled region, I saw it clearly—with all of its problems and possibilities. This was one of the world's red-hot crucibles of change. Here in Detroit, ingenuity and industry were forging a whole new world.

In Detroit, we had it all—international waterways, global industrial leaders, bare-knuckle conflicts and enclaves of world-class wealth. What an exciting place to start a new life! At least, that's how Detroit looked to an ambitious young student from India. I wanted my shot at following in the footsteps of the giants who had amassed fortunes before me. I could be part of this city's still-unfolding history. I could see clearly that Detroit's landscape would continue to change in dramatic ways in the years ahead, so I was in the right place.

The moment I began walking these streets, the very foundations of my world—from language and culture to my assumptions about others—began to shift in minor and major ways. I was open to changing right along with this city—and that started with the way I talked.

Each day was full of new lessons. In my first semester, a classmate in my MBA program asked me, "How far do you live from campus?"

"Just a furlong," I said.

He looked confused, then he explained: "I guess you might hear that word in horse racing, but no one else is going to understand that way of talking! Just say, 'a block or two.' That's how we talk about walking distances in a city here—the number of blocks."

Those kinds of lessons popped up repeatedly. My British-Indian style of speaking tripped me up, partly because I wasn't shy about putting myself out there in a public way. Like other would-be titans of business before me, I wasn't afraid of starting out with dirty hands! I knew that my savings from Saudi Arabia could only stretch so far, so I got a permit that allowed me to work a few hours each week.

I started at Willy's Boron gas station, which was walking distance from the University of Detroit (UofD). This was before the oil crises of the mid-1970s, when gas prices soared and many full-service gas stations were forced out of business. Willy was a big, gruff guy and proudly maintained a full-service station. I quickly became his No. 1 gas jockey—running to get the gas pumping, clean car windows and check that engine oil. Even pumping gas, I had an entrepreneur's eye. I knew that selling quarts of oil meant commissions and a bigger paycheck.

One busy morning, a guy walked up to me as I was bent over a car, cleaning the windshield. He looked at me anxiously and asked: "You got a john, man?"

I had no idea what he was asking, and I was busy. "No," I said, shaking my head and returning to the windshield. I thought he'd walk away.

Finishing the windshield, I turned back and saw him still standing there.

Now he was even more urgent. "I got to pee, man!"

Again, I had no idea what that meant. Slang is a steep learning curve! Finally, Big Willy caught on to what was happening and rescued both of us. He handed the guy the men's room key.

In 1970, Detroit was a checkerboard of segregated neighborhoods. Even today, half a century later, southeast Michigan still has one of the most racially divided patterns of housing in the U.S. There were many willing defenders of those separations. Since the end of World War II, the Catholic Archdiocese of Detroit had been ushering their faithful out of Detroit and into big, new parishes opening in the rural and suburban counties north of the city. The core city was falling on hard times, and most of Detroit's business leaders seemed content to rapidly rebuild their businesses in a ring of booming communities around the city.

Four years after I arrived, Coleman Young was elected Detroit's first black mayor and uttered his now-infamous Inauguration Day challenge. The context of those remarks was his pledge to get tough on urban crime. He said: "I issue an open warning to all dope pushers, to all rip-off artists, to all muggers. It is time to leave Detroit. Hit Eight Mile Road. And I don't give a damn if they are black or white, if they wear Superfly suits or blue uniforms with silver badges. Hit the road."

Fighting crime is a good thing, but that's not what suburbanites heard in Young's proclamation that day. They thought he was drawing a line in the sand around Detroit and would be hostile toward suburbanites. Misunderstandings and tensions continued for years. There were some major successes. Henry Ford II, the original automaker's grandson, opened the city's landmark Renaissance Center along the Detroit River in 1977, with Young's encouragement. And there were failures. By the 1990s, the city had lost nearly half of its peak population of the 1950s. Detroit was one of the world's most diverse metropolitan areas, but that didn't mean it was a harmonious community.

At the University of Detroit in 1970, I had the luck of landing in one of Detroit's few comfortably multicultural niches. The Jesuits who founded the school had an enduring commitment to promoting diversity. My first residence was a small, brick Victorian two blocks from campus, shared by four guys. When I first arrived, there was one surprise after another in even the smallest details of my new home. I had never seen wall-to-wall carpeting in bedrooms or a hardwood floor in a living room. From our front steps, the line of nicely maintained brick homes and neatly trimmed greenery was a delicious experience. When I walked into our backyard, I discovered unfamiliar sights: a chain-link fence and a passageway behind the house called an alley.

My roommates mirrored India's diversity. Ramesh was Hindu. Cyrus was Parsee, a people with ancient Zoroastrian roots who migrated to India more than a millennium ago. Mujahid was a somewhat observant Shia Muslim—and I was a similarly flexible Sunni. Together, we were a self-contained interfaith community. Our casual observance of our traditions made life easier. I can't recall any cultural or religious differences that arose. We all ate meat, but we agreed not to include pork in the groceries we jointly purchased each week.

We divided the household chores. Three of us cooked twice a week. And the fourth? Initially, Cyrus declared, "I don't know how to cook!" He told us he preferred to wash dishes and clean up the house, instead. That prompted us to dump all our dishes in the sink and to leave our clutter around the house—until poor Cyrus finally begged us to reconsider our arrangement. In Urdu, he cried, *"May'ray ko kha'na puck'ana sikha'tho bhai!"*

In English, that's: "Brother, teach me how to cook!"

I was familiar with this kind of friendly diversity from my school days in India. But I quickly learned enough about America's history of internal strife to appreciate the rare cooperative spirit of our interreligious living arrangements. We might not have understood many of the finer points of American culture, but we knew something valuable about successfully living together. I was beginning to appreciate some of the assets I had brought with me to this new land—and that inspiring vision of our friendly little household at UofD has stayed with me for many years.

That's not to say we never had challenges. Mujahid was a health nut and exercise freak, and we always griped that, when he did the shopping, he spent too much of our grocery budget on milk. Although he took his turn as chief cook, his idea of acceptable cuisine was hamburgers wrapped in tinfoil, thrown into the oven and claimed as his version of a kabob. Hardly! Sometimes, when Mujahid cooked, we were forced to eat out!

Yet Mujahid also was a helpful advisor. He suggested I start with three supposedly easier courses, totaling nine credits—the minimum required for full-time foreign students. As it turned out, that was all I could handle. I understood immediately that I needed help to improve my "Hinglish"— Hindi-Urdu-influenced English with its legacy of British idioms. I would continue working on that challenge for years, enrolling in courses on speech and articulation. I even completed the Dale Carnegie course to conquer my fear of public speaking.

On one hand, America seemed to welcome me with wide-open arms. I was part of the Woodstock generation, with all the freedoms that followed.

On the other hand, American culture was shockingly myopic. As the home of Hollywood-style entertainment and some of the world's most popular music and TV series, I quickly realized that the U.S. entertainment industry had a huge blind spot. American producers were only in the media export business. They paid little attention to important stories from other parts of the world, including many news events that directly affected me. At first, I didn't see the problem. American TV promptly hooked me on. I remember rushing home at night so I wouldn't miss the most popular TV series, including the wonderful variety shows of that era. I will never forget a live TV performance by Cat Stevens, before he became Yusuf Islam.

It took a while for me to understand the narrowness of the nearly all-white, middle-class slice of the world Americans were seeing night after night in their living rooms. The top 20 TV shows during my first two years in the U.S. included *Marcus Welby MD*, *Here's Lucy*, *Gunsmoke*, *Bonanza*, *Hee Haw*, *My Three Sons* and *The Mary Tyler Moore Show*. The real cutting edge for those of us concerned about diversity were Flip Wilson, who got his own TV show in 1970, and *All in the Family*, which hit the airwaves in 1971. They were rare exceptions—a narrow edge of diversity just barely cracking America's all-white prime-time vision of the world.

That tunnel vision eventually became heartbreaking for me, when Americans showed no interest in a war that was tearing apart my extended family. This was the war involving Pakistan, India and what had been the eastern half of Pakistan. In 1971, that eastern territory became Bangladesh, in a devastating war between Bengali nationalists and Pakistani forces. Sitting in Detroit, far away from my family, I looked everywhere for some media acknowledgment that people were dying and fleeing their homes. I knew that Americans loved war stories. Hollywood kept pumping out one World War II movie after another. Vietnam was on the nightly network news. But this war in my country of origin was killing thousands of vulnerable people and displacing many more—and it remained almost invisible in the U.S. This weighed heavily on my heart, because people I loved were caught up in the violence. One of my favorite cousins was shot. Then, my sister and her family found themselves interned in a POW camp. My brother-in-law had become a Pakistani citizen and had been working as a civil engineer at a power plant in Dacca when the city changed hands. Civil servants and their families were taken, along with surrendering members of the Pakistani army, to a POW camp in Allahabad. The bitter irony was that my uncle, H.U. Begg, was chief justice of the Provincial High Court in the region where the camp was located—and even he was powerless to pull them out of that prison. The details of this conflict were complex—perhaps too complex for American TV producers to turn into a neat little capsule on the nightly news. Most Americans remained unaware of the conflict, until George Harrison and his friend Ravi Shankar organized a huge benefit concert for Bangladesh in New York City in the summer of 1971. At least their young American fans began to learn about the conflict.

For many immigrants like me, living in the U.S. was a painful awareness of our adopted country's blind spots. This was a land of enormous opportunities—and equally huge challenges. For the most part, other than my anxiety over the tragedy in Bangladesh, I rolled with the prevailing culture in those days. Among my friends at the University of Detroit, I gained a reputation as an outgoing guy who enjoyed socializing with other young people, no matter their ethnic origin or background.

Then, in 1972, I found myself attracted to a girl from home. A beautiful girl, named Lata, sat down in my accounting class in her sari and caught my eye.

I didn't waste time. I walked up to her and said, "Hi."

A fellow classmate pulled me aside and warned, "She's married."

"How do you know?" I whispered.

"Look at her forehead," he said. He had seen Lata's bindi, the dot on her forehead, and assumed it was a sign of marriage. In fact, that's not universally the case. Bindis have a long spiritual tradition in Hinduism aside from marriage. And I certainly wasn't shy, so I didn't go away.

I pursued a conversation with her, getting directly to the point. "What does your husband do?" I asked.

Fortunately, she didn't take offense at my pointed question. She looked at me with her greenish eyes and clarified, "I'm single."

We got to know each other, and our friendship grew into love. Lata lived with her brother, Ramesh, in Oak Park, a small suburb not far from UofD. Ramesh was a well-established aeronautical engineer and felt responsible for Lata, like a father.

When I found out that Lata was eager to learn to drive, I offered lessons. Ramesh liked that idea, too, because he had been chauffeuring her to school. Soon, she was behind the wheel of a junky old car Ramesh owned, even though its license plates had expired. She began driving it back and forth to school, even though it made her anxious any time she took that heap out onto the streets. One day, she was driving home and spotted a police cruiser approaching from the opposite direction. Expecting to hear a siren wailing and lights flashing at any moment, her eyes were glued to that cruiser. As the police drove past, her eyes zeroed in on the image of that car in her rear-view mirror. What would those officers do? That's how she ran straight into a utility pole. Her radiator was shot! She was too afraid to even call her brother and admit what had happened.

She called me for help.

I rang Ramesh. "Lata was driving down McNichol and had an accident." I continued, trying my best to add a little wit to the somber news. "No fault of hers! A pole ran into her car." Not everyone found it funny.

While it obviously wasn't wise to be driving an unlicensed car, that's the kind of corners we all cut in those hand-to-mouth days as students. I can't recall banking any savings while I was at UofD. I didn't have funds for health insurance. To pay the bills, I was outside pumping gas and cleaning windshields until the Michigan winter finally forced me to look for indoor work.

What I found was a much warmer job washing dishes and busing tables at the 24 Carat Club on a main highway, Telegraph Road. The Lebanese-American owner booked bands and a floorshow, so it became a hotspot for couples. Once again, I learned that the key to success was speed and efficiency. I was so good at cleaning tables and keeping water glasses full that servers fought over me. There is always something to learn wherever you work, so at the 24 Carat Club, I befriended the old bartender, Bill. He taught me about cocktails—drinks I'd never heard of with names that sounded so exotic to me: Manhattan, Black Russian, Grasshopper, Screwdriver.

Then, I got another rude reminder that surprises never stop in America, especially in Detroit! One day, I showed up for work and the club was gone—quite literally. Only the charred remains were left. I never did learn how that club burned down, but I was out of work without warning.

UofD's placement center helped me to find what I assumed would be a much better opportunity at the Chrysler Foundry in Warren, just north of Detroit. My eyes were focused on the $8 an hour I could earn on the assembly line—big money for me! I could also boast to friends in business school that I had landed a job with the Big Three, never needing to mention my humble job classification. No special skills were required. My shift started at 6 a.m.—an ungodly hour for a university student—but I wanted that paycheck. On the first day, I got up very early and made it to the plant on Mound Road, punching the clock on time. I was already planning how I would spend my first fat paycheck.

I was guided to a position on the line and told that I would insert a pin into each engine mold that passed my station. I couldn't conceive how these parts might function inside a car. The materials in front of me looked like lumps of metal, but I knew the supervisor had not hired me as an engineer. I was content to perform my repetitive motion. Everything ran smoothly for a couple of hours. I sat on a metal stool as I inserted my pins. Then, my butt and forefinger began to hurt. My finger turned pink. My mind was numbing, too, from the relentlessly noisy rhythm of the production line. I was restless and aching, trapped on that stool. My ears began ringing. Walking around to get some relief wasn't permitted until a brief break every couple of hours to hit the john or sip a drink. I rubbed and even sucked on my finger, trying to relieve the discomfort. Instead of soothing the pain, my finger began to turn blue. As a drastic measure, I wrapped some duct tape around the finger, which didn't help at all. By the end of my first day, it was a relief simply to walk outside and suck in a deep breath of fresh air!

I certainly wasn't afraid of hard work, but the next day my finger was so swollen, I couldn't go to work. I hated to let $8 an hour slip away from me, but I had no choice. I stayed home, skipping my shift. By the next day, I still wasn't ready to go back, so I decided to call in sick.

I dialed the factory. "I'm *siiiick*," I said, trying to convey my condition in that one drawn-out word. I gave my name and said, "I work the 6 a.m. shift."

My dramatic skill at conveying my illness was completely lost on the woman at the other end of the phone line. She did not know me. She could not even seem to locate my employee information, which could be a real challenge before computer networks. She asked questions and I tried to answer, but my Hinglish and her Detroit slang didn't mesh. I repeatedly tried to correct her spelling of my name. She complained, accusing me of mumbling.

On and on this miscommunication went until she found my file. "According to this, you *used* to work here," she said.

That was the end of my career in the automobile industry. I had survived one day.

In my next visit to the student placement center, an advertisement caught my attention: "Earn $5,000 this summer and also qualify for a college scholarship!"

I eagerly wrote down that number! Trotting back to my apartment, I made the call and heard four words: "Good afternoon. Electrolux. Louise."

Today, the idea of selling vacuum cleaners door to door might sound like the punch line to a bad joke—a non-starter on most people's list of prospective jobs. In fact, Electrolux began selling vacuums from its base in

Sweden just after World War I and, to this day, remains a big player in the home-appliance industry, with dozens of brand names around the world. But Electrolux had not been a well-known brand in my part of India.

The truth is: The morning I carefully donned my button-down shirt and tie and polished my shoes for the interview, I didn't have a clue what Electrolux sold.

That first day, Louise greeted me with a smile. She introduced me to the store manager, Dave, a big guy with a square pink face and short grey-ing hair. In front of him was a low, shiny, cylindrical machine with little wheels that seemed to be hugging the carpet. A long hose was attached to one end. The other end was in Dave's hand. Showing all his teeth as he smiled at me, he reminded me of a standup comedian about to perform. I wanted that job, whatever Electrolux was selling. For his part, Dave didn't ask me a single question about my qualifications, experience or interests. He simply shook my hand in a friendly way, waiting for me to introduce myself.

That was a challenge. I took a deep breath. "I'm Ghalib," I said.

No reaction at all. Dave didn't seem to have a clue what I had just said—so I repeated my name and, this time, I spelled it.

Still, it was clear he had no idea what I was saying. So, I said my name a third time.

Nope! This time, I spelled it—*very slowly.*

Ultimately, I caught on that Dave didn't care who I was or what I called myself. I was simply the latest prospective salesman. I don't think he ever understood my name, but soon he was performing his act.

A handful of dirt was scattered across the carpeting, ready for Dave to demonstrate "the spectacular cleaning power of the Electrolux!" Right on cue, that dirt disappeared into the machine's belly.

But, wait! There was so much more. "Lower your head please," Dave instructed.

Having no idea what came next, I bowed my head. Dave popped a special attachment onto the end of the long hose and began to vacuum my scalp!

What was happening? Dave showed me. A fine screen inside the vac-uum attachment caught dandruff, which I didn't know I had. Amazing!

Then, Dave hit me with the punch line: The job opening was for a door-to-door salesman. Not until that moment had I dreamed that such a job existed! But I needed money and I suspected that I had a talent for sales. I tried not to look as astonished as I was and that must have worked, because I passed Dave's inspection.

I was turned over for further training to Roy, a rotund, bald-headed man. I wondered: Had he demonstrated that scalp-suction trick too many times?

The moment we met, I discovered that Roy had a very discerning eye. He could read people and he could tell that I was skeptical. Roy suggested that I ride along with him to see the potential in this line of work.

"What have you got to lose?" he asked.

This began to sound like an adventure. I also immediately learned another lesson: Never assume you know a person's talents or limitations until you see them in action. As it turned out, Roy was a retired automotive engineer who was an expert salesman. In that first day's training mission, he sold a machine and Roy generously put my name on the sales report. At that time, a $295 sale paid $95 in commission to the salesman. I was hooked!

Roy became a good friend, like an uncle. Roy's introduction to the salesman's lifestyle suited me perfectly. I liked the independence—working out and about and keeping my own schedule.

Knowing I was used to living a student's life, Roy sometimes went out of his way to help me. I still remember his voice in a morning phone call: "Are you up, Mr. Begg?" He was a wonderful mentor and encouraged me to attend a series of morning sessions at which salespeople described their selling experiences and lessons learned.

That whole summer, I drove my little old Ford Cortina around affluent suburban neighborhoods, knocking on doors, talking to housewives, and offering to clean their carpets. I was discovering a whole array of talents.

One of those talents was adaptability. The confusion over my name, when I was first introduced to Dave, haunted me frequently. I realized that I was wasting time essentially having to sell my name before I even started selling my machines. Not everyone had a problem with my name. In Jewish neighborhoods with a background in Hebrew and Yiddish, the guttural "gh" in Ghalib was a familiar sound. I was reminded that, despite our differences, there are a lot of connections that bind us as people of faith. But most Americans could not seem to make their mouths produce the "gh" sound. They would stumble. I would repeat. With real regret, I had to admit that my given name was a barrier, and I began introducing myself as "Victor." That moved the focus immediately from establishing my identity to demonstrating the vacuum that I was confident I could sell. To this day, I am sad that I gave up Ghalib at that point in my life—but it was the right thing to do from a salesman's point of view. The moment I made the change, the benefits were obvious. Even at the home office, Dave had taken to calling me "Buddy," or sometimes a more formal "Mr. Begg." Now, he was happy to greet me as "Victor."

I soon caught on to all of the opportunities in this trade. Beyond making an individual sale, customers could help me expand the business if they were willing to recommend a friend or relative for me to visit. I also realized that my commissions grew if I sold additional supplies, like vacuum cleaner bags.

In three summer months, I sold more than $10,000 worth of machines and accessories. On top of my commissions and bonuses, my sales record won a $500 bonus toward my university fees. A corporate newsletter featured my picture: a smiling young man with a full head of shoulder-length, dark, curly hair, wearing the official company blazer that I had earned as another perk of the job. Proudly, I mailed a copy of the article to my parents back home.

I laughed over my father's reply: "You look like a *wahshi*," which meant "wild man." Friends and relatives back in India could never understand how I could be so proud of what they considered a silly thing to do. Some thought this kind of work was demeaning, others thought it was hilarious.

I was proud of my accomplishments and my appearance. I thought my hair was stylish. My new job had boosted my confidence in talking to people. I learned how to engage strangers in a conversation, to hustle to make the sale and even to push a bit to close the deal, if things looked shaky.

During those early years, I sold a lot of products—even insurance, at one point. Later, I sold management consulting for what is now George S. May International.

My most unusual job was analyzing costs and potential profits for Mr. Ansari, the owner of an Indian grocery store. He was considering a deal to produce roti, Indian flat bread. In that case, I also got UofD class credit for the project. Initially, this seemed like a good idea. Roti is a staple in an Indian diet. What I learned is that Mr. Ansari would have to sell a whole lot of roti before he could expect a decent return on his investment. Indian cuisine was not as popular and widespread as it has become today. Mr. Ansari thanked me and dropped the idea. I was paid in free groceries, which helped with my meager household budget. More importantly, Mr. Ansari gave me my first experience getting up on stage at public events, because he and his wife had a secondary activity sponsoring popular Indian movie stars and singers to come to the Detroit area. I agreed to organize Bollywood movie nights and other events at the campus theater for the Ansaris through the Indian student organization, where I was an active member. Sometimes, I served as emcee and became more comfortable working with a crowd.

After I graduated from UofD in March 1974, I was hired by an international lumber company to revamp their accounting systems, which were outdated and relied on old-fashioned machines. When I dove into that new assignment, I looked at the challenge ahead of me and thought: Now you've landed in a real mess! I was the first to begin automating their systems, although today's computer networks were not yet available. In that era, my major step was moving from manual bookkeeping machines to electronic equipment. Working with two staff members, we vastly improved the accounting department—to the point that management doubled sales by keeping a tighter control on the company's financial systems. That experience mainly convinced me that I had to become an entrepreneur myself. As I watched the executives' annual incomes rise dramatically, I knew that I didn't want to remain a glorified bookkeeper.

The other huge influence on my decision to leap into starting a business was Lata, who chose the new name Shahina as she wholeheartedly accepted Islam. I had not asked her to do that. Neither one of us was especially observant at the time, but she told me that it was right thing to do so that we could raise our children in a harmonious household.

As it turned out, navigating our cross-cultural, interfaith union took some careful planning. First, we had a private *nikah* (Islamic wedding), officiated by my old friend Syed Salman on a park bench in the presence of my sister and brother-in-law. Then, since her parents were coming from India to bless our union—and we already had friends from every religious background—we scheduled a civil marriage. We did not want anyone to feel left out. What became our "family wedding" was a prophetic sign of the interfaith work that both of us would pursue in the years ahead. Shahina lived in Oak Park, which has a sizeable Jewish community. So, our new Hindu and Muslim family members came together at a civil ceremony in 1975 conducted by the Jewish mayor of Oak Park.

We had our first child, Sami, four years later.

Toward the end of that year, Shahina and I agreed that it was time to start a business. My catalytic role at the lumber company had convinced both of us that I needed to be at the helm of our next business, not just a part of someone else's crew. To this day, I am thankful Shahina has been such a solid partner, supporting the daring decisions we have made. More than once in those early years, we packed up all our belongings and moved to a new home—enormous challenges we both accepted.

I can still remember Shahina sitting next to me in our car, with our worldly possessions loaded up for yet another move—my green card in hand and major risks ahead of us down the road we had chosen to travel.

From the start, we were a family of all-American pioneers.

CHAPTER 5

Naked Furniture

He taught the youth the need of industry;
He taught the public mind the need of art;
He taught the narrow soul the need of heart;
He taught the land the need of loyalty.

An epitaph for lumber baron Charles Hackley in 1905

Long before Michigan became world-famous as the realm of automakers, our Great Lakes State was known as the land of lumber barons. To this day, tourists travel to mid-Michigan to tour the lumber barons' mansions just as they travel to metro Detroit for tours of automotive landmarks. From the moment the Old and New World collided in 1492, European hopes were fueled by gold fever. Early Spanish explorers in the New World were able to grab relatively little of that precious metal in South America—but the North American colonists struck it rich with their own "green" Gold Rush. This new continent's old-growth forests seemed limitless, at a time when Europe desperately needed wood to build ships and could find few suitable forests left on their continent. America quickly became known as the place for European businessmen to shop for everything from quality planks to some of the best ship masts on the planet. The strike-it-rich lumber boom spread westward across North America, along with the ever-expanding settlements of European immigrants.

Michigan's lumber barons arrived at the Great Lakes well before the Civil War. By the end of that conflict, Michigan was poised to produce more lumber than any other state in the U.S. The state's official tree, the white pine, was a bonanza for those early companies. Some white pines were more than 200 years old and stood ramrod straight—sometimes 200 feet tall! Trunks could measure 5 feet in diameter. The best thing about

Michigan's lumber industry was that land in the 1800s sometimes was as cheap as pennies per acre.

Like me, these lumber barons were risk-takers who were not afraid to get their hands dirty. Charles Hackley's family was so poor that, as a boy, he had to spend as many hours working as attending school. Eventually he became a carpenter, then he worked repairing public roads, which at that time were made of planks. He got a job on a lumber crew in Michigan and finally risked everything to start his own lumber company. Hackley lived long enough to amass a huge fortune—and to see Michigan's vast forests completely cut down. But, also like me, Hackley always believed that his calling ultimately was to contribute to a healthy community. Hackley gave millions back to his adopted home of Muskegon. Before his death in 1905, he had built schools, a hospital, a library, an art gallery and a public park.

When I arrived in Michigan, full of ambition, I shared one more essential quality with the would-be barons before me. We were young dreamers—and our dreams were as big as the state!

I boasted that I would make my first million by age 40.

When I launched my entrepreneurial career, I was 32. Shahina and I had both worked full time after leaving school, so we had managed to save $50,000. I realized that I was never going to make it in the auto industry. Other than my one ill-fated day on the assembly line, I knew nothing about manufacturing autos. But my work in the finance department of a lumber company had given me some perspective on that industry. So, I drove to Lansing, Michigan's capital, and registered my first enterprise: International Forest Products, Inc. I also opened a commercial account, depositing our life savings in the National Bank of Detroit.

More than a century ago, lumber barons lived and worked right in the Great Lakes State. Unfortunately, Michigan's "green" Gold Rush had panned out long ago. Decades after Michigan was clear-cut, foresters did replant millions of trees across both of Michigan's vast peninsulas; today, our forests are popular tourist destinations. But, from a business perspective, only tiny patches of old-growth forest remain in Michigan. By the time I launched my career, the forest industry had moved far to the West.

To jump into the lumber industry in the mid-1970s, I flew first to Canada's lumber capital: Vancouver, British Columbia. I enrolled in a seminar on the forest industry and visited lumber mills. My earlier work in the industry had been limited to the business offices. So, I made a grand sweep of all points in my new venture. I traveled next to Seattle, where I explored American shipping alternatives to Asia-Pacific countries. That looked very expensive, complicated and downright too risky without well-established customers. I decided that I should start closer to home by selling lumber in the Caribbean market. From Seattle, I traveled deeper into the heart of America's lumber country. In Oregon, I met with a Potlach Corp. sales manager and arranged to purchase a trailer-load of lumber for export to Trinidad. I put my order on hold, with a final shipping address to be confirmed later.

Starting a new business, I had to understand every part of my supply chain, so I flew to Trinidad. Trinidad and Tobago had gained independence from Great Britain in 1962 and, at that time, was known as a booming center of the Caribbean economy. Everyone seemed to be interested in new construction on the islands, so my supplies were needed. I had no idea what connections I could make in these islands, but kismet was in play. On the plane, I met a Muslim businessman returning home to the islands from an Islamic convention in the U.S. I still wasn't especially religious, but we became friends on that flight and he offered to introduce me to a lumberyard owner he knew. At his invitation, I also wound up at a mosque shortly after we landed. There I met more Muslims, including the owner of Nabi's Hardware Store, who promptly placed an order and gave me valuable background on doing business in the islands. Within a few days, I had sold my entire trailer-load of Oregon pine. So far, smooth sailing!

I had invested more than half of our life savings in this one shipment, which covered the cost of material and transportation. At that time, international banking was far different than it is today. I had to settle for an unsecured sight draft, which meant that I had to trust the buyer to pay upon receipt of the merchandise. My strong drive for a business startup drove me to take unreasonable risks like this. I was so intensely focused on establishing a business that nothing was going to stop me.

Returning to the U.S., I arranged to ship the goods on barges from the Port of Savannah, Georgia, to the Port of Spain, Trinidad. After the load left the Oregon mill, I received the shocking news that my shipping company had shut down. I nearly had a heart attack! This was my first big gamble—and disaster was looming. Under the terms of my agreement, this shipment could wind up going back to Oregon with no refund. Shahina and I could be facing ruin without ever having made a sale!

Frantically researching solutions, I found that my trailer of lumber could be rerouted while already in transit to Halifax on Canada's eastern seaboard. Although more costly than my original plan, that port was my only shipping alternative. In the midst of this crisis, my friends' secure jobs with well-established companies suddenly started to look very inviting. As I look back, I was taking crazy risks. I had not even figured out how to get health insurance for my family. But I knew that starting a new business takes more guts than money. Achieving the American Dream is not for weak hearts.

Deeply worried, I was turning toward my faith in a new way. I was thankful that I could count on Shahina as a bedrock of support. Prophet Muhammad's wife Khadijah had supported him when he faced insurmountable crises. Together, they endured hardships with patience. After a long time of ignoring prayer, I found myself praying once again. God listened. The journey of that lumber to its destination was sheer agony as I awaited news at each stage of the shipment. Eventually, the load reached the barge and headed to the islands. I began the long wait to see if payment would actually be made. When the money arrived, I had made a substantial profit on the deal. That confidence pushed me to expand.

However, the high stakes of my first venture came into glaring focus when I met with an officer of the National Bank of Detroit. I thought I was arriving at that meeting with a solid plan of a functioning business and a splendid future. Instead, the man scoffed at me. My reliance on sight drafts was far too risky, he told me. I was deflated. Angry. I assumed my business was on the verge of taking off. He left me rudderless. I had hoped to export a whole series of these loads from the Northwest, turning a handsome profit on each one. Without financial backing, I would have to resort to one agonizing shipment after another, which was no way to build a company.

At that time, Shahina was in India with little Sami, enjoying an extended visit with family we had not seen since our wedding. I took that opportunity to head toward India myself, stopping off in Kuwait along the way. Perhaps I could strike a deal to ship lumber to the Middle East.

Immediately, I ran into a disappointing legacy of predatory American businessmen before me. The Kuwaitis I met didn't trust any Americans. They showed me a pile of bad lumber that an American company had unloaded for a quick profit. Instead, Kuwaitis bought most of their wood from Russia and Eastern Europe. I could see a real opportunity in the region, because the quality of the hardwood and the technology of the American lumber industry had far surpassed the government-run industries of the Soviet Bloc. After the disastrous clear-cutting policies of the 1800s, the American forest industry had developed renewable practices that will keep our green gold flowing forever. But I was not able to overcome that long-simmering distrust in Kuwait and couldn't make a deal. I left for India, empty-handed. America's main concern seemed to be exporting arms to the Middle East instead of our other national products.

We celebrated Sami's first birthday in Hyderabad at my parents' home. When we returned to the U.S., we settled back into Oak Park, which had a vibrant Jewish community with an ethnic and religious diversity that we liked.

I scrambled to make use of my accumulated knowledge. I talked with the owner of a Detroit lumber business about expanding his business overseas. I met with one executive after another. I was a talented salesman and I had a solid proposal based on trends in the lumber industry and emerging markets, but no one seemed to be buying. The 1970s had been rocked by one financial crisis after another. Everyone was talking about "stagflation," an economic meltdown in which inflation is high, economic growth slows and unemployment soars. As usual, when the American economy was in trouble, Detroit got the worst of it.

I had not even considered a retail business until I ran across Naked Furniture, a franchise operation that intrigued me because it was closely related to the lumber industry. In marketing, the word "naked" had a daring, catchy appeal. I ignored what else it may imply; it was amusing to some, but interesting to others. The company's basic concept—selling furniture without a finish—had a solid connection with the popular do-it-yourself home décor trend in that era. I began analyzing this niche in the market, visiting similar stores, observing customers, studying the displays of merchandise, and weighing costs vs. potential revenue. In my gut, I could see that this was my shot at that American Dream.

I visited the franchise office in Naperville, near Chicago, where I met with Michael Busch. For years, Michael retold the story of our first meeting to prospective franchisees: "Victor bought the franchise before I finished my sales presentation."

That's true. I had done my due diligence and my ambition was sky-high. I decided to build my own retail furniture chain, so I negotiated a lock on franchise royalty payments and rights to the Detroit market for five years. I put all of our savings into the new venture, borrowing a little from a cousin.

Although I was aggressive, I wasn't foolish. My MBA training had taught me to keep the overhead low to reach the break-even point as quickly as possible. I found a location, negotiating a couple of months of free rent with new carpeting and painting as part of the deal. I minimized my startup costs—and that began with staffing. I decided not to hire anyone, at first.

To build a sales counter, the carpenter I contacted wanted a small fortune. So, I decided to tackle that challenge, as well. The problem was: I had about as much talent in woodworking as I had in auto manufacturing. I purchased a workbench and an electric saw, preparing to trim a big sheet of wood for the counter. Instead, I promptly managed to saw my workbench in half! I had to find some metal plates and jerry-rig the workbench before I could begin again. Even though I had no aptitude for the work, I produced a masterpiece: a uniquely designed sales counter in unfinished, aromatic cedar. On the back wall, I displayed our "Shop Naked" T-shirts in a variety of colors. When the president of the franchise operation visited our store, he decided to recommend that basic design to his shops nationwide. My first and last carpentry project made me proud.

In April 1981, we opened our doors with mixed feelings. That store—from the new merchandise on display to the stacks of inventory in the back—represented our life savings. I have to admit that I still was not observant enough as a Muslim to ask God to bless this new venture. Fortunately, God looked after us. One savvy early step I had taken was purchasing space in the Yellow Pages long before our opening day, scheduling that ad buy for an edition that hit front porches just about the time we opened. Before the internet, the Yellow Pages was a shopper's bible.

The first customer who walked through our doors announced that she had found us in the Yellow Pages. She bought two room dividers, a total sale of $700, and we loaded up the merchandise.

"I had seen these room dividers in another store," she told us, "but in the phone book I found that you were closer."

I was thrilled. On our first day, we made a big sale—and had taken that sale from a competitor. We would become a force in the market. The dream was realizing.

With no employees at first, Shahina and I both worked at the store. I traded a Mustang I loved for a cargo van that doubled as our delivery vehicle. Each day, as we closed the store, we would pick up Sami from day care and deliver furniture. Shahina even helped me carry furniture into our customers' homes. That was no easy task! I remember one delivery of a heavy dresser that had to be lifted up a tight stairway to a third-floor apartment. The man had paid for us to deliver that dresser, so he stood to one side as Shahina and I struggled all the way—straining at every step. I could see tears in Shahina's eyes from the heavy load. But we both knew: That was our business and business wasn't easy.

We worked the customers as a team. I already knew how to make a sale, but I quickly discovered that Shahina had talent, too. As customers walked through the door, she would flash a broad, welcoming smile—a silent pitch that worked as well as any verbal patter. She also made a point of remembering our customers' names. If someone returned to the store, her warm, personal greeting was all that was needed to make a second sale. She did that naturally—and I understood its value from my Dale Carnegie course, where we were taught that greeting people by name is the sweetest sound to their ears.

The course also taught us various mnemonic tricks to remember names, but I didn't have the knack for that. I remember a customer, Lisa, who told me point-blank: "Just remember Mona Lisa."

When she turned up a second time, I did remember—or so I thought. I called out, "Hi, Mona!"

Shahina and I were a good team. In addition to the trademark "naked" pieces, we also offered custom finishing in the customer's choice of colors. Initially, Shahina enjoyed that part of the business—she had a talent for that, as well. That wasn't my skill. Never, in my entire career with the stores, did I agree to finish a piece of furniture—with one exception.

Once, a customer who was buying a bench insisted. "I want Victor to finish it for me," he declared—and wouldn't budge.

To make the sale, I agreed.

He returned to pick up the finished piece. "What do you think?" I asked.

He carefully eyed that bench, looked back at me, inspected the finish and shook his head. He was a friendly fellow, so he weighed his answer carefully. At length, he said, "Well, I plan to use it in my garage. Where it's headed, it'll do fine."

I learned my lesson. My experience as a finisher was also as brief as my tenure on the auto assembly line. As we expanded to multiple locations, we would set up a full finishing shop with a staff of skilled craftsmen—but that was down the road.

Our first employee was Roy—the ace Electrolux salesman who had been so kind to me that summer I sold door to door. Roy loved all aspects of the business. Some of the furniture arrived in pieces and he happily assembled them. He was so helpful that he even took some projects home and finished them in his garage.

For the first year, both Shahina and I worked for the store day and night. We brought some of little Sami's toys into a play area we set up in the back room. He was just old enough that occasionally he would toddle out onto the sales floor. He liked to ask customers, "Are you looking for anything in particular?" A preschooler with a talent for sales!

Shahina and I both were experienced in managing business accounts, but it was not until we sat down at tax time, at the end of our first year, that we realized: We've done very well!

That meant it was time to set up a second store. Shortly after Ronald Reagan took office in January 1981, the last of the price controls of the 1970s were phased out. Over the next year, the economy seemed to be booming again. I was able to secure a reasonable lease for a much bigger store in Sterling Heights, a growing suburb north of Detroit. To get the new store off on solid footing, I used a General Electric (GE) inventory financing program, which paid for shipments and gave me 90 days to pay off GE, with no interest. That meant I could open the new store on cash flow. My only initial outlay was for some fixtures, signage and the cost of the launch. This time, I hired a carpenter to make the sales counter.

I was on a roll. Having two locations spread across the metro-Detroit area made regional advertising affordable. My initial decision to negotiate a cap on franchise royalties now turned out to have been an especially smart move. As our operations grew, both the franchise fees and royalty rates would have risen, as well, if I had not nailed down that cap.

In 1983, I took my mom to visit my father's grave at the Roseland Park Cemetery on Woodward Avenue, the major northwest artery from Detroit's waterfront into the suburbs of prosperous Oakland County. Near the cemetery, just four miles north of Detroit in Royal Oak, I spotted a "for lease" sign in a storefront. I leased that building with a first-right-of-refusal option to buy if the owner ever received a written offer to purchase the site. As it turned out, I had to exercise that right and, in the end, became a commercial property owner. That was our third location, and it launched with our most successful grand opening so far. As sales rose, we achieved the highest sales volume in the entire franchise chain.

I remembered from my earlier experience with the lumber company that controlling financial systems was the key to optimizing sales. As early as 1982, I invested in an IBM computer with two floppy disks, plus an inventory program and spreadsheet. It was inefficient, but we had started to computerize our data. We added a central warehouse, office space, and the centralized custom-finishing operation. When a more robust computer system became available, with terminals for each store, I bought and installed it myself.

Finally, I decided that while we had outlets in three regions of the metro area—north, east and west—we needed a southern location, and Dearborn looked ideal to me. An old building on Michigan Avenue became available, with a showroom on the first floor and four apartments on the second. I purchased it at a bargain price, and upgraded it to bring the building up to code. It turned out to be a profitable real estate deal, with rental revenues from the apartments covering a good portion of the overhead.

While Naked Furniture was expanding, my competition seemed to be retreating. I considered four other companies my competitors when I first opened in Farmington. Over the years, two of them closed and a third owner approached me about buying his holdings. He operated out of a large facility with huge inventory. I bought the building and the operation. I realigned the products with much lower inventory and display space. The rest of the building was divided up and rented out. In addition to my role as furniture baron, I was now becoming a regional real estate mogul. At our peak, I had five company-owned stores. There also was a franchised store in Ann Arbor. Naked Furniture became a household name—and regional advertising dollars paid off.

Wherever I go, I tell people that America rewards hard work, ambition, drive and willingness to sacrifice. I believe that no other country in the world would have offered these wide-open opportunities to a newcomer. I had achieved my American Dream at age 36, four years ahead of the target age of 40.

In 1984, Sami was ready for school and we wanted to ensure he was in a top-ranked school district. Shahina and I bought a hilltop residence in Bloomfield Hills. Yusuf, our second son, was born the year we moved to the bigger house. Sofi, our daughter, was born a year and half later. Eventually, my mother moved in with us.

Like other successful business pioneers before me, the relentless pressure took its toll. Shahina and I often spent nearly every day at the warehouse—including evenings. We were making money, but we were unable to enjoy it. I also was diagnosed with ulcerative colitis, which my doctor described as a Western disorder sparked by stress.

The national office of Naked Furniture had set up a central warehousing system in Chicago and offered to supply that service for our stores—at a fee. We ran the numbers, and the cost of running my own warehouse system turned out to be higher than having someone else do the job. The centralized system also meant that our stores would have access to a substantially broader stock compared to my own, much-smaller inventory. The arrangement also would free up some cash and save the headache of buying, warehousing and distributing to our stores. With that deal, Shahina and I could now afford to enjoy our family and focus on managing a retail chain, not a distribution center.

The Great Lakes also were calling me. As a student in the early 1970s, boats cruising up and down the Detroit River fascinated me. I dreamt of owning one someday. With the reduced workload, we were able to purchase a 28-foot cruiser with enough time to actually enjoy it. Among other adventures, we used the cruiser to take our kids to Cedar Point, an amusement park on the shores of Lake Erie. The kids would spend three days in the park, until they had had enough of the rides. Then, we could cruise to other favorite spots like Put-in-Bay and Kelleys Island.

Of course, my life-long affliction was always wanting more. I always dreamed of expanding, and I caught the disease that, along the Great Lakes, we call "2-foot-itis." That's a perennial desire to keep exchanging boats to gain "just another 2 feet." I was so vulnerable that we wound up with a 40-footer, complete with three staterooms, a full galley, a command bridge and two inboard diesel engines. At that point, we could explore the Great Lakes' many treasures at our leisure. For a while, I dreamed of sailing all the way from Michigan to Florida in a grand two-year cruise—a plan that never materialized.

My love of the Great Lakes also collided with the ominous dawn of the 21st century. Until 9/11/2001, I could hop on my boat, cruise across the river to a Canadian marina restaurant and then quickly pop back across the river. After 9/11, new security measures ended that easy life on the Detroit River.

Over the years, that red-hot trend of do-it-yourself furniture finishing cooled off considerably. We also rode the ups and downs of Detroit's auto industry, sometimes rising and sometimes sinking with the unemployment rate. Global trade played a role, as well, with cheap wood—and wood-like products—flowing in from China and other points in the East. Eventually, the IKEA concept of inexpensive, almost-disposable furniture caught on with young adults, replacing their parents' taste for quality hardwood furniture that would last through the generations. I closed one store, then another. My real estate holdings kept me in the black as I downsized. Then, I wound up with a single store. I was getting older, too—and my focus was moving from my own business interests to helping the entire community. After 33 years in business, we locked up our last store in 2014.

The *Detroit Free Press*, the statewide newspaper, published a huge color photo and a story chronicling my career. It was a nice farewell for a furniture baron.

CHAPTER 6

Path of the Pen

The pen is mightier than the sword.
Assyrian sage Ahiqar in 7th Century BC

Read!
Your Lord, Most Generous, Who taught by the pen.
Quran 96:3-4

As my investments across southeast Michigan grew, I naturally became a community leader, interacting with all of the issues that well-established business owners encounter in a major metropolitan area. Looking back, I know that God also was guiding me along a path as a peacemaker and an advocate for justice. Step by step, I found myself reaching out to neighbors, cooperating with other local leaders and making a contribution toward building a healthier, diverse community. But I see the steps in that pathway now in the clarity of hindsight. At the time I took my first steps toward such activism, I was not particularly observant as a Muslim. World events—one after another—seemed to almost accidentally push me toward my eventual calling.

My first decade in America was marked by many challenges because of my immigrant roots. My foreign origins were obvious to anyone I met from my manner of speaking. Then, in early 1979, the Shah of Iran was sent into exile—and, throughout that year, Ayatollah Khomeini's followers unleashed what they called an Islamic Revolution. On November 4 that year, Americans suddenly were riveted to the latest news from Iran as a mob, calling themselves "Muslim students," stormed the U.S. Embassy in Tehran and took 52 hostages. I will never forget the daily broadcasts by Ted Koppel on ABC's Nightline, counting the number of days our diplomats remained imprisoned. Suddenly—in the eyes of my neighbors—my

Muslim faith eclipsed all other aspects of my identity.

Can you even recall the world before that stormy autumn of 1979? Can you remember—or perhaps envision, from accounts in history books—the terrifying era of the Cold War? You may have seen videos of American school children performing "duck and cover" drills in their classrooms to prepare for an atomic attack. On many classroom walls hung world maps indicating which nations were "free" and which were caught "behind the Iron Curtain." The globe had been reduced to a chessboard with two sides. On one side were the Soviets, and across the board were American allies. All that mattered, beyond our U.S. borders, was supporting our American friends—and confronting the Soviet Bloc. The Berlin Wall wasn't torn down until 1989.

Most Westerners had not even considered Islam as an emerging global force before 1979. "Islamophobia" was an unknown word. For many years, the U.S. government was willing to support Muslim militias—as long as they were fighting Soviet forces. In Afghanistan, we actively backed armed militias that we regarded as courageous *mujahidin*. People around the world were still weighing news events on a Cold War fulcrum well into the 1990s.

Watching anti-shah protests unfolding in Iran in 1978 and early 1979, global responses were mixed and colored by the Cold War anxiety. I agreed with many other Westerners in that the Iranian people had lots of grievances against the shah. In fact, even as his regime was crumbling around him, the shah lashed out publicly at the BBC news network because its reporters seemed to openly encourage the protests against his regime. It was obvious to people around the world that the American CIA had been meddling in that country for years. We had been propping up the shah's U.S.-friendly puppet regime—even though he was guilty of excesses on many levels.

Events in the autumn of 1979 took this revolution in directions that deeply disturbed Americans, myself included. I was outraged—even as a cultural Muslim with little spiritual commitment to the faith at that point. I certainly knew that our Islamic principles of justice forbid the humiliating mistreatment of diplomats that we were watching on our TV screens week after week. As a result of this jarring juxtaposition of violence and counter claims about Islam, I began to question the emerging global role of Islam.

After years of ignoring my own Muslim studies, I was compelled to learn more. First, I learned that the Prophet had granted immunity to and had extended the highest levels of hospitality and protection to foreign emissaries. He never would have sanctioned the actions of Khomeini's so-called Islamic Revolutionary Guard Corps.

In the Quran, I re-read the story of King Solomon, who was offended by emissaries of the Queen of Sheba and yet did not punish this diplomatic entourage. The clear message of the Quran, in this story, is that diplomatic protection must be observed even in the face of looming conflict.

Repeatedly during the life of the Prophet Muhammad, he demonstrated this principle. On one occasion, confronted by a terribly rude envoy of an enemy head of state, an upset Prophet is reported to have said, "I swear by God, if emissaries were not immune from harm, I would have ordered you to be killed." At another time, the Prophet received kindly the representative of the people of Taif, Wahshi, knowing that they had targeted and killed his uncle, Hamza.

I learned that both the Quran and the Prophetic tradition contradicted Khomeini's policies. I was realizing that so-called Muslim voices around the world were twisting Islam to their own political ends. Compounding that confusion was a rising tide of American anger at those committing the outrages. At the time, our nation's collective anger was aimed primarily at Khomeini and the Iranian revolutionaries, in general. But all too soon, in the 1980s, their mistaken claims about Islamic justice turned the global awareness of my faith into an often-toxic shouting match. Over and over, debates about Islam were full of more misconceptions and bigotry than constructive responses.

My background in business and my entrepreneurial skills were talents that I could use in the defense of both my faith and the entire community of families who were facing this emerging hostility. At the time, these steps toward activism simply fell one after the other—an accidental tangent in my life's journey. I felt that I was slowly affirming a new mission. There was no moment at which the sky opened, and I saw a bright ray of light or heard a voice. I was not suddenly enlightened. I had to learn a great deal to prepare for the ever-growing challenges that lay ahead. I had no single spiritual guide—but the Quran did keep educating me. I was especially guided by the basic Quranic principle of choosing to enact what is good and prevent what is bad (Quran, 3:104). Islam is a very practical way of life. Shahina and I became compulsive volunteers in living out those values—a commitment that has remained throughout our lives.

As the 1980s dawned, I embarked on my first efforts to organize the Muslim community. I committed myself to publicly countering misinformation about Islam—from whatever quarter that confusion arose. I worked with others to develop diverse community networks that could defuse tensions, protect the vulnerable and build strong relationships that could withstand future crises. Thankfully, my entire family supported me in my growing activism to lift up what Dr. Martin Luther King, Jr. envisioned as a "Beloved Community."

The first lesson I learned is that Muslims are called to the ancient wisdom: The pen is mightier than the sword. The Quran stresses that core principle. The idea was taught and modeled by the Prophet, as well. The first words of the Quran revealed to Muhammad emphasize the power of *qalam*, the pen. One entire chapter of the Quran is called *Al-Qalam*, the Pen. Another common phrase used to describe the Quran is *Kalam Allah*, Word of God. The use of "the Word" or "words" to defend the faith is a core value from the Prophet's earliest revelation. I have been heartbroken again and again, in recent decades, to see Muslims on the nightly news in some corner of the world resorting to deadly mob violence against vulnerable people—claiming to act on behalf of a faith that condemns such actions!

Unfortunately, in 1989—a decade after the start of the Tehran hostage crisis—Khomeini compounded the confusion by issuing a *fatwa*, an interpretation of Islamic teachings, calling for the death of Salman Rushdie for writing *The Satanic Verses*. From his *fatwa*, cascading calls for Rushdie's death followed—echoing through our American newspapers and nightly TV news from far corners of the planet. Watching it all, I thought that this was a foolish, tragic wave of hostility against a novel that no one was likely to read in the first place! In many cases, protests were violent and showcased the worst of mob mentality masquerading as Muslim values. The situation made no sense to me! I am an avid reader and love nearly all genres, but I wasn't able to make it through Rushdie's dense and confusing book. I read enough to understand that the author's primary motive was to wave an angry fist in the face of Islam. He packed the book with deliberately offensive passages. But who would have ever heard of his book, let alone read it, if these protests had not erupted?

During his own lifetime, the Prophet Muhammad faced indignities. He was scorned and called names. Some of his companions were tortured. Yet the Prophet never reacted like the hooligans I saw in world news reports. All that these self-proclaimed defenders of the faith were doing was deepening well-established biases in the West about Islam as a faith of dangerous, uneducated people. They also were turning an obscure book into a best-seller.

So, for the first time in my life, I took up my pen—not to write a business plan or advertising copy for my stores, but to write what I hoped would be an eloquent essay for newspaper op-ed pages, bringing clarity to this tragic situation. I assumed that the newspapers would welcome this. What community-minded journalist would not share such a noble goal? Like me, they valued the pen's power to bring truth out of confusion. Certainly, we would be allies.

As it turned out, executives at both of the major daily newspapers in Michigan rejected my idea. Newspapers had huge circulation at that time and, even more importantly, they had enormous "penetration," which meant that most households in southeast Michigan paid to have a newspaper land on their doorstep each day. Today, I have good relationships with journalists from coast to coast and I have organized countless opportunities for reporters and editors to learn more about Islam. Back in the 1980s, however, Muslims did not have that kind of well-organized professional network—and journalists had little interest in reaching out.

Even though I was a significant advertiser in the newspapers, I was treated disrespectfully at both major dailies. Finally, frustrated by this utter rejection, I offered to purchase space to print the essay I had written with support from Muslim colleagues. Although we made the offer through a nonprofit group, the newspaper representatives added insult to injury by rejecting our application for a nonprofit rate. They held us up for $13,000 for less than a quarter of a page. Having no choice, I organized a handful of Muslim leaders in the community to pool our funds and buy the space. I had no experience with this kind of public relations, at that point. In fact, I got so angry at our treatment that, when the bill arrived on my desk, I held the payment until it became overdue. Only when the newspapers threatened to contact a collection agency did I finally turn over the money.

Along with my Muslim colleagues, however, we did understand enough about marketing that we wanted an eye-catching headline for our essay. We chose: "Fanatic Muslims!"

What we presented in this essay was our model of a peaceful and properly Islamic way of responding to Rushdie's book. Such an offensive publication should not be met with violence but with a reasoned, persuasive counter argument. The telephone number in our advertisement reached an answering machine at my home. Hundreds called, many in support, but other callers got quite nasty. More than 500 people requested a copy of the Quran. This was my first exposure to advocacy—and my first experience in responding to conflict and confusion through the use of that powerful resource: the pen.

Here is what we published in *The Detroit News* and the *Detroit Free Press* on March 3, 1989:

FANATIC MUSLIMS!

Words have power, and therefore they have to be used carefully. Words can wound, and they can heal. It is naive to say that freedom to use words of hate and destruction can be unlimited. No civilized society allows this. That is why Penguin or any other mainstream publisher does not publish Ku Klux Klan or the neo-Nazi literature. The physical injuries can heal faster, but the emotional wounds caused by pen/words leave deep-rooted scars.

We Muslims believe that it is highly imprudent and inconsiderate for an individual to completely ignore the religious sensitivities of his/her fellow citizen while exercising freedom of speech. Right of individuals is undoubtedly guaranteed by the state, but it is the spirit of harmony, goodwill, and mutual respect among the members of the society that ensures the full enjoyment of these rights by all.

The recent media attention to Mr. Rushdie's book, The Satanic Verses, and worldwide condemnation of the book by the Muslims have given rise to talks on such issues as freedom of expression, decency, and intolerance. We feel truth and honesty have been the real casualties in the nightly drama of the evening news. We draw attention to these facts here, so that you may hear the Muslim side of the debate and form your own opinion.

What is in The Satanic Verses?

Nearly everyone agrees on one thing about the book; it contains offensive material. But to say this is to put it very mildly. The facts are much harsher. By depicting Prophet Abraham (Peace be upon him), and his family in a highly defamatory, obscene and derogatory manner, Rushdie, author of the book, has grievously offended many Muslims.

Rushdie describes Prophet Abraham (Peace be upon him), the patriarch prophet common to Judaism, Christianity and Islam, as "the bastard" (p. 95). An African companion is painted as "an enormous black monster," a remark which is both racist and monstrous. Rushdie's so-called "scholarship" is further evidenced when he describes other companions of the Prophet as "those goons and f******clowns" (P. 101)."

No, Mr. Rushdie's case is not at all "intellectual," nor are Muslims trying to counter "scholarship with a box of matches." Several "intellectual" works that take a less-than-favorable view of Islam are being and have been published all over the world. We Muslims do not throw such works into the incinerator. We buy them for our libraries and universities and at times invite their authors to give a lecture or seminar on their "studies."

Indeed the very first verses revealed in our Qur'an to Prophet Muhammad (Peace be upon him) are: "Read: In the name of thy Lord who created; and thy Lord is the Most Bountiful, who taught the use of the pen." (Chapter 96: verses 1–4.)

Islamic civilization and Muslims cherish scholarship whether it favors them religiously or not. But The Satanic Verses does not indulge itself in the intellectual criticism of Islam, it scandalizes and maligns.

Slander and libel are nothing new to Mr. Rushdie. In a previous novel, Midnight's Children, he tried his hand at the late Indian Prime Minister Mrs. Indira Gandhi. She had to be given a public apology by both the author and the publishers in answer to her libel action. They also paid costs and gave an undertaking to remove from all future editions the passages objected by her.

In The Satanic Verses, Rushdie is not libeling an individual; he insults and libels a whole community. It is obscene. It has self-hating, racist undertones. And it incites racial as well as religious passions against the Muslim community and any decent human being.

Once the book was published in England, it was strongly criticized by Muslims and non-Muslims alike. It failed to win the Man Booker Prize. In British parliament the members backing a motion condemning the Rushdie book has swelled to 33.

For the last four months, tens of thousands of Muslims from all over the USA wrote and called Penguin/Viking requesting that the book be withdrawn from Britain, and not be published in the USA.

Are Muslims Intolerant?

The above points establish that Muslims in the country have politely sought to diffuse the situation. Yet ironically it is the Muslims who are now blamed for intolerance.

Yes, we are intolerant of hypocrisy and hate; yes, we are fanatic about morality, goodwill and decency. If that is a crime, we admit to being guilty. Muslims are exercising their freedom only to express their feeling of disgust that some should abuse freedom of expression in order to blaspheme their sacred beliefs and were insistent on doing so. We have rights to peaceful protest. Islam stands for peace and tranquility.

The Muslim community in America is strong. We are here to stay and prosper. A vast majority of us are taxpaying professionals, scientists and educators. We trust that Penguin would not publish any slanderous material condemning Martin Luther King, Jr., any work of so-called art from an author like Rushdie declaring that Hitler was an Angel and his actions heavenly, because it will be against the sensitivities of racial relations and it would cause emotional injuries. Penguin should have exercised better judgment in selecting and printing a book which is offensive to one-fifth of the human race, a billion Muslims and many other decent human beings.

It is not unusual in our Western democratic societies for the media and the publishing industry to exercise self-restraint in the interest of social order as well as in consideration of moral and ethical norms and racial and religious sensitivities of the society. The Muslims would like the people in media and the publishing industry to extend to them the same courtesy which has generally been extended to other ethnic, racial and religious groups threatened by stereotypical portrayal, innuendoes and false characterization.

In raising their objections to The Satanic Verses, Muslims are only trying to underscore the difference between the sacred and the profane, and between liberty and license. We see it basically as a moral issue, one about decency and civility across all religious or ethnic lines. It is not civilized to insult the sanctities of any people. And that is why Muslims joined with Christians in the protest march against the movie The Last Temptation of Christ.

For more information on Islam watch Islam at a Glance every Sunday (and we listed the time and channel). For a free copy of the English translation of the Holy Qur'an, and information on Islam, please call (a number was listed) or write to (an address was provided).

We have presented the facts: You be the judge!

PAID FOR BY THE CONCERNED MUSLIM CITIZENS

CHAPTER 7

Bringing Us Together

And hold firmly to the rope of God all together and do not become divided.

Quran 3:103

As a business owner, used to developing a plan and managing a staff, one of the toughest truths I had to learn in my work throughout the larger Islamic community was this: Muslims are an impossible people to organize.

That's not a criticism of individual Muslims. This truth stems from the roots of our religious tradition. The five pillars of Islam—faith in one God, prayer, fasting, charity and pilgrimage—make no commitment to an organized religious group. Since its founding, the religious appeal of Islam is that nothing stands between an individual and God. Most Muslims around the world respect imams for their scholarship and preaching ability, but imams do not have the same authority as Christian pastors or bishops. In 2019, the world's nearly 2 billion Muslims are approaching the size of the Christian population, which is 2.3 billion. The vast majority of those Christians are organized into hundreds of denominations with hierarchies based on canon law or other books of discipline, enforced by powerful entities such as the pope, patriarchs, bishops, synods and dioceses. When Christians officially join a congregation, they make solemn promises to follow their chosen church's leadership. In contrast, a Muslim has the Quran as a guide and approaches God directly on a daily basis. Our mosques have board members, supporters and regular attendees, but Muslims do not join a mosque in the way that Christians join their congregations. In Islam, no one can simply develop a plan and expect adherents even to pay attention to what is being proposed—let alone follow the plan as written.

In America's colonial era, individual Muslims and their families began settling in the New World, but not in any significant numbers. The first major wave of Muslim arrivals was impossible to organize, because these men and women were African slaves. Slave owners actively suppressed public expressions of Islam, along with other African religious traditions. If any religious freedom was allowed among slaves in the South, Christianity was their only choice. The founder of Methodism, John Wesley, eventually became an outspoken anti-slavery activist from his home base in England late in his life, but he did visit the Southern colonies as a young clergyman. At that time, Wesley's main concern for slaves was that churches should send more Christian missionaries to them. Islam did not have a chance to take root in the South's slave-based society.

This country's first nationally famous convert to Islam was an entrepreneur, newspaperman and diplomat who called himself Mohammed Alexander Russell Webb. Webb was serving as a U.S. diplomat in the Philippines in 1887 when he began reading about Islam. He was so inspired that he contacted Muslims in India. Webb eagerly sought interfaith assistance and eventually, a Parsee businessman played a key role in connecting him with Muslims. By 1888, Webb had publicly declared his conversion.

Thanks to research by California State University historian Brent Singleton, author of Webb's biography *Yankee Muslim*, I recently learned that at the heart of Webb's pilgrimage to India was a month he spent with the Nizam's household in Hyderabad. My great-grandfather must have been fascinated to meet this astute and outspoken American visitor. More than half a century before the Nizam finally was deposed by military force, Webb could clearly see the danger the Nizam was facing. In his journal, Webb noted that eventually, larger powers would "coolly pull him out of his position, send him away and quietly gobble up his property." As Webb spent time with the leading figures in the Nizam's entourage, he was saddened that these Muslims had "fallen deeply into English customs." He could see the trap these Muslims had carved out for themselves. Webb even looked over the Nizam's modest military force and could concur that it was poorly equipped and trained, compared with British forces. The eventual fate of the Nizam was obvious to him.

Nevertheless, Webb loved much of the culture of Hyderabad. He wrote about its custom of firing the canon as a call to prayer. He described the grandeur of the local mosque. The only thing he truly detested was a small handful of Christian missionaries who hung about the city, trying to convert people. He took pleasure, one day, in chiding one of those missionaries and then sending him away "humbled." Webb wrote in his journal that he wished he could remain longer in this city.

The high point of his visit was a public address he delivered to 2,000 in Hyderabad's main park. As he describes the event, he mentions that poetry was read to the crowd before he spoke. We don't know for sure what verses were read, but I like to think it might have been lines from Ghalib. Webb gave a lengthy talk about the genius of Islam and its great promise in the modern world. He closed by describing his vision of returning home and spreading global Muslim unity from coast to coast in the United States. In his written text, Webb felt free to vary his spellings of terms for "Muslims" in a quaint, 19th century style. Here is the conclusion of his talk:

> *"In carrying out this project, I want to feel that the prayers and good wishes of the Mussulmans of the East are with us; that they are interested in the work and will do all they can to help it along. I want to take your hand and carry it across the sea to be seized in an earnest, fraternal grasp by the people of America. I want the Mussulmans of the East to be united with those of the West in that true spirit of fraternity which our Prophet so plainly taught. The Moslem brotherhood should extend to the four corners of the earth, not in name only, but in the true spirit of perfect unity. There was a time when Islam was the glory of the world, when it was the centre and inspiration of all that was grand and noble and exalting; the heart and soul of the arts and sciences; the civilizer and teacher of mankind. Will history ever repeat itself in this respect? I hope so."*

The crowd was so inspired that a local judge arranged to have printed copies of his address distributed after the talk.

As soon as he returned home to the U.S., Webb attempted realizing his vision of a unified Muslim community, starting with the American South.

In early 1893, he wrote to land owners in Florida, Georgia and Alabama about purchasing property to establish Indian-Muslim communities. This idea seems outlandish to me today, but it seemed quite logical to Webb, at the time. This was the method many Christian missionaries used to successfully plant new churches. Muslim immigrants were likely to do better in their own small communities, far from the big cities of the Northeast.

The crescendo of his career was the first World's Parliament of Religions, organized under the umbrella of the 1893 Chicago World's Fair.

Earlier, an exhibition that is now regarded as the first official world's fair in the U.S.—the Centennial International Exhibition of 1876 in Philadelphia—had put Islamic culture on public display for the first time in the U.S. The highlight was Islamic calligraphy, built around some famous samples of Islamic script from the collection of Queen Victoria. These were such beautiful artworks that they remain in the collection of the Philadelphia Museum of Art to this day. Tunisia, Egypt and the Ottoman Empire collectively shipped 140 cases of materials to Philadelphia for exhibits that were presented to crowds, much like P.T. Barnum's museum drew tourists, as exotic curiosities. In one of many tableaux that comprised the exhibit, two "Moorish" individuals were put on display and photographers eagerly arranged bulky equipment to capture sepia photos of these turbaned figures. The photographers did not even bother to record their names as they turned images of these "Moors" into photo-postcards and stereopticon slides, some of which are still in the archives of the Library of Congress.

By 1893, the Parliament's organizers in Chicago wanted to do far more than gawk at religious curiosities. They sought out authentic spokesmen from the world's great faiths to talk to the crowd of 8,000 attendees. Historians now mark that 18-day conference as the formal debut of Hinduism in America because Swami Vivekananda journeyed to Chicago from India and was an enormous hit with the audience. Historians also note that Webb was the only featured speaker on Islam. Unlike the truly authentic representative of Hinduism, Webb was a recent convert who still had a lot to learn about our faith. For example, he was billed with the Barnum-style nickname, "the Yankee Mohammedan."

Webb also was well received, newspapers reported, although he once again ran into the perennial thorn in his side: Christian missionaries. One fat evangelical preacher from Boston insisted on loudly heckling him during his talk—a detail that was noted in daily newspapers. The most widely reported line in Webb's address echoed what he had proclaimed in Hyderabad. He told the crowd that Americans should welcome Muslims and would find that Islamic principles dovetail perfectly with American values. He said, "I have faith in the American intellect, in the American intelligence, and in the American love of fair play, and will defy any intelligent man to understand Islam and not love it."

Even his evangelical heckler seemed to add to the high drama of his appearance. For a time, Webb seemed to be on the verge of success. He even received invitations from famous Americans, including Mark Twain, who wanted to learn about Islam.

With his titanic enthusiasm and at least a moment of American celebrity, one would think that Webb's quest for Muslim unity surely would find a welcome audience. But, despite Webb's best efforts, Muslim immigrant families turned a deaf ear. His campaign to start Islamic centers across the American South, despite its noble motives, turned out to be a dud. His Southern communities never even broke ground. Webb faced bankruptcy.

"At his height, Webb was a huge sensation. He was covered from the biggest daily newspapers to the little newspapers in corners of America you've never heard of like small towns in North Dakota," says Brent Singleton. "For a while, he was red hot—then Webb's efforts to organize Muslims hit a dead end. By the 20th century, other people did start to make their own fresh efforts to organize Muslim communities, but really everything Webb himself tried to accomplish seems to have faded away. Ultimately, Webb's work looks like a dead end in American Muslim history."

What happened to Webb doesn't surprise me at all. Webb was a Euro-American convert trying to reach immigrant communities of Muslims who preferred to keep to themselves and avoid the public spotlight that Webb craved. While he was running around the country like a missionary, other Muslims were quietly sinking their own roots in the U.S.

Webb was right about one thing: Many Muslims settled in big cities. But other immigrant families didn't like the risky prospect of a giant metropolis like New York City or Chicago. They wanted a fresh opportunity to settle in the American heartland. So, in the late 1800s, a group of immigrant families from Lebanon and Syria found their own ideal parcels of land in Cedar Rapids, Iowa. That community built a mosque in 1934, and claims it is the oldest surviving mosque in the U.S., since the Highland Park mosque in Michigan failed and vanished. The National Park Service has listed it on the National Register of Historic Places.

Whichever claim you regard as the "first," I admire those Iowa pioneers and their relentless efforts to bring Muslims together. In 1952, they organized the first truly nationwide Muslim conference in Cedar Rapids. That gathering resulted in the formation of the Federation of Islamic Associations (FIA). The leaders were American-born, educated, successful individuals. Some were military veterans. To preserve their traditions and identity for future generations, they also hoped to organize a united voice for Muslims. They wanted to build a strong consensus around a program promoting education and public relations. After that 1952 conference, regional chapters formed, as did an ongoing series of gatherings from coast to coast. I first connected with the FIA as a student, when an assembly was held in Detroit in the 1970s.

In every one of these campaigns launched on American soil, unity proved to be a tough sell among Muslim families. The very idea of organizational allegiance is not a good fit with the deep ethnic and cultural divisions among them.

Even in the 1980s, among Michigan's burgeoning Muslim neighborhoods, no one was commonly grouping us with the phrase "Muslim Americans." That was the main reason I encountered such a bruising response from Michigan's two major newspapers when I tried to publish our first collective statement. The editors simply did not see us as a unified constituency—and they were not alone. Nearly all of the university-sponsored studies and articles in popular media about diversity in Detroit that were published back in that era focused on ethnic and cultural divisions. We were seen through lenses such as Indians, Pakistanis, Lebanese, Egyptians, Yemenis or Iraqis. The one Muslim group most Americans could name was "Black Muslims," but that was a label for followers of Elijah Muhammad. Despite a century of attempts, a common bond among American Muslims didn't exist.

The largest Muslim organization today struggled through many challenges in the 1980s. The Islamic Society of North America (ISNA), the biggest Muslim umbrella group in North America, officially lists its origin as 1963. But the ISNA really was reborn in the mid-1980s. To its credit, the ISNA now has established a tradition for North American Muslims that is unique in the world—a huge, family-friendly gathering on Labor Day weekend every year. This kind of event for men, women and young people is unheard of in the rest of the Islamic world. It's an all-American festival of famous speakers, panel discussions, classes, performances and a huge bazaar. In American terms, we might say that Muslim families look forward to this big event each year like many rural Americans look eagerly toward their annual state fair.

I first attended an ISNA event as a student in the 1970s; I went back years later with my family. What an eye-opener! Forty thousand men, women and young people! The bazaar seemed to go on forever, with row after row of booths selling everything from books to music, clothes to calligraphy. The music of Yusuf Islam, perhaps better known as Cat Stevens, floated in the air. There was a parallel event for children, the Muslim Youth of North America (MYNA). At night, there was entertainment. Our three kids had a ball and made new friends. As an adult, I was inspired by the fabulous opportunities to learn and converse with others. Leading scholars addressed a myriad of topics—so many different subjects that it was difficult to choose what to attend. After sessions closed, I enjoyed standing in line to ask the speakers additional questions. This was a wonderful learning experience. Afterward, I carried home both audio and print books that I could enjoy week by week. I remember enthusiastically diving into topics such as the finer points of Islam's five pillars, the meaning of prophethood, Jesus in Islam and a host of issues in daily life, from business to parenthood.

Through the years, the most important impact of the ISNA on my life is as a reminder that I'm part of a large and growing Muslim presence in America. After an ISNA gathering, I come home with fresh enthusiasm for my own work.

Just as I owe a debt to organizations like the ISNA, I also owe a great deal to giants in the interfaith movement who were working in southeast Michigan before I took a seat at this expanding table.

One of my mentors was Hajj Khalil Alawan, a Muslim community leader who always introduced himself as "Chuck." Like me, he was an accomplished businessman—a regional representative for an industrial-supply company. Chuck also had the enormous advantage of looking and sounding like a twin to country-western superstar Kenny Rogers—right down to his carefully manicured beard. Chuck was a big man who towered over the people he met and, as a proud veteran of the U.S. Army, he had a military bearing that seemed to command respect. When he was invited to a conference or a newspaper interview to discuss religious stereotypes—all he had to do was walk into the room and extend his warm, country-style greeting.

More than once, when journalists first met Chuck, their jaws dropped and they would double-check that they were greeting the right visitor. "You're the Muslim representative?"

Chuck would grin and say, "I sure am." He knew exactly what he was doing. Chuck was busting every biased assumption about Muslims before anyone had taken a seat in the room.

Another supportive friend was Rabbi Sherwin Wine, who founded the international movement of Humanistic Judaism in southeast Michigan in 1963 and was one of the nation's leading rabbis by the 1980s. The three of us came together at a gathering Wine hosted with the goal of redefining the term "religious terrorism." Chuck and I agreed to represent Islam at Wine's meeting.

Beyond Chuck's disarming warmth, I saw him in action as a negotiator that day and realized that he was a very astute spokesman for Islam. He promptly countered any effort to link the religion of Islam itself with terrorists who claimed to be part of our faith. Individuals may *claim* a religious motive for terrorist acts, Chuck reasoned, but they are tragically distorting the faith. We should not let them succeed in hijacking our faith. In interfaith settings, one of Chuck's favorite arguments was posed as a question. He would slowly say: "Aww, come on now! Get serious! Do you mean to tell me that because a Ku Klux Klan firebomber claims to be a Christian Knight that you're going to start calling them 'Christian terrorists'? I don't think so, do you? Just doesn't make sense!" Chuck was very persuasive and, on that day with Wine, I served mainly as his sideman. I distributed the materials we had brought that explained Islam to the other participants. That day, we made our point. Our joint actions changed the direction of that conversation. This was an eye-opening experience for me in the value of interfaith dialogue.

These mentors forever shaped my own positive approach to promoting harmony. In the passing of Sherwin Wine, the Jewish community lost a great scholar, and in the passing of Chuck, our community lost a great ambassador and a talented advocate. Visitors to the Arab American National Museum in Dearborn, today, pass a large photo of Chuck in one of the galleries dedicated to proud Americans from Arab families. His ancestors were Lebanese.

These historic milestones taught me that I should not always expect to be successful in my organizational efforts. I have plenty of gray hair from the unexpected objections and barriers I encountered along the way— some from angry bigots and some from faithful Muslims.

My first experience in trying to gather Michigan's Muslims under a single banner arose from a simple idea. Each year, newspapers reported that even inactive Christians liked to show up at church for Christmas and Easter. The same thing was true in the Jewish community. Men and women who would never darken a synagogue door throughout the year would make a point of showing up for the Jewish High Holy Days. This is true in Islam, as well, revolving mainly around the two big observances that we call Eid, which simply means "festival" or "celebration." One Eid celebrates the completion of the annual Hajj to Mecca, while the other marks the end of the fasting month of Ramadan.

My simple idea was: "Why not have a tri-county, metro-Detroit united prayer service?" After all, the Prophet Muhammad himself encouraged Muslims to gather together on religious holidays. I assumed this would be widely welcomed as a way of reviving Islamic tradition in America.

The first problem was that there were not as many mosques in the mid-1980s as there are today. Many people traveled quite a distance to the mosque they preferred to attend for these holiday prayers. Existing mosques had limited space. So, we rented a far larger space along the Detroit River in a well-known Detroit landmark: the cavernous Cobo Hall. We advertised the event and attracted a broad diversity of Muslims from across southeast Michigan. When everyone streamed into the hall and formed the lines for prayer, we counted thousands!

I certainly did not accomplish this on my own. My friend Syed Salman and Imam Abdullah El-Amin—head of the main African-American Muslim center in Detroit— also were major supporters, along with many volunteers. We were relieved, first of all, that a good-sized crowd showed up. But we all shared a larger dream. By coming together for Eid in downtown Detroit, we were uniting Muslims who lived in distant suburbs with inner-city Muslims. Families who rarely had an opportunity to mix in this region's deeply divided geography were joining in the long lines for Eid prayers at Cobo.

News reporters did agree to cover that event—although it was obvious that many of these journalists were encountering Islam for the first time. For example, they were fascinated that we remove our shoes before prayer, which is a universal custom in Islam that isn't remarkable in other parts of the world. News reports focused on the big pile of shoes outside our makeshift prayer hall. We didn't mind. All of us were grateful that day for the coverage of such a peaceful, colorful festival of prayer. The ABC-TV affiliate covered our Eid as part of the evening news. The next morning, *The Detroit News* featured our story on the front page. Within days, my colleagues across the Muslim community were buzzing with pride over what we had accomplished.

"We've never seen such positive attention for our community!" said more than one friend. My heart was warmed every time I heard a Muslim use those words: "our community."

That was the good part of this effort, but the warm feeling certainly was not unanimous. The leaders of one suburban mosque north of Detroit were outspoken in their disapproval of our Cobo event. Their argument was pragmatic: We were encouraging families who would usually show up at their mosque for the big holiday to drive to Detroit, instead. Among other things, that meant these families were not bringing their Eid donations to the suburban mosque. To be fair, my Christian colleagues tell me that donations at Christmas Eve services often balance the year-end budget for congregations—so we almost never hear of community-wide Christmas Eve services. Pastors know they need to draw the faithful to their own individual houses of worship. Suddenly, I was hearing that same argument from some imams and board members. In my sincere quest to

pursue Islamic unity, I was learning my first lessons about the thorny controversies that can divide Muslim centers.

Those united Eid prayers we organized became an annual event for a
few years—until more mosques sprang up and the population grew to
a point that it simply made sense for families to gravitate toward their
own chosen mosque on the holiday. After all, that's how my Jewish and
Christian friends had always handled the big holidays. Each congregation
takes pride in celebrating in its own way with its own families.

That's when I first began dreaming of an entirely new congregation: a
model of community-wide unity. At that point, so early in my organizational work, that had to remain a dream. It was such an ambitious idea
that it even scared me. I wasn't ready to be the founder of a full-scale
congregation in the 1980s.

I also learned that, if my goal was unity, I was smart to avoid perennial
controversies. For example, community members asked me to propose a
holiday for school children on Eid in an area with many Muslim families. I knew that public schools cannot operate if attendance falls below
a minimum, which can occur on major holidays. So, school districts and
teacher unions negotiate a common-sense calendar that does make room
for some religious holidays. One could argue that, in predominantly
Muslim communities, attendance would plummet at Eid. The problem is
that Muslims historically do not agree on the dates for upcoming holidays,
which are determined by sightings of the moon. Today, these calendars are
becoming standardized across entire regions of the world, but at that time,
the scheduling of Eid was always discussed among Muslim leaders—and,
even so, individual families might start or end Ramadan a day or so different than their neighbors. Given my own shortage of patience with delays
due to insurmountable disagreements, I had little interest in fighting the
uphill battle of negotiating a unified Eid holiday for a school district.

As I was learning more about my faith and deepening my own commitment to Islam, I kept thinking about the Quran's wisdom in 13:11:
"God won't change the condition of a people until they change what is in
themselves." I was confident of my talents as a businessman. I was persuasive, outgoing and understood the complex challenges of launching an
organization. After all, I had launched multiple locations for my furniture stores. I was also unafraid of diving into uncharted waters. Obstacles

did not deter me. But, I was learning through successes—and occasional bruising criticism, as well—that I needed to connect my efforts with core values in Islam to motivate my colleagues throughout the community.

Clearly, a century of efforts to organize American Muslims had left many futile dead ends in its wake—but unity is, indeed, a core value in Islam. From the first revelation to the Prophet, Islam has prized the *umma*, or community. The Quran tells us that Muslims are a community called by God to serve as a light to the world. We know that none of the five pillars call on a Muslim to take vows to follow a particular religious leader, as Christians commonly do. But the pilgrimage to Mecca is a pillar of our faith. That worldwide gathering of Muslims forms a visible and inspiring *umma* of millions of pilgrims each year. The Hajj reminds us not only of the roots of our faith, but also that we are a truly global community. Of course, in the 1980s, most Muslims in America weren't thinking much about the implications of this basic Islamic value. They certainly had not formed bonds across southeast Michigan. That's why the troubling news events of the 1980s were a mixed blessing. An awareness of our need for joint protection and collective advocacy finally pushed us all to think about the larger *umma*.

My thinking crystalized into a plan for an umbrella group—perhaps a council that could represent the growing number of Muslims living in metropolitan Detroit. Christian denominations had various committees, councils and spokespeople. Jewish groups contributed to a highly respected umbrella group, called a federation, as well as a public relations council and other shared institutions.

Teaming up once again with my friend Sayed Salman, I reached out to the leadership of mosques—including board members, long-time supporters and imams. Salman and I were a good team. My reputation as an advocate and organizer was growing, but I certainly would never claim to be a religious scholar. As my colleague, Salman was pious, mild-mannered and the model of polite hospitality. He was bearded; I was clean-shaven. Salman opened doors and warmed people's hearts; I pushed for action. Despite the contrast in our approaches, people responded to our sincerity. Behind our obviously different styles, we were both experienced with large organizations. Salman was an auto executive with years of experience in dealing with corporate politics; I was a hard-nosed businessman with a no-nonsense reputation. Together, we logged countless miles in his Chrysler van—a Muslim odd couple traveling anywhere we might open a new dialogue and inspire action. If the board of a mosque or a Muslim center would put us on their agenda, we would show up and make our case.

The timing helped us immeasurably. I pushed; Salman facilitated. Ears were receptive; hearts were moved. Key to our success was our timely message. Everyone recognized that news events were raising uncomfortable and often unfair new challenges for Muslim families.

In the late 1980s, we organized a community-wide meeting of representatives from a diverse array of mosques at the Islamic Center of America (ICoA). We recognized our achievement when we saw that Sunni imams were willing to take part in the meeting even though the ICoA is a Shia mosque. We brainstormed a name, and Islamic Diversity Forum was suggested—then rejected, because the initials would have been IDF, and anyone with a background in the Middle East associated that with the Israeli Defense Forces. The second proposal was Council of Islamic Organizations (CIO). That almost was approved until someone objected, complaining, "It sounds too close to the CIA."

Finally, we settled on the Council of Islamic Organizations of Michigan (CIOM). A logo subsequently was designed, with a map of Michigan inside a large letter C in a crescent shape. The logo was green—a color the Prophet was known to have liked. Our bylaws were drawn up. We agreed that council meetings would rotate among the mosques. The legal paperwork and all of the legwork involved in setting up a new nonprofit fell on my shoulders, which did not surprise me. At the time, the council address was simply a post office box in Bloomfield Hills at the same post office where I collected my mail. Our official goal was to participate in civic, interfaith, media and other forums, representing a "singular" community voice. For our new letterhead, we chose the Quranic verse 3:103: "And hold firmly to the rope of God all together and do not become divided." I smiled to myself at the all-American tone of that line! Benjamin Franklin is credited with coining the line: "We must, indeed, all hang together or, most assuredly, we shall all hang separately." The Quran and an American Founding Father were both echoed in our stationery. We were doing everything we could to demonstrate our good citizenship in the civic arena.

It took a while for reporters from the major newspapers, TV and radio outlets to become aware of our new role—and then to accept our offer to call upon us for help with news reports. But, over time, journalists learned that they had an official Muslim source to contact if they wanted to include all of the major religious perspectives on an issue. For years, journalists reporting stories on religion knew they could call official spokespeople at the Catholic Archdiocese of Detroit and the Jewish community council. In the past, if a reporter wanted to include a Muslim opinion, they tended to grab the first Muslim they could find. Now, just like Catholics and Jews, we collectively had an official spokesman who could talk to reporters. I served as that spokesman for many years, often fielding reporters' questions at all hours of the day and night.

That's not to say that every Muslim community leader became an avid supporter of the council. Some were committed and rarely missed a meeting; others were overwhelmed with the daily demands of running their own centers and gave us token support at best. That's when my retailer's instinct kicked in again. What would motivate our potential supporters to feel that they were an active part of this enterprise? We needed a hook, a unifying appeal, a project that we could market to prompt a solid buy-in.

As a businessman, I knew that marketing involves media. I connected with Dr. Nazir Khwaja, a Los Angeles physician who was producing an Islamic TV program, *Islam at a Glance*. Khwaja wisely chose Nasiha Al-Sakina—a tall, attractive, all-American—for a host. She was a convert to Islam and an actress. I knew that, if we could syndicate that show into the Detroit media market, we would have a rallying point for our new council. Next, I contacted what was then a small local TV station that primarily hosted religious programming: Detroit's Channel-62. I was anxious about whether the staff would even listen to our proposal. At that time, Channel-62's programming schedule seemed to be a wall-to-wall parade of overwrought TV evangelists. Would the station's management even consider an Islamic show? I was relieved to find that airtime was simply a matter of good business to the station's management. Our money was as green as anyone else's. The cost of a weekly half-hour of Channel-62's airtime was $1,000, requiring a year's commitment. I negotiated a Sunday slot at 6:30 p.m., knowing that that was prime viewing time for most of our families.

Truth be told, this was one more enormous risk in my already risk-prone career. I signed that $52,000 contract with only $2,000 in the bank! What saved us was that this step truly did awaken a real excitement throughout the Muslim community. This was long before the internet and smartphones let anyone launch broadcasts at virtually no cost. This was even before widespread access to cable TV. At that time, most television shows came through the air to individual antennae. Just a few channels had access to that powerful technology. So, Salman and I invited families to come and watch the first broadcast of this TV series at a mosque. Fortuitously, this was during Ramadan, when men and women were used to gathering at Muslim centers in the evening. So, we drew a good crowd. We set up a big TV set, adjusted its antenna, and thanked God that we were able to tune in the broadcast! This particular show featured Yusuf Islam, Cat Stephens, who performed an Islamic song at the end of the broadcast.

As that first episode came to an end, our TV host signed off. There was a brief moment of silence as we all reflected on what we had just witnessed. Then, a huge "*Allahu Akbar!*" erupted from the crowd.

Until that debut, anyone living in southeast Michigan thought of religious TV shows exclusively as a parade of televangelists pleading for donations. Of course, the Christians could do that—but Muslims? I will never forget how Salman stepped so naturally into his own fundraising appeal that night. He didn't miss a beat in tapping into the widespread assumption that religious TV requires donations. The pride and excitement sweeping through our audience produced another $3,000 on the spot. I thought: Whew! We've just paid for the next three weeks. What a relief! We learned a lot that night. Soon, we actually inserted a brief appeal for donations in the middle and at the end of each show.

I was on a roll. During a visit with family in California, I attended a conference on *Sharia*, Islamic law, held in a Los Angeles hotel ballroom with a fancy dinner. This was new to me. I had logged countless hours at Muslim gatherings—but I was used to meeting in mosques or rented halls with folding chairs, paper plates, plastic silverware and, often, screaming kids running around us as we tried to listen to speakers. In Los Angeles, the Muslim organizers had booked a nice hotel and a comfortable meeting space with great food—and they had planned ahead for day care, including a clown who performed magic tricks to entertain the kids.

The best entrepreneurs are always looking for good ideas to borrow. I flew back to Michigan, describing this event to friends and urging them: "We need this in Michigan!"

Every project I launched, now, was aimed at bringing people together, so a phrase began to roll around in my mind: "Unity Banquet." I spotted the fundraising opportunities of such an event, if we could truly bring together the leading lights of our far-flung Muslim community. That meant including religious leaders, of course, but a quality banquet also had a natural appeal to the many successful professionals who wanted to show their support for Islam. And, if we could convince them to appear, we could invite major power brokers in Michigan who would want to shore up their own support with our audience. We already had a presence on local television. We knew that Ramadan was an auspicious season for a debut. We brought all of these elements together in plans for a gala at the Novi Hilton, to celebrate the end of Ramadan and raise funds for our TV series—all in a single, glittering night of celebration. More than 400 tickets were sold for our first Unity Banquet. We pulled out all the stops. We even had the TV crew from Los Angeles pay a visit. Dr. Jamal Badawi, a highly respected Muslim scholar, was the first keynote speaker. Civic, political, interfaith and media leaders were among the guests. In the audience that night, we even recognized Michigan Senate Republican Majority Leader John Engler, who was contemplating a run for governor. The following year, he launched his campaign and won—and became a friend to our community for many years.

Muslims who walked into the Hilton that night were stunned! They had never seen a Muslim-sponsored event of that size and quality with so many local celebrities in attendance. We netted $4,000 for the TV series that night. Plus, we received many pledges for monthly donations that we arranged to receive through (what was then) a high-tech system called Check-o-matic, an early method of electronic bank transfers.

The euphoria spilled over into the following days. A strong supporter of my efforts, Hisham Rushdy rang me excitedly.

"Ghalib!" he greeted me.

I greeted him in return. And, he got straight to the point: "I've got a check for you." He promised to pass along a check from an anonymous donor who wanted to underwrite the TV show. And what a donation it was! That check would underwrite more than a year of the broadcasts.

Unfortunately, that turned out to be the entire run of our TV series, because CBS made a major move in the Detroit market and bought the sleepy little Channel-62. CBS wanted to transform it into a network hub in Michigan. Immediately, all contracts for religious programming were terminated.

That did not seem to slow us down, however. Our influence was growing, and that was partly because we, as a council, were careful about remaining politically nonpartisan. For our second annual banquet, we welcomed U.S. Rep. David Bonior, who would become a Democratic whip in Congress and also would become a good friend to our community. Eventually, Muslims from out-state cities, away from the major Detroit hub—including Flint, Lansing and Port Huron—were regularly buying tickets to these major gatherings. Unity Banquet became an essential campaign stop for major candidates, a place for media professionals to make an appearance and a required annual event for top businesspeople who hoped to maintain a warm relationship with our community. Like most annual banquets, we also began a tradition of honoring important men and women. I am so pleased that my late friend is named each year when we present the Sayed Salman Community Service Award. At the 34th annual gala, the community added the presentation of one more honor: The Victor and Shahina Begg Interfaith Partner Award.

With a firm foundation and widespread acceptance of our work, I was able to address one other issue that concerned me. Our original council was constrained by its dependence on the various representatives who served on our board. We were supposed to be working on media relations, coalition-building and civic engagement, but our board members were not authorizing very much action in those crucial areas. So, I did what I always did throughout my career—I began making plans to expand. I had other models in the religious realm that I could follow in this kind of expansion. Catholics had various departments within the Archdiocese of Detroit working on a wide range of issues, as well as a host of other semi-independent Catholic organizations and advocacy groups. The Jewish community also had overlapping nonprofits working on specialized issues and projects. If we were to follow suit in becoming an effective part of the American landscape, we needed more than a single forum. I initiated the Muslim American Alliance (MAA) with a tight focus on media, networking and advocacy. The money we had left from the TV series set up the MAA's first office. This group's membership was less institutional and more focused around emerging leaders such as Suzanne Sereini, the first female Muslim member of the Dearborn City Council, and Adam Shakur, the African-American chief judge of Detroit's 36th District Court, who later became deputy mayor of Detroit. Like me, other business owners immediately understood the value of joining the MAA. These were movers and shakers who encouraged me to push our collective voice in the media and in partnership with other like-minded allies.

As we developed this overall organization, we envisioned CIOM as our overall umbrella. Then, for the new MAA, we hired Zana Makki, a veteran media personality, as our first executive director. Yahya Basha, a prominent Syrian businessman, provided the office space in his Royal Oak office building. Press releases were issued. Journalists covered the launch of this new Muslim organization. Civic leaders took notice. A newsletter called *Michigan Muslim* was published by MAA and copies were delivered to mosques. Coalitions were developed with the Dearborn Lebanese-American Club, the Pakistan-American Friendship Society, Detroit's Muslim PAC, the Indian Muslim and other ethnic organizations engaged in political advocacy. We organized voter registration drives and held regular meetings with news outlets. Politicians running for office learned that, especially during campaign season, they should try to attend one of our town hall gatherings.

Truth be told, we were following the same playbook used by Catholics and Jews to develop their public presence and advocate for causes close to their community values. Of course, they were decades ahead of us in developing this multi-faceted approach. I was not reinventing the wheel; I was using proven strategies to develop broad-based opportunities for Muslims to join in religious advocacy. This work was as American as apple pie. And, over many years, the other religious groups recognized us as like-minded colleagues. Often, I found myself working cooperatively with Christian and Jewish networks on projects.

Throughout these many efforts, I knew that at least some of the other leaders across southeast Michigan's civic life still regarded me as a pushy businessman, trying to leverage the principles of my trade to promote the value of religious diversity. The emergence of Muslim voices in the public square was a surprise to many people. After all, for decades, newspaper readers and TV viewers had been used to hearing about religious issues from cardinals or bishops, pastors or rabbis—or those emotionally charged TV evangelists. Now, we were emerging as a new kind of religious voice—and, in particular, I was a new kind of religious activist. I wasn't an ordained religious scholar, like a bishop or a rabbi. Sometimes I encountered resistance, and even outright opposition, because of this new kind of role I was playing. But I knew that what I had accomplished in these early years—and what I was going to develop in the future—sprang from the very roots of our faith.

In 622, when the Prophet Muhammad and his close followers moved from Mecca to Medina in the *Hegira*, or exodus, one of his first concerns was to end the perennial fighting among clans in the region. The *Hegira* became the start of the Islamic calendar—a foundational moment in our faith. The Prophet drafted a treaty that, in English, is known as the Constitution of Medina. This remains one of the most important documents from the origins of Islam, because in its text the Prophet was summoning a cooperative sense of the *umma*. In that constitution, he organized and bound the eight warring clans around Medina to shared principles for resolving disputes and for their collective defense. Religious scholars and historians have far more expertise than I have in interpreting that constitution. But, as I look back across 1,400 years, I see myself not as a pushy businessman trying to invent some new concept in Islam—I see myself as a humble follower of the Prophet's example.

In this troubling and turbulent world, we truly need each other. Unity certainly is an elusive goal in Islam, yet from the time of the Prophet, it has been one of our core values.

Chapter 8

Little Mosque in the Suburbs

In the mosques which God has ordered to be built, in them God's name is honored and celebrated. Therein glorify God in the mornings and in the evenings.

Quran 24:36

"Victor, you must check it out—this property on Square Lake Road would be perfect for an Islamic center!" Joyce Kafi was excited to share this news with me. She had made small donations to our TV program and I had gotten to know her as a serious supporter of our initiatives. When Joyce spotted a real estate sign in front of a former public school on a spring afternoon in 1993, she dreamed of a Muslim community center.

This was a boom time for religious pioneers all across America. The Iron Curtain had fallen. Pope John Paul II had drawn millions of Catholics during his triumphant 1987 tour of North America, partly because of his role in toppling communism in Poland. American televangelists like Jerry Falwell and Pat Robertson had become major players in American politics. And, in this era of high hopes and prosperity, a new generation of young evangelicals had borrowed a page from the rising stars of Wall Street. These young pastors were bullish on religion in America and were eager to launch multi-million-dollar expansions.

Back in the 1980s, the Willow Creek Community Church near Chicago had purchased 90 acres and, eventually, expanded to 150 acres. The worship center held, at capacity, 7,000 people—which its young pastors filled on Sundays. By the 1990s, the Willow Creek phenomenon had been covered in all of the major newspapers and magazines. Suddenly, everyone seemed to be talking about the potential of these "megachurches." Willow Creek's vast campus became a Christian mecca for evangelicals who wanted in on this hot new trend. The Willow Creek staff even launched a side business, teaching others how to launch similar suburban congregations. That boom spread across southeast Michigan in the 1990s. The leaders of at least a half-dozen would-be megachurches bought sizeable tracts of suburban land and made expansive public proclamations. Then, in several cases, these same church leaders found themselves mired in years of protests and legal wrangling with local residents, government officials and the courts. One giant evangelical church wound up spending 15 years on its development, between purchasing property northwest of Detroit and officially opening the doors of its giant new home. The urge to expand wasn't limited to evangelicals, either: Countless mainline Christian congregations were advised that they could attract more young men and women if they built multi-million-dollar family life centers—usually designed with a gymnasium, fitness center and banquet hall. The facilities turned out to be harder to build than most church leaders envisioned, sometimes sparking neighbors' objections. Once built, they often wound up sinking the congregations into decades of debt. *The Detroit News* and *Detroit Free Press* reported on these thorny suburban disputes over the height of church towers; legal wrangling over the capacity of parking lots; and battles with neighbors over traffic jams and late-night crowds.

In the midst of that era of religious expansion, Muslims had an added burden: general suspicion about our faith and our ethnic roots. For the most part, the mid-1990s was an era of high hopes for the West. Democracy seemed to be taking Eastern Europe by storm. Prosperity was breaking out in many unlikely corners of the globe. Iran was fading from American newspaper headlines—until the February 26, 1993 World Trade Center bombing freshly awakened American anxieties about fanatics who claimed to be acting in the name of Islam. Then, in the spring of 1995, the homegrown Oklahoma City bombers reminded Americans that terrorists pop up with a lot of crazy claims. This was pre-9/11 America. Anxiety was in the air, but the hopes of religious groups were sky-high as well.

In many ways, that decade—the 1990s—was the best of times to build a house of worship in America. But, in other ways, it was the worst of times to wade into the host of financial, legal and public relations challenges. Suburban leaders nationwide were on high alert for any signs of a religious or cultural group trying to sink new roots in their neighborhoods. Nowhere in Michigan was that radar as finely tuned toward outsiders as in the wealthy area of Oakland County, northwest of Detroit. Bloomfield Township, where that former school building was situated, was ranked among the wealthiest communities in Michigan. The neighboring city of Bloomfield and West Bloomfield Township were similarly high-income communities with their own tough barriers against expansion. In 1989, Chaldeans—Iraqi Christians—wanted to buy a country club in West Bloomfield and suddenly faced a costly battle with local residents when the news broke in local media. Before the deal was finally sealed, *The New York Times* reported that the Chaldeans were required to spend more than $1 million in upgrades to calm neighbors' fears. Eventually, they were accepted by those neighbors—and the banquet hall was a popular destination. By 2017, that country club also became the site of the world's only Chaldean museum. But, their tough initial experience with neighbors was a costly cautionary tale for us.

To say that founding a suburban Muslim center was a high-stakes venture in the 1990s is to understate the long-shot odds. The idea of trying to establish one in the heart of restrictive Bloomfield Township was so daring that it verged on insane.

But, after Joyce's call, I had started dreaming, too. That site was in walking distance of our home, which was just over the township line in nearby Bloomfield Township. My family was dissatisfied with the narrowness of vision and the internal politics of the mosque we had been attending.

I just couldn't get Joyce's call out of my mind. I was caught up in the high hopes of the 1990s, like so many others. I kept reading in newspapers and magazines that religious pioneers from coast to coast were taking their best shot at making dramatic expansions. I was already a successful entrepreneur in one arena of American life. I became convinced that I should now take a shot at helping my religious community to grow in a creative, diverse new way. That lovely 11.5-acre lot, with its 16,500-square-foot building, was calling me. In my mind's eye I could just see it transformed into an Islamic center—virtually in my backyard—and organized under a whole new approach to welcoming Muslims of all backgrounds. What a dream!

I wasn't naïve about the challenge. I had weathered my own share of public attacks in some of my earlier attempts at speaking out on American-Muslim perspectives.

With the expansion of the global oil industry after World War II, questions about traditional Muslim approaches to finance arose around the world. In the 1970s, some predominantly Muslim countries experimented with financial institutions that tried to adapt to Muslim values. In the 1980s, the world was buzzing about a Bengali Muslim banker named Muhammad Yunus who was encouraging a movement toward microfinance loans that could help the underprivileged. Much later, in 2006, he was awarded the Nobel Peace Prize for his efforts. In the midst of the emerging global dialogue among Muslim business leaders, Sheikh Ahmed Zaki Yamani, president of the Islamic Society of North America, invited me to speak at the first American-based Islamic Finance Conference, in Kansas City. I eagerly accepted. This fit with my own vision of encouraging Muslims to get involved in a positive way in our pluralistic society by engaging governments, businesses, media and the civil society.

At that Kansas City conference, I began my talk by describing the Prophet Muhammad's role as a merchant prior to accepting his mission. I emphasized that business continues to be *Sunna*, the way of the Prophet. When he moved to Medina, he constructed the first mosque and had his companions set up a market nearby. His vision encompassed the economic welfare of the entire community. Another example I used was Indonesia, which has the world's largest Muslim population. I cited examples of honest, pious businessmen who were famous for spreading the faith in Indonesia. I even quoted the Prophet: "The truthful and honest merchant is with the prophets." When I finished, the crowd applauded. I left the podium confident that I had properly addressed the issue with solid examples and a grounding in Muslim theology.

I didn't notice the few faces that were frowning at me.

The next speaker was Dr. Mahmoud Abu Saud, an internationally respected economist, author and religious scholar who had helped establish banks in the Middle East. He also was known for addressing hot-button concepts such as "interest and usury." In his presentation, he further emphasized the importance of trade in Islamic societies and cited the Quranic verse 61:10: "O you who believe! Shall I guide you to a trade that will save you from a painful torment?" He even suggested that God

Almighty trades heavenly rewards for good deeds—implying that God means business. He was stretching his point a bit too far, I thought, but overall it was a successful talk.

Then, even as the applause subsided, the few grim-faced individuals in the audience became obvious to all of us. One of them leapt to his feet—visibly upset. He pointed a finger at me, angrily saying, "First, he calls the Prophet a businessman!"

That accusatory finger moved toward Abu Saud. "Then, this one doubles down, calling Allah a trader. Where we come from, such language is disrespectful to Allah and his messenger!" Only later did I learn that this man was a Saudi traditionalist. Whatever his background, his fury certainly was startling!

I was astonished. I wanted to say, "Please, calm down, man!" But I was speechless for a long moment. Neither of us had said anything revolutionary in our talks to the crowd. It's a well-established tradition to talk about Muhammad as a successful merchant.

Until that verbal attack, I had not been exposed to such passionate disagreements among believers on what I considered to be trivial matters. This also rubbed me the wrong way because I have such huge respect for the right of free speech. I could shrug off this man's emotional attempt to silence us, but I knew that such outbursts were counterproductive to encouraging the emergence of a vigorous, diverse Muslim community in this country. We need to hear from more perspectives, not less. We need Muslims to feel free to express creative ideas, not shout them down.

Despite that incident, I was well enough received by the conference sponsors that I was asked to hold a second, similar conference in Detroit. These two conferences opened my eyes to how contentious the Muslim values concerning Sharia can be. Sharia is the way to worship, based on the Quran, traditions of Muhammad and human reasoning. Similar to Jewish Mosaic Law Halacha or the Catholic Canon Law. At the Detroit gathering, we tackled the thorny issue of charging interest and the sin of usury. That's when I began to study the concept of *riba*, which the Quran condemns—exploitive gains made in business through certain practices, including interest on loans. However, the Prophet Muhammad never clarified whether all forms of interest amount to *riba* or only predatory practices. He seems to have left this issue to future generations to clarify.

To this day, some Muslim scholars believe that all financial arrangements involving "interest" are *riba*; others disagree, taking what I think is a more common-sense approach. This is a very difficult issue because in the Prophet's era there were no modern banks, the concept of inflation was unknown and modern corporations weren't yet invented. The Prophet could not specifically address our current challenges in carrying out international transfers of funds, business loans and global trade.

As a Muslim businessman, I had used inventory financing offered by an offshoot of the General Electric Company to expand my retail business; I had to accept credit cards to sell my merchandise; and I had offered consumer financing plans to qualifying customers. Without such interest-bearing financial instruments, it would have been impossible to run my business. Today, there now are more widely available Islamic banking systems for the faithful who want to go a step further with these issues. But a strict adherence to a no-interest policy would doom most American entrepreneurs, even today.

I looked into these issues in a serious way. I discovered that all of the Abrahamic faiths—Judaism, Christianity and Islam—traditionally considered usury a sin. The biblical books of Exodus, Leviticus and Deuteronomy all condemn charging interest in language very similar to warnings in the Quran. As it turns out, the followers of all three faiths have shared this ancient challenge when developing modern business practices. Christians and Jews found pragmatic solutions. I consulted a Muslim-American jurist about our modern Islamic approaches to the issue. He advised me that a reasonable return, even if it is designated as "interest," is allowed in business. Usury—the sinful abuse of interest—refers to predatory financial arrangements. That is how America's lawmakers, down through the centuries, have sorted out the issue. Unfair loans with excessive interest—such as loan sharking—are illegal, but home mortgages and business loans are not. In the end, I was reminded that Islam is a very practical faith—encouraging common-sense solutions to the problems we face. Muslim scholars refer to this process as *ijtihad*, or "independent reasoning."

The Prophet Muhammad was a clear-eyed, compassionate leader who looked after the life of the entire community—not only in the narrow issues of theology and worship. Just as I had described in my Kansas City talk, his first order of business upon moving to Medina was to lay the foundations of a mosque, which has become known as Al-Masjid an-Nabawi, or the Prophet's Mosque. This was truly a gathering place, a center where the nascent Muslim community could come together for prayer and work together to sustain everyday life. This is a founding example that continues to encourage Muslim immigrants to build their own Muslim centers wherever they settle around the world.

All of these perspectives were shaping my dream for that building on Square Lake Road. Questions swirled in my mind every day. Doesn't the Prophet's example encourage us to establish a mosque in our community? If we managed to do that, what angry voices would be raised against us? On the other hand, what positive examples could we set if we dared to develop this center? Wouldn't it be wonderful to have a facility where a unique Muslim-American spirit could emerge and be shaped by the families who would gather to share their lives? In this new center, I was hoping, we could free ourselves of the burdens of foreign cultures—even as we celebrated the best in our diverse traditions. No longer would our community be divided by each family's ethnic customs. Islam would unite us—even with all of our differences.

Privately, I began floating the idea among colleagues who I figured would support a progressive house of worship. To my surprise, there was little pushback. If I was getting such immediate encouragement from these people who I considered my longtime supporters, then I was confident we could find more people willing to join this collective effort. I was careful to enlist supporters whose family origins circled the Muslim world.

The owner of the school was the old Pontiac school district, a legacy of Michigan's patchwork quilt of cities, townships and school systems that often overlap. The broker listing the property informed me that the deadline for closed bids on the property was rapidly approaching and that a deposit was required with each proposal.

A deposit?

I did not have any kind of solid fundraising committee behind me. I knew from my supporters that we could leverage the $15,000 left over from the TV series, but I also knew that the weight of this financial commitment would fall on me, Shahina and our family. Like other religious groups moving into the suburbs in the 1990s, I knew we would face an uphill battle in rezoning the property and winning the right to turn this into a house of worship—and a Muslim one, at that! If we somehow managed to buy this property, then could not get zoning approval for our site plan, we would be stuck with a white elephant—an empty school and acres of land we couldn't use. In a life of high-risk ventures, this would be one of the biggest risks our family had ever dared to shoulder.

I couldn't help myself. I had completely fallen in love with the property. A couple of times each day, I would drive by Irving School, as it was known at the time. I would park my Jeep and walk the grounds. I explored the landscape and the neighborhood. In fact, there weren't many homes nearby. I could see a new Islamic center taking shape, surrounded by lakes, rolling meadows and well-kept mansions. Towering walnut trees bordered one side of the acreage. More than the beauty of the site, my own faith had been deepening with each passing year. I trusted that God would help us build this house of worship. I was reminded of the Prophet Muhammad once encountering a Bedouin who turned his camel loose, trusting in divine protection that he wouldn't lose this animal that was his lifeline. The Prophet wisely advised: "Tether your camel, *then* trust in Allah." It wasn't enough for me merely to pray that this dream would become reality. I was going to have to accept the huge challenge of securing this property, winning local approvals and making the renovations.

I knew what I had to do. I had to invite more people to walk across the landscape of our future home. The site sold itself, though, and this dream was catchy.

In fact, a lot of people were walking these grounds and catching their own dreams on the site. One Sunday afternoon, I stopped by the school and found a church bus in the parking lot. All across America, Christian congregations were dreaming of laying down new suburban roots. I parked my Jeep and chatted with some of the church members milling around. They told me they were excited that this could be the new home of their church.

There were many more. I learned that a Jewish day school was considering a bid, a Pakistani group wanted to establish a cultural center—even an Iraqi group had an eye on this property. Clearly, our bid would go up against competitive offers from some highly motivated parties.

As I drew support for this new idea, I also faced competition from other

Muslim leaders. Our site would be springing up between two other existing Muslim congregations, each about a dozen miles from this Square Lake Road site. The Islamic Association of Greater Detroit (IAGD) in Rochester Hills was directly east of us; the Islamic Cultural Association (ICA) was the same distance, but southwest of us. At the time, leaders from these two groups told me they were concerned that we might draw away some of their supporters, many of whom lived in the very communities where we hoped to find our own new families. As a businessman, I understood those fears. Neither of these existing congregations was excited by my vision of establishing this "21st-century mosque." I also faced run-ins with a few community leaders who disliked me for various reasons, sometimes simply because my aggressive personality had rubbed them the wrong way.

My main focus was the deadline for that sealed bid—a huge hurdle, especially considering that we had almost no money for such a grand project.

"I need advice—and anything else you can do to assist us," I told Ghassan Beydoun, a real estate broker and former head of the American-Arab Anti-Discrimination Committee in Michigan. We had worked together on issues through the years. He agreed to act as our agent in the purchase and generously donated most of his share of earned commissions. Beyond helping me to prepare the bid, he encouraged me personally at just the right moment.

"Victor, with your reputation for community service, there'll be many supporters for this project," he said. Those were just the kind of words I needed to hear as I was facing such a daunting challenge.

After a lot of research and discussion, we agreed to offer $675,000 for the acreage and the school. We placed no contingencies, which we knew was a desirable provision for anyone selling an old building. We considered our bid aggressive—comparatively high for this property, even in these wealthy suburbs. Every step in this process was conducted with lots of consultation—known as *shura* in Arabic—which is the traditional Muslim way of making such community decisions.

Ghassan's connections were very helpful. His brother-in-law, attorney Jamal Hamood—whom I once supported as a candidate for Dearborn City Council—offered pro bono legal help in our efforts. With very little money in the bank, these were crucial gifts. Senior partners in Jamal's law firm, Stone, Biber and O'Toole, were invaluable in their advice.

Everyone was surprised when our bid won! City of Pontiac officials seemed to be ecstatic, admitting that they had not expected that much money for the property. I received the news with mixed feelings. I had been running on adrenaline to meet that deadline for the bid. Now I had to live with what we had achieved. I felt like I was waking up from a deep sleep. We still owed more than $600,000. The reality was that, other than verbal commitments from our handful of key supporters, we did not have money in the bank to pay the balance. Thank God that Shahina was a rock behind me. We had nothing personal to gain in this effort—only an enormous debt to shoulder. Comerica Bank knew me as a client from my business ventures and approved a loan, guaranteed with our home as collateral.

As I was reeling from the full responsibility of what I had just done, I began to hear from many supporters that they would stand beside us. They became more committed to the cause when they learned how much that Shahina and I had laid on the line.

To secure these financial commitments, Jamal and I developed an attractive proposal for an Islamic center, with facilities for the entire family—unlike any other mosque in our area. At that time, Christian churches were including family life centers in their expansion plans. Jamal and I similarly emphasized that our new center would be a place where men, women and children could gather to enjoy all aspects of community life. Of course, the heart of this new center would be the mosque—for prayers, worship and other religious services—but we also would accommodate lifecycle events. For recreation, we would start with the school's gymnasium and later add amenities like tennis courts and a swimming pool.

Jamal also was key in organizing the financial side of the campaign. He designed a limited liability corporation (LLC) and an entity we referred to as the I-Comp, or Islamic Company, which had room for multiple shareholders in purchasing the property. Once we successfully developed the property into a Muslim center, those I-Comp shares would be donated to the mosque and the participating investors would get a tax deduction. But, if the project was stalled with legal challenges or general red tape, then the investors would be reassured that we could try to use the property as an investment. This way, even if we did hit some kind of a brick wall after winning the bid, they would not have risked their money. With this arrangement, we were able to get promises of $250,000. The bank loan would cover the balance. I knew that the issue of interest on such a loan would be controversial among some Muslim traditionalists, but my own earlier research into these matters gave me confidence in explaining to other Muslims that such a mortgage was not a forbidden practice.

I was overjoyed at the diversity among our major supporters. A Shia Lebanese group from Dearborn—including Ned Fawaz, Jamal and Ghassan—pledged 30 percent of what we needed. Donations also came from South African native Dr. Farook Tootla, Syrian American Dr. Ghalia Katranji and Indian American Dr. Yusuf Siddique. I visited the Lebanese-American Club in Dearborn to solicit an investment from Ali Jawad, a prominent businessman. He dug his hand into his pocket, pulled out a checkbook and bought a share on the spot. I also got support from Pakistani American Zubair Rathur and my lifelong friend Syed Salman. Khalid Baghdadi joined later, at a critical juncture when our operational cash flow was running low. I also bought a share. This group would become the board of trustees for the proposed mosque and remained involved in the ongoing *shura*, or collective decision-making process.

There were others, as well. Hisham Rushdy, an Egyptian-born entrepreneur who had secured the large donation for the TV series a few years earlier, met me in the Irving School parking lot one day to learn about the new venture. When I explained to him what we were doing, he countersigned a third-party check made out to him and handed it to me.

"I had this money coming from the settlement of a lawsuit. I'd like to donate this to your project," he said. Hisham passed away of a heart attack soon afterward, while swimming near Egypt's Alexandria coast—may God bless his soul.

Yusuf Johnson, an African-American entrepreneur who lived not far from the mosque, offered a substantial monthly donation to defray operational expenses during the early days. We made a point of describing our new suburban mosque as a sister congregation to the Muslim Center of Detroit on Davison Avenue, near the Lodge Freeway. That center, founded by Imam Abdullah El-Amin and Mitchell Shams-Uddin, is a Detroit landmark. The Muslims associated with that mosque proudly claimed to be followers of Imam Warith Deen Muhammad, the son of Elijah Muhammad. When Elijah died, Warith publicly encouraged Nation of Islam members to embrace mainstream Islam. From the beginning, we wanted to establish ties with our brothers and sisters in the city. Our association with that nationally respected African-American mosque in Detroit was a strong statement of Islamic unity across racial lines.

This commitment to diversity was our unique appeal. The broad array of our early donors showed us how compelling that vision was. People were ready for this. This was going to be the first mosque in Michigan committed to a non-sectarian approach to worship, programming and operations. No ethnicity, race or sect would dominate. Shia and Sunni came together to encourage us. So, it was quite natural to call this new home the Muslim Unity Center.

Supporters flocked to the project whether they had deep pockets or not. I will never forget a Bosnian refugee and an African-American maintenance man from the Pontiac schools who volunteered to keep the grass cut and the building clean. They could not afford to make cash donations, but encouraged us with their commitment of sweat equity.

However, all of these donations, promises and plans didn't mean a thing if the building could not be put to our intended use. Unfortunately, we had the least control over this next hurdle: winning approval from the township for our plans. I was not naïve about this. As a businessman, I had scars from other battles with municipal codes and building inspectors, trying to secure occupancy permits for new furniture stores—and then a host of other clearances, from signage to sewage. I knew that winning approval for this mosque was going to be an absolutely vital step in the process. Anyone following newspapers in the 1990s had seen the headlines about congregations frustrated in their suburban expansion plans. I was also aware that most of those groups were Christian. I knew that we faced the added burden of neighbors' anxieties about our ethnicities and our faith.

I approached this challenge in a serious way, mainly by trying to win over the hearts and reassure the minds of local officials. I had helped U.S. Rep. Joe Knollenberg win his seat in Congress, so I asked Joe for his advice. We all knew that the key figure in this process was the township's tough-as-nails supervisor Joe Korzon, who had a reputation for protecting residents' rights against any development that might threaten property values. Joe Knollenberg advised me not to be afraid. "Joe Korzon is a fair man," he said.

When I finally approached Korzon, I found him smiling, receptive and willing to talk. I took heart from that warm reception. I remember thinking: The loving God is showing us mercy. With no signs of serious concern, we scheduled a public hearing on the matter before the local zoning board. The letterhead we used for our proposal bore the formal name of the nonprofit we had established, even though that group had no formal headquarters: the American Society for Religious and Cultural Understanding (ASRCU). The mailing address on the letterhead was a post office box held by my company. We already had distributed to potential supporters our promotional literature, promising what we understood to be expansions that would unfold over a number of years. In particular, the recreational facilities—tennis courts, a swimming pool and so on—showed the breadth of our overall vision, and not what we planned to build any time soon.

Jamal Hamood, Syed Salman and I thought we had done our homework before the hearing and we arrived with high hopes. In addition to my friendly reception with Knollenberg and Korzon, I also knew a number of the Republicans on the zoning board and we assumed that we were very close to success.

Then, as I parked and made my way to the hearing room, I realized that a whole lot of people were heading in the same direction. A crowd was forming.

"What's going on?" I asked someone as I walked into the room. That's when I got a look at the agenda for the evening. There was only one item: the Irving property.

I couldn't believe what I was seeing all around me. I turned to someone else: "Why are all these people here?"

He confirmed: "Irving School."

I soon learned that many of these people were part of something called the Square Lake Neighborhood Association—and their goal was nothing short of killing our project.

What a shock! I remember swearing softly to myself in utter surprise. Why hadn't I envisioned this? Clearly, I had been overly confident. Near me, Syed Salman was more devout. He was whispering a *dua*, praying for God's assistance. I saw a few of my friends filtering into the room among the stern-faced neighbors. Not one of my friends was smiling.

What made me angry was my own lack of preparation. I had been blindsided. Had I known this kind of outpouring might materialize, I could have organized a neighborhood-wide effort to educate people and respond to their concerns. As a businessman, I knew a lot about reaching the public with a positive message. But, I'd had no warning we would need such outreach.

One reason I had missed this essential step was the fact that there were relatively few neighbors surrounding our site. I still remember whispering to a friend that night: "Where on God's earth did all these people come from?"

I wondered how so many people could claim to be concerned neighbors when there was so much open land surrounding the school. Standing at the front door of Irving School, I didn't even need the fingers on one hand to count the homes I could see. A single neighbor lived along Square Lake near a curve in the road, barely visible from the school's front door. On one side, woods totally shielded homes from our view. There were a few nearby homes to the east of us, and construction of a new subdivision was underway in the general area. But none of those homes were close to the building.

I discovered that this neighborhood association circled the entire lake, which comprised the more than 100 homeowners who seemed to be opposed to any kind of new development on the school property. Those residents also had encouraged homeowners surrounding Hammond Lake, which was west of our property, to join them that evening in trying to kill our proposal, using the sheer force of a concerted public outcry.

I will never forget the discomfort as I walked through that room and slumped into one of two seats reserved for us near the board. Jamal sat next to me. My enthusiasm had fizzled. I could see my other friends searching for empty seats. A couple of them had to settle for standing uncomfortably along the wall.

The officials who held our project in their hands sat on high-backed leather chairs along a stage with microphones poised in front of each seat. All of those nail-biting courtroom dramas I had seen on TV flashed through my mind.

Township Clerk Wilma Cotton banged the gavel and we began with the Pledge of Allegiance. The slow cadence of the reading of the minutes and other routine business was sheer agony. All I could see was the stern faces of our opponents, ready to pounce.

Then, we were asked to present our plans. Jamal rose and did a marvelous job of outlining our project. Somehow, he managed a warm smile. He seemed cool and confident as he talked about our sincere desire for this new house of worship—and our hopes to welcome families to use other facilities we would add later. He finished. He sat down.

The room was too quiet, I thought. I grimaced, bracing for what I knew would come next.

Two microphones had been set up for public comments, and one speaker after another charged that our project would ruin the neighborhood. They talked about traffic. Public safety. Parking problems. Noise. At first, I was surprised that none of the neighbors brought up our faith or ethnicity; I then realized that the opposition was smart about not tipping their hand to potential bigotry. We all knew that an underlying hatred still existed in at least some quarters of the community. Research into the title of the property had revealed an old racist, anti-Semitic exclusionary clause from an earlier era, barring any sale to "people of color or non-gentile." Such language is unenforceable today but showed the legacy of assumptions made by the longest-standing residents in the area.

One speaker after another came at us—head on—in classic arguments used to block suburban expansion. We sat through a long litany of concerns about safety, congestion and property values.

This actually made me feel worse. These arguments would have been relatively easy to deflect, if only I had seen them coming. The questions about traffic and parking were bogus. After all, this site had been a school for many years! In fact, our use of the facility would involve fewer hours, each week, then the school had used at the site. I also realized that we had been foolish to talk about future expansions—tennis courts and a swimming pool. Those were distant dreams, but they proved to be potent ammunition for the neighbors. Had I only laid the groundwork through conversations with neighbors, we could have reassured residents and even revised our plans to soften their opposition. We might have also encouraged people to admit any anxieties they had about our faith or ethnic background—and then found ways to reassure them on those matters, as well.

Instead, we had this confrontational showdown like a climactic scene from *Law & Order*. Although the opponents did not overtly raise anti-Muslim bias, they certainly went for my jugular. In fact, I was impressed at their due diligence as they came at me. They had prepared for this meeting better than I had. They had traced the post office box on our letterhead to my company. No one asked me why we listed that address, which I easily could have explained. It was just a matter of convenience. Instead, our opponents leapt to their own conclusions. They were suspicious of my motives and had contacted the Michigan Department of Commerce, in Lansing. They dug into the public information about my business and real estate investments. They tried to portray me, as the group's leader, as an opportunist with an ulterior motive of somehow profiteering on the deal. In doing so, however, they overplayed their hand. My retail business was reputable, and I was well known to public officials in the area. As I closely watched the back-and-forth that evening, I could sense that these attacks—while personally painful—weren't landing with the commission. They didn't seem to be impressed by such claims.

The assault was so relentless that I remember looking stunned when the officials finally turned their faces toward me. "What do you have to say?"

I still was stunned, but I realized that the tidal wave of objections apparently had ended. It was my turn.

My turn to—to say what? I take pride in my ability to address people. But that evening, I had been surprised by the crowd, annoyed at my own lack of preparation and deeply upset by the endless verbal salvos. Beyond all of that, I felt terrible for the busy professionals who were so sincere in supporting our project, including doctors, engineers and business executives. They deserved far more respect than the sneering claims made by this crowd. I still remember a couple of the speakers who spoke derisively of us as a "society"—a word that was part of our formal name on the letterhead—and stressing that word as they talked about us, as if we were somehow an ominous secret society.

I was not at my best. I paused. I turned to Jamal. He reminded me to smile, as he had done earlier. Clearly, we needed some time to regroup and regain our momentum in adapting this plan for approval.

Row upon row of angry faces looked my way. An empty microphone awaited me.

As I rose and walked forward, my heart sank to see the sadness on the faces of my handful of friends. That just made me mad. I'm tough. I can shoulder rough opposition. But my friends were good, solid members of the community who had just faced a humiliating assault for their good-hearted support of a house of worship. It just wasn't fair!

I remember forcing a smile. I shook my head in disbelief as I began. "There is clearly some misunderstanding," I said, dramatically unfolding a piece of paper I had used to take notes during the session. "I started to write down the points I would need to address, but you can see—I ran out of paper."

I kept my remarks very short. I concluded: "We ask for the decision on this matter to be moved to the next scheduled meeting date for us to work with our good neighbors, clarify matters and allay their concerns. There are too many misunderstandings about us, our goals and the ways we intend to use this property. We wish we had known about these concerns earlier, and we now need time to address these issues in a helpful way."

The officials voted to give us three weeks.

We had survived that confrontation. Now I saw clearly what I should have done in the first place. I knew exactly how to proceed. We could have planned a legal challenge, but that approach can take years, cost untold amounts of money—and, in the end, winning in the courts can entrench an ill will throughout the region.

We needed to change the neighbors' attitudes toward us. I quickly concluded that we would need to make concessions to sway this group. We also needed to educate them about our faith and soothe their fears.

Now we also had the glare of a public spotlight. News of that showdown reached reporters. I had known Tarek Hamada, the religion writer at *The Detroit News*, for some time, and he filed a solid story the very next day. In Tarek's story, I was moved to read the kind words of Rabbi Ernst Conrad, of nearby Temple Kol Ami. The revelation of the racist and anti-Semitic covenant in the property's title was evidence of past bigotry, even if speakers in the public hearing had scrupulously avoided such claims. In the newspaper, Conrad said, "When we too moved into a WASPY neighborhood, we weren't welcome." That broadened our base of allies in the community and publicly identified an underlying issue. Conrad, who died in 2009, was a giant in the interfaith movement—all the more impressive because he did his work with little fanfare until his voice was needed. Then he would speak out, as he did in the pages of *The Detroit News*. Born in Germany in the 1920s, Conrad had experienced childhood persecution before moving to America at age 18. Like me, he found that many events throughout his life compelled him to defend his community—and other minorities, as well. In 2003, he received the Michigan Coalition for Human Rights' Lifetime Commitment Award.

Through the courage of people like Rabbi Conrad, I was coming to appreciate the strength of the larger interfaith community in southeast Michigan. There were allies all around me who were courageous enough to defend Muslims—not because they were Muslims themselves, but because they knew that diversity is America's greatest strength. We needed to stand together. Sam Yono, a prominent Iraqi Christian, told me recently, recalling those days, "Victor, when I found out your community is interested in that property, we pulled out our bid." Such comments continue to warm my heart even today.

A reporter from the *Oakland Press*, which was heavily distributed in the cities and townships surrounding our site, took an even more ambitious approach to the story. He met me at a local restaurant for an interview and I noticed that reporting on Islam was new to him. I explained that we are an Abrahamic faith—stemming from the legacy of the patriarch Abraham, like our Jewish and Christian brothers and sisters. I described how a mosque functions as the heart of community worship, much like a church or synagogue. An *Oakland Press* photographer visited a mosque in a nearby city, to show families at prayer. The resulting full-page article presented an overview of Islam, but that was exactly what people needed to see in the neighborhoods surrounding our site. That made our public relations effort a whole lot easier.

Then, we took to heart the board's suggestion of meeting with neighbors. We invited them to meet with us at the school, and this time, I had carefully prepared. I asked Syed Salman and Dr. Tootla, both of them mild-mannered professionals, to join me in listening to questions and concerns. It worked.

One neighbor suggested: "Why not create a buffer of residential lots on two sides of the proposed mosque, which would still leave you more than 5 acres for your center?" In effect, this would reduce the overall footprint of our center by nearly half and reassure the surrounding home-owners that—whatever our future plans might be—we could not expand our facilities across the original 11.5-acre parcel.

This had not occurred to me. I jumped at the idea. The more I consid-ered this suggestion, the more it made good financial sense. We could spin off and sell a significant chunk of the property to help pay off our loan. I was so surprised at how this meeting was unfolding that I was happy to let our neighbors take credit for pushing this concept. This was a win-win-win solution, guaranteed to please a third party as well. By turning those acres into residential property, the township would add to its tax base.

Armed with this consensus plan, we returned to the board. This time, there were no surprises. Jamal presented the new plan. We also added some allies to our presentation: Rabbi Conrad, as well as another giant of the interfaith movement, the late Rev. Bill Gepford. They talked about the value of houses of worship, including mosques, to the well-being of the whole community. To this day, I miss those noble souls. I intentionally kept a low profile at this second hearing. I let our allies speak for us.

When the entire deal was laid out, there were other accommodations, as well. We had to compromise our happy dreams of tennis courts and a pool. That was a longer-term vision of a center catering to family life. If it materialized, we would have invited our neighbors to enjoy the amenities.

The other restriction was a ban on an amplified *adhan*, the call to prayer. Some of our neighbors had visited Muslim countries and knew about broadcasts from minarets. Again, we were happy to agree. This was a moot point for us. The purpose of the *adhan* is to announce prayer times for the faithful within earshot—similar to churches ringing bells at service times. For Muslims living in dense urban settings, the *adhan* is a practical part of daily life—but none of us lived close enough to the new site to hear such a broadcast. So, we complied with the neighbors' request.

The board voted. We won!

At least, we had won the right to undertake the enormous work needed to launch a Muslim center. As soon as possible, we had to build up our base of supporters by initiating services on Fridays, the Muslim equivalent of the Sabbath. Syed Salman took charge of organizing Friday prayers. A classroom equipped with a comfortable expanse of carpeting was chosen to become our prayer room, since Muslims form rows and bend down onto the floor in prayer. Members of the community pitched in to furnish the building's other rooms. Because I was in the furniture business, I was responsible for tables and chairs. Just like churches and synagogues, Muslim centers have weekend classes for children. My sister and brother-in-law from Chicago, Shahnawaz and Akhtar Khan, picked up children's furniture for our classrooms from a rummage sale at a school. Dr. Nakadar paid for new basketball hoops to be installed in the gym.

We had to fix a long list of issues to meet the building code—and we completed enough of those upgrades to receive a temporary occupancy permit that went into effect one day before the start of the holy month of Ramadan, in February 1994. That seemed to be a blessing from the heavens. Suddenly, our new challenge became trying to find a *hafiz*, a person who had memorized the Quran and was expert in reciting it in melodic tones. That seemed like an impossible quest on such short notice—but we spread the word that we were looking.

Another sign of God's gracious mercy: I received an unexpected call from Washington, D.C. "Do you need a *hafiz* for Ramadan?"

"Yes!" I said eagerly. "We're looking."

As it turned out, this was an international connection. The caller explained that a Pakistani *hafiz* had been invited to a Salt Lake City mosque to lead nightly prayers during Ramadan, "But it looked like the *hafiz* would be delayed, so the Utah mosque got another one."

Then, the *hafiz* showed up, after all!

"We'd love to have him," I said. So, the *hafiz* was re-routed onto a Greyhound bus, despite a blizzard that was snarling traffic across much of the northern U.S. I thanked God that his bus was able to make the trek—and that I was able to make it through the snow to the downtown Detroit bus station to get him. That poor man got no rest! I brought him home, provided a quick meal and took him straight to the mosque to lead that night's prayers. For Ramadan, the Quran's text is divided into equal parts so that the entire Quran can be recited during the month's nightly prayers. Throughout those weeks, the *hafiz* stayed in our home. What a blessing it was to hear him warming up during the day with the verses he would recite that night!

Once the fasting month ended with the Eid celebration and the weather began to warm in Michigan, we turned to the other projects necessary to gain full clearance for occupancy. That checklist included a landscaped berm—a buffer screening the residential lots bordering the mosque. Newly planted evergreens, maples and dogwood shrubs were watered by our own kids, along with other youth from our congregation. We had to repair and expand the existing parking lot. There was a long list of cosmetic and building-code issues, as well.

The grand opening was held on a hot summer day with a carnival-like festival for all ages. We even brought in a dunk tank. Our son, Yusuf, got a chance to drop Dad into the water. He was surprisingly good with his left hand!

Then, there was an emotional blow. Joyce Kafi, the woman who first told me about the site, died. Her son, Yusuf Kafi, rode his bicycle over to the center with the news. When he found me, he told me about his mother's death and then surprised me with a check. "Mom willed this as a donation to the mosque," he said.

Tears ran down my cheeks as I took that check. In the heat of everything else over the past year, I had nearly forgotten about Joyce. I prayed that she was resting in peace in paradise.

That reminder of Joyce's crucial role was an exclamation point on a truth that was so clear to me now: We were a community! This Muslim center was a collective dream. For all of the debt and anxiety and hard work I had shouldered personally, none of this would have been possible without our friends and allies—men, women and even children surrounding us.

This was a critical milestone in my life. I kept thinking of the Quran 47:7, "O you who believe, if you will aid the cause of God—God will aid you and plant your feet firmly."

The story of our visionary, inclusive dream has crossed the continent. When the CBS network produced a documentary, *Islam in America*, they included a 20-minute segment on the formation of the Unity Center. The central point of the CBS story was showing that an Islamic house of worship could, indeed, fit into a conservative suburban area. How was this accomplished? The interfaith community rose up to help, CBS reported, describing this as America at its best: Jewish and Christian neighbors coming to the aid of our minority, because everyone deserves equal access in this country.

Millions of other Americans saw our story in *U.S. News & World Report*, in a major cover story about the rapidly changing religious landscape in this country. In that issue, a group of stories by various reporters was headlined collectively: *In God We Trust—Testing Personal Faith in a Cynical Age*. A photographer from the magazine, Brian Palmer, spent two days photographing me as I engaged in my daily routine at work and at the mosque. The editors chose to feature photos of many different people in the midst of prayer—so my photo showed me in a traditional Muslim gesture during daily prayers. The reporter chosen to write our story within that overall package was Tarek Hamada, which I appreciated. Tarek wrote that I pushed for the name Unity Center, "because he believes the mosque must be a multicultural intuition. Too many mosques in the United States are focused narrowly on the ancestry and ethnicity of their members, Begg feels." Already, we had attracted families of Syrian, Lebanese, Egyptian and Indian descent, he reported. As Tarek's sharp eye scanned our prayer room, he caught the sign that said, "Please respect all variations."

In that story, I expressed my highest hopes for the future. "To me, America is the most Islamic country in the world," I told *U.S. News & World Report* readers. "Islam stands for democracy, for free enterprise. Prophet Muhammad was a businessman. It's very easy to be a Muslim in the United States."

CHAPTER 9

Why We Serve

Said Prophet Joseph as he became a vizier in his adopted land: "Appoint me over the store-houses of the land. I will indeed guard them."

Quran 12:55

"You new citizens are a beautiful sight to behold!" U.S. Senator Carl Levin told our crowd along the Detroit River on the Fourth of July, 1987. "Leave your old fears and scars behind as you begin a new destiny that embodies hope."

Shahina and I wanted to take the citizenship oath at this special event in Detroit's downtown Hart Plaza, the riverside landmark where Antoine de la Mothe Cadillac landed in 1701. He founded Fort Pontchartrain du Detroit, a settlement that became Michigan's main metropolis. We requested to be part of this particular ceremony because so many people we admired were coming to celebrate with us, including Levin and U.S. Secretary of State George Shultz.

It turned out to be a beautiful summer morning for us and our three children. Our daughter Sofia was in a stroller. Yusuf, who was 2, was tempted to stray, so I held his hand tightly as Shahina and I placed our hands on our hearts, ready to recite the Pledge of Allegiance. Our oldest són, Sami, was so caught up in the pageantry that he mirrored our pose and proudly recited the pledge with us. Then, when it was time to take the oath, he raised his right hand, too.

Photographer Stephen Cantrell spotted Sami's solemn participation in the pledge to the flag. He moved around the crowd until we appeared to be in the foreground and Detroit's Renaissance Center was squarely in the background. Then, he took his picture. Cantrell's photo became the main image of that special Fourth of July event in the Observer & Eccentric newspapers, a chain that served the suburbs. This was obviously an emotional event for many of us in the crowd. I had tears in my eyes.

Detroit's NBC affiliate, WDIV-Channel 4, interviewed me in front of the Detroit River. The crew lined up the shot so that I was facing the international border. Just across the river was Windsor, a Canadian city that maintains elements of both its British and French heritage. The camera also was able to pan across the Detroit skyline behind me. It was a truly international setting, and I shared a few words about my pride in contributing to this wonderful nation where I was now a citizen. That little video was such an iconic snapshot of pride in America that WDIV turned it into a 10-second public service announcement that aired repeatedly, celebrating both patriotism and diversity.

With citizenship, I became entitled to vote—a right that I am well aware is not enjoyed in many other parts of the world. And I could now carry a U.S. passport, with all of its prestige, in international travel—once again, a right that I was thankful to receive. Whenever I pull out my passport, to this day, I think of the millions around the world who cannot move so freely.

Just as the WDIV producers realized in their brief video clip, this was all preparation for expanded public service. The rights America bestows on its citizens are powerful, but our thanks for those rights should be expressed in the way we reach out to help others.

That's why I played a key role in the freeing of a man who, today, is remembered as Ahmad A. Rahman, a noted scholar in African-American history who served as a University of Michigan professor for many years. The time I first met him, he was an inmate serving a life sentence for murder. Rahman, born in 1951 in Chicago, showed such promise as a student that his teachers urged him to aim for Harvard. He was exceptionally brilliant and, at an early age, also developed such a strong commitment to social justice that he joined the Black Panthers under Fred Hampton. At the time, Hampton was considered a dangerous "militant" by law enforcement agencies. In books and two documentary films, today, Hampton is portrayed as an inspiring black leader who was tragically slain in 1969 in a raid that amounted to his execution by police. His death did not scare away Rahman, though, who further dedicated himself to combating injustice.

By 1971, Rahman had moved to the Panthers' Detroit group and wound up going on what he and several colleagues thought was a citizens' intervention into a notorious drug den. Unfortunately, everything about the action went wrong, mainly because of the provocative involvement of an FBI unit that was working secretly to trap young African-American "militants" in Detroit. Rahman and his friends wound up confronting not the drug dealers they expected, but some college students. In the chaos, a 23-year-old resident of the house was killed by one of Rahman's companions. Three of the four accused men pleaded guilty and received relatively modest sentences. The actual shooter was released by 1983. Rahman was a victim of the wildly unfair judicial imbalances in that era any time that race was a provocative factor. He argued that he was innocent. He risked going to trial—and he was convicted. The judge sentenced him to live out his life behind bars, even though he was not responsible for the violence that night. This is not my own opinion about these events—this is the story *Detroit Free Press* investigative reporter James Ricci unfolded in a series of front-page reports, trying to correct the historical record and campaign for Rahman's release.

In prison, Rahman embraced Islam. His supporters on the outside knew that I was both a prominent Muslim and had connections with Republican leaders, including John Engler. When I first got involved in this case, Engler was the Michigan Senate majority leader. The more I heard about Rahman's plight, the more I became convinced that I had to help. To this day, I am frustrated at the rate at which American courts sentence young black men to prison, whether they are Muslim or not. The American rate of incarceration is an international scandal.

As I looked into Rahman's case and Ricci's reporting, I was impressed by this man's whole approach to life behind bars. He was the first person allowed to enroll in a University of Michigan graduate program while incarcerated—and he earned a master's degree. I went to see him in prison and will never forget what he told me: "I'm in prison, but the prison is not in me."

As Ricci's stories in the *Detroit Free Press* landed week after week, people began to refer to Rahman as "the Mandela of Michigan." Many people joined the effort and, before he left office, Gov. James Blanchard was bombarded with thousands of signatures on a petition to commute his sentence. Blanchard refused. That's why Engler wound up playing such a crucial role and my lobbying was especially effective. I supported Engler's long-shot campaign against Blanchard in 1990 and built on my already solid relationship with him. I was among those who celebrated with Engler after his hair's breadth victory of less than 1 percentage point. Then, I helped with the preparation of Rahman's appeal to Engler. His legal team advised me that we would need to secure a full report on Rahman's behavior behind bars, a parole board recommendation and a statement from the victim's family.

Reaching that family was a challenge. The only living relative was a sister based in Florida. Rahman had reached out to her. She said that she simply wanted to put the memories behind her, but she did believe Rahman to be innocent. We needed her to come to Michigan to be a visible part of the effort to free him; my role was arranging a plane ticket to bring her to Michigan. She stayed in our home.

The next morning, Shahina, my sister, Nilo and I drove her to a meeting of the parole board at the Lakeland Correctional Facility, a prison in Coldwater, Michigan. The hearing went well. Lots of favorable testimony was offered by people, including elected officials and other community leaders, who made emotional appeals for his freedom. I remember one man, who once had served with Rahman in prison, talked about how Rahman remained a positive influence in his life. "The dude keeps me out of trouble," the former inmate said. "Even behind bars, he gives me these regular calls to keep me straight!"

Engler finally signed his commutation in 1992. Rahman became a free man—after more than two decades behind bars—on the day before Thanksgiving. He had gone into the prison system as a teenager and he came out at age 41. Like Mandela, from this very unlikely beginning and the trauma of so many years of imprisonment, Rahman immediately stepped up as a community leader pushing for peace and justice. He earned his doctorate and became a beloved teacher who inspired thousands of university students. The first Fairness in Media award at our Unity Banquet went to James Ricci for launching the whole effort to free Rahman. Before Rahman died of a heart attack in 2015, he also won many honors, including the 2013 College Professor of the Year from the Michigan Council for Social Studies.

When he was given that prize, Rahman talked about what had motivated him through such a painful and remarkable life. He said, "I am motivated by a drive to make a difference for those persons I see in need. They are quite often 'the least of these.' Much of the energy of us academics goes toward achieving status within academia. Many of the best minds that could challenge and solve problems in the inner city are exclusively occupied, writing academic books and articles that have no impact on the most important issues facing black America. I have sought to avoid this ivory tower phenomenon. I have always worked to balance academic achievement with what I regard as the more important goals for Detroit of achieving real solutions. At one time during my youth I called myself a revolutionary. Now I see myself as more of a *solutionary*."

The connection with Islam was obvious to me. While the Prophet Muhammad was one of the world's greatest spiritual leaders, he always was concerned with the entire well-being of the community. He was truly a religious revolutionary—but he also was a solutionary. Throughout the Prophet's teaching runs a passion for social justice—for helping the vulnerable—that many Muslims feel to this day. As a Muslim, that is why I got involved in helping to free Rahman. That is why Islam moves so many of us to serve in so many ways.

That is not to say that all Muslims share this grand vision. There are many personal and ethnic agendas that can separate us. My own assumption was that the Republican Party represented many of our values in the 1990s. By that time, many Muslims of Indo-Pakistani and Arab descent were professionals living in the suburbs—at least, many of the Muslims I regularly worked with in the various groups I supported. In that era, I often invited Muslim friends to political events. I remember attending my first Lincoln Day dinner, a popular annual Republican fundraiser across the northern states, at a posh hotel in the upscale suburb of Troy. A friend who was prominent in the party offered me a ticket to a special event with President George H.W. Bush at Detroit's Renaissance Center. That was my first experience of seeing a president in person, and it inspired me to get even more involved in the party. I got started at the grassroots, becoming an active member of the Bloomfield Hills Area Republican Club. In the next election cycle, my name appeared on the ballot as a precinct delegate—an entry-level position for those who wanted to give serious support to the party. My name did not draw enough votes to become a delegate, but then realized that I simply wasn't widely known among GOP voters at that point.

That changed after I got involved in backing Joe Knollenberg, whose support was crucial when we launched the Muslim Unity Center. Initially, Joe was a long-shot candidate with little money, running in my home congressional district. I met him and found that we shared a lot of political and social values. I also found that some of my friends already had agreed to endorse him. No one expected him to win, but Shahina and I threw our full support behind him and worked hard throughout his campaign. His win was such an upset that, when Shahina and I showed up at the venue for his election-night reception, the place was absolutely dead. All the Republican big shots were heading to other venues, wanting to celebrate with candidates who were sure to win. But we stayed at the Knollenberg reception, watching the results on big-screen TVs. As the numbers stacked up for Joe in the TV reports, one couple after another began to arrive until the place was packed. Mobile vans from every local TV station finally camped outside, wanting to interview the dark-horse winner. What a thrill it was to bet against the odds and win with Joe!

In addition to helping with the mosque, Joe named me to his new finance committee. In 1994, I was invited to Washington, D.C. to attend the public signing of the Contract with America—a master stroke of GOP political theater held six weeks before the congressional elections that year. Echoing lines from President Reagan's 1985 State of the Union address, the contract signing was orchestrated on the steps of the U.S. Capitol.

After that, Shahina and I went back and forth from Michigan to D.C. several times (including one spring trip during which we especially enjoyed the city's cherry blossoms in full bloom). True to his word, Joe kept lifting up issues of concern to Muslim voters, although this is where we began to run into some conflict. For example, the newly empowered Republicans wanted to push legislation authorizing formal prayer in public schools—a policy that I strongly opposed. While Muslims welcome talking about God in all settings, that particular campaign for what was called "school prayer" was something else altogether. It was an effort by evangelical Christians to have their prayers recited in our classrooms. I am a strong supporter of our separation of church and state in such matters.

On many issues, we agreed. On some, we disagreed. That's the nature of politics.

By 1994, I knew that I was gaining acceptance as a national voice for Islamic perspectives on politics. I hosted a retreat for major Muslim leaders who wanted to discuss civic engagement, and participants came to our new Muslim Unity Center for the event. There, we featured one of the most important Islamic leaders in the country: Imam Warith Deen (W. D.) Muhammad. Born in 1933, son of the late Elijah Muhammad, who founded the Nation of Islam. At that time, Elijah and his family were living in the city of Hamtramck—that enclave adjacent to Highland Park where Ford built his first factory and Muslims built the first mosque in the U.S. By the time our gathering occurred, in the mid-1990s, Imam W. D. Muhammad had been based in Chicago for many years—but he publicly talked about his trip to participate in our gathering as a personal homecoming. Newspapers had been covering his courageous work since 1975, when his father died and Warith announced that he would be moving the separatist Nation of Islam back into mainline Islam. Among other things, he gave up the hereditary title that his father wanted to bestow on him: supreme minister. Instead, he took a more proper Muslim title, "imam." Of course, not everyone followed his example. Minister Louis Farrakhan broke away in 1977. But the vast majority of African-American Muslims today are Sunni largely because of Imam W. D. Muhammad's example. The Muslim Unity Center's sister congregation in Detroit, which is situated not far from where Imam Muhammad was born, is a nationally respected example of the mainstream practice of Islam among black Americans.

As we gathered at the Muslim Unity Center for our political dialogues, the future looked bright for all American Muslims. But potential divisions also were obvious. I personally liked most of the Republican political agenda, but some GOP issues were non-starters for others who joined us for the conference. Some of us had worked for GOP candidates. Other Muslims backed Democrats. Race and ethnicity and income tended to separate us. African-American Muslims had different political perspectives than South-Asian-American Muslims.

Beyond specific candidates and issues, there also were thorny issues to discuss regarding the Quran and the Prophet's own teachings about political involvement. These discussions were animated. Some Muslim traditionalists argued that any participation in Western democracies was *haram*, meaning forbidden. Others vigorously disagreed. As we talked about these foundational values, the story of Prophet Yusuf—known as Joseph to Jews and Christians—emerged as a prime example. His story is told in the book of Genesis as well as the hit Broadway musical, *Joseph and the Amazing Technicolor Dreamcoat*. An entire *surah*, or chapter of the Quran, also is dedicated to Prophet Yusuf's life. He was a newcomer to Egypt, brought there against his will. Irrespective of his religious belief or nationality, he selflessly served his adopted country despite the maltreatment and injustice he suffered.

Muslims whose families came from the Indian sub-continent or whose families had lived in the U.S. for generations had no trouble understanding Prophet Yusuf's example. This made perfect sense to us. The Prophet Muhammad said, "The best of people are those who benefit other people." We have so much to offer. But we need to be civically engaged. We had always adapted as minorities in nations where other religious groups controlled the levers of power. But Muslims who came from undemocratic regions of the Middle East tried to counter our perspective. They were used to living under Muslim-majority governments.

This was exactly the kind of spirited discussion I had hoped would unfold. Of course, I was already one of the strongest supporters of participatory democracy. We needed this kind of broad-based debate if we hoped to emerge as effective leaders. I cited passages from the Quran's chapter on *Shura*, which explains the importance of widely consulting on policies with the people who will be affected by them. Muslims also are required by Muslim tradition to obey the law of the land in which they live. Then, if we identify injustices, we are instructed to speak out publicly and to work for change. Americans have embraced that process for two centuries. Our original U.S. Constitution had many moral flaws, including its suppression of women's and African-Americans' rights. Amendments were passed through public activism and a democratic process. This is one of my favorite subjects. I can clearly see the Islamic imperative to serve as a good U.S. citizen, vote in elections, run for office and take part in vigorous debates about overcoming the injustices we continually encounter. In my view, participatory democracy is an Islamic form of government.

While I have publicly associated myself with the Republican Party, I also urge Muslims to establish warm bipartisan relationships. I had worked closely with John Engler, among other GOP officials, but Shahina and I also had established a close friendship with U.S. Rep. David Bonior and his wife, Judy. He was first elected to Congress in 1976 and became one of the most important Democrats in Washington, D.C., serving as House minority whip from 1995 to 2002. David and Judy are wonderful people whom Shahina and I enjoyed seeing through the years. Our political connections arose because of shared values. David was deeply involved in human rights and social justice.

I do not blindly follow a party slate. In 1998, Jennifer Granholm ran as a Democrat for attorney general of Michigan against a Republican candidate whom many of us did not like. He seemed cold toward minority concerns. So I organized a meeting for Granholm with some Muslim leaders, and she was very engaging. She had moved to the U.S. from Canada as a child, so she talked about her own immigrant experience. Eventually, she was elected governor of Michigan, when Engler retired. I continued to have at least some access to the governor's office in Lansing, even though I was kept at more of an arm's length as a prominent Republican.

Nationally, I had backed successful lobbying campaigns for a number of bipartisan issues. I supported the creation of a Muslim military chaplaincy at the Pentagon and I publicly talked about the need to maintain cordial relationships with the U.S. State Department and the FBI.

I also supported the Clintons' efforts to establish an annual Eid celebration at the White House in 1996. First Lady Hillary Clinton hosted that first Eid festival, and our family was invited. Michigan news media covered the historic event, and our family was featured in *The Detroit News* and on *WWJ*, a news radio station. We were pleased to find that, year after year, a White House Eid reception at the end of Ramadan became a tradition. Unfortunately, President Trump discontinued the time-honored practice in 2017—sending a hostile message both to Muslim Americans and to our Muslim allies around the world. In 2018, Trump re-established the White House Eid observance, but he limited his guest list to foreign diplomats. No Muslim-American leaders were invited.

My purpose in all of this activism was to lift up Muslim concerns and to encourage many other Muslim men and women to engage in the public square. Some may prefer to do that through political campaigns. Others may prefer donating time in community service; giving money to a good cause; showing up at a local school board meeting; or writing a letter to a newspaper. I'm pleased to see that many of the young professionals in our next generation see this as a natural part of their lives.

But sometimes, this effort to bring others into the public square is a challenge. For example, other Muslims would call me for help in approaching Gov. Engler. He had appointed me to the Michigan Community Service Commission and, during one of the commission's retreats on Mackinac Island, I was invited to Engler's summer home on the historic island. Engler wanted to know more about how the GOP might attract Muslim support. At his request, I put together a brief analysis for the party about how to draw more voters. In particular, I recommended that he establish a new minority commission, which would include a diverse array of Muslim community leaders who could share their perspectives. There already were other ethnic and religious minorities who had well-established groups that counseled political leaders. The GOP should invite us to organize a new one, I argued. I did not get quite what I hoped to see. Instead, a broader Arab-American council was formed that included Muslim issues as well as Arab-Christian issues within its portfolio. For a time, I served on that council, even though it had frustrating disagreements built into its makeup. At one of these meetings that Engler attended, a Chaldean and a Syrian representative began arguing in front of the governor. A Chaldean—a Christian with Iraqi roots—naturally would have some goals that were different from the perspective of a Syrian Muslim. The argument that day grew heated—and then spilled over into an emotional confrontation.

Finally, one of Engler's aides leaned over and whispered to me: "Victor, if Arabs could only learn to get along, they wouldn't have to worry about Israel."

That spoke volumes about the Middle East stalemate. I was embarrassed that we were fighting in front of a powerful political leader—at a time when we were supposed to be impressing the governor with our shared goals. Obviously, we didn't share anything of value in that meeting.

For many years, Shahina and I did everything we could from the sidelines. We donated to candidates, showed up at events, served on committees and volunteered our time. It got to the point that, at the end of a year, I did not even want to total up all of the tickets we had bought to political fundraisers! Some years, the total donations were jaw-dropping.

Eventually, I decided to throw my own hat into the ring.

Mindy Nathan, the vice president of the Bloomfield Hills School Board, called me one day and urged me to launch a campaign. "Victor, you ought to run for the school board."

Here is what prompted that call: Mindy thought of me following a public uproar in the high school, after a Jewish student wrote an unpleasant article about Arabs in the school newspaper. When that controversy spilled over into the larger community, I had gotten involved to bring peaceful resolution. She thus became aware of my longstanding interfaith work. Two of our children were still in the school district. At Mindy's urging, I said that I would organize an interfaith panel involving students. Our daughter, Sofi, agreed to be the Muslim speaker that day. The program went so well that Gary Doyle, the school superintendent, thought my perspective would be helpful to the school district in an ongoing way.

That's why Mindy urged me to run for a seat on the board and also add diversity. She was up for re-election herself, and we agreed to jointly campaign on a Muslim-Jewish ticket. That proved to be a winning strategy. Our joint campaign advertisements appeared in both *The Jewish News* and *The Muslim Observer*, the two regional newspapers serving our religious communities. We also displayed our lawn-signs side by side on supporters' properties all over the district.

How did we readily form such an alliance? We agreed to promote our shared religious perspectives on the value of good public education—and our concern for the next generation. Our views on the Middle East conflict may have differed, but our own kid's welfare was paramount to us.

It was a tough campaign with some nasty moments. At one point, my lawn sign was pulled up and replaced with with a competitor's. One day, while Shahina was grocery shopping, someone tore off the campaign poster on the side of our Ford van. But, I continued with my joint campaign. Shahina and I didn't back off. Although we knew people were personally targeting us, we allowed our kids to go out and distribute fliers. Even the teachers' association endorsed me. I considered that a miracle because I also had the endorsement of the local Republican club and, in Michigan, teachers' groups and the GOP tend to be like oil and water. Before it was all over, I also had some high-powered national support behind me, including a leading figure in the Bush Michigan campaign, and our Republican Congressman Joe Knollenberg. The Observer & Eccentric newspapers endorsed both Mindy and me, citing in my case my business background and my connections in Lansing as assets for the school district. I spent over $4,000 on printing, mailings, lawn signs and campaign events for a volunteer position, which takes immeasurable time, efforts, energy and occasional heat from the public; while paying zero. I fully appreciate now how critical fundraising is to election campaigns. It is only getting worse.

We won. I began serving a four-year term with Mindy, and we learned that people across the country had been watching our school board election. I was invited to appear at a Reformed rabbis' conference in Dallas to tell the story of our Muslim-Jewish cooperation. I was delighted to make the trip, and talked about the potential of Jews and Muslims building ties for our common good.

A few months later, I ran into Gov. Engler in Lansing and told him, "I'm a school board member now."

He hadn't heard. Surprised, he asked, "Were you appointed?"

"No," I said. "I ran and got elected—just like you."

Fast-forward to 2018 and we find young Muslims exceeded my expectations, as two of our young people in Detroit and Minnesota won Democratic primaries for the U.S. House of Representatives. Another Muslim, who grew up with our son Yusuf, came second after running a spirited progressive campaign for the Governor of Michigan, making national headlines. Nationwide, young Muslims in 2018 ran for all types of public offices.

When I talk to young adults, now, I always urge them to consider public office if they really want to shape the future. While high office is a common goal, it can become such an expensive unattainable goal that it amounts to an easy excuse for giving up on public service.

As I am making that point to a group, I explain that one can make a difference in any public service position. When our celebrated Superintendent Gary Doyle retired—I played an important role in hiring his successor. That meant I had an enduring influence on the local schools for years afterward. An important perspective I learned during my tenure on the board is: "A school district is not only a lamp, it's a mirror reflecting the community it serves."

At that point in my talk, I pause to let that point sink in—and then ask: "How can our schools reflect the entire community, if we don't participate?"

Occasionally, even in a small school district like ours, there is an opportunity to lift up an issue that echoes nationwide. In my case, I realized that one school board member liked to send provocative emails to the rest of the members. My main role was, as a mediator, trying to calm some of the more raucous debates about tough issues so that we could focus on shared solutions. Those emails offended me. I thought that they were a counterproductive irritant. So, one night, I thought I would help resolve the situation.

I was recognized to speak, and I asked: "Do email communications— among elected members as a group—constitute a violation of the Open Meetings Act?"

Michigan has a strong law requiring government business to be conducted in the open at public meetings, with advance notice and with minutes that must be kept as a permanent record. The goal is to avoid behind-the-scenes bullying or private deals that can fuel political abuse or corruption. Apparently, no one had posed this particular question about the Michigan law, because *The Detroit News* immediately ran a story, headlined: "Bloomfield Hills School Board Member Questions Open Meetings Act." As a result of that story, the Michigan Legislature in Lansing discussed the issue. This made its way to *USA Today*, where the headline became: "Public Officials Look to Limit Email that May Violate Open Meetings Act." My question at the board meeting, and my perspectives on the issue, were included in that nationally distributed newspaper.

There I was—just one school board member in a small regional district—but I had raised a timely question that sparked a national conversation about the official use of email in government bodies.

At the turn of the millennium, I was sure, Muslim political involvement in America was becoming widely accepted. We had a rosy future. In 2001, the crowning achievement of my public service was going to be a meeting at the White House with President George W. Bush. His campaign advisors were well aware that in the hotly contested race for Florida, 60,000 Muslim votes were cast. According to an American Muslim Alliance exit poll, 70 percent of registered non-African-American Muslim voters opted for George W. Bush. In building our case for Bush's special attention, we had managed to demonstrate the crucial tipping point represented by our community. We argued that the GOP could make more headway among Muslim communities if they would welcome us and listen to our concerns. The Bush team was impressed. A White House meeting with American-Muslim leaders was promised for late 2001. I was eager to participate. I knew it would be a truly historic occasion in which Islamic voices were sincerely welcomed in the Oval Office.

I remember telling people in early September 2001, "Our political future in America is about to change forever."

CHAPTER 10

The First Day of a New Calendar

If anyone kills an innocent human being,
it shall be as though he had killed all humankind;
If anyone saves a life,
it shall be as though he had saved the lives of all humankind.

Quran 5:32

Tuesday, September 11, 2001

7:59 a.m.

At Boston's Logan International Airport, 76 unsuspecting travelers, a flight crew of 11 and five hijackers took off on American Airlines Flight 11, a giant Boeing 767.

In the little village of Augusta near Kalamazoo, a sunny autumn morning was unfolding on the last day of my eight-year term with the Michigan Community Service Commission (MCSC). We were starting the second day of our planning retreat at Brook Lodge, a lavish conference center that once had been the estate of the founder of the Upjohn Company. We greeted each other warmly and took our seats. On one side of me sat Michigan's first lady, Michelle Engler; on the other side was Tom Watkins, the state's superintendent of schools.

8:14 a.m.

Another Boeing 767 took off from Logan, carrying five more hijackers. That was followed, minutes later, by a 757 taking off from Washington's Dulles International Airport; five terrorists were on board. Soon after that, a 757 left Newark, with the final group of four hijackers hidden among the passengers. On board each flight, the terrorists almost immediately began unfolding their grand strategy of crashing these planes into American landmarks.

At that same moment, I was thinking about the positive contributions Muslim Americans must make to our communities—and what I might do next to help promote that. I was proud of having served for eight years with this group of remarkable men and women whose mission was to use volunteerism and public service to address some of Michigan's most pressing issues. As our program began that morning, Russ Mawby, president of the W.K. Kellogg Foundation, rose to present a certificate from Gov. Engler that recognized my years of service. The text read: "Victor Begg has provided thoughtful leadership and steadfast dedication ... enabling all Michigan's citizens to engage in public problem solving through service and volunteerism, and Victor's strong commitment to promoting the mission of the MCSC has strengthened and improved the wellbeing of communities throughout our great state."

I rose to accept the honor from Russ.

There was a real sense of progress that morning. All of us at the retreat center shared the same thought: believing that together we make our State stronger, as we unite in service for the common good.

8:46 a.m.

Hijackers flew American Airlines Flight 11 into the north tower of the World Trade Center in New York City.

8:49 a.m.

The CNN network cut short an advertisement to broadcast a headline in all capital letters: "WORLD TRADE CENTER DISASTER." The video showed smoke billowing from the north tower. Anchor Carol Lin told viewers, "This just in. You are looking at obviously a very disturbing live shot there."

Two minutes later, NBC's Matt Lauer cut short an interview and reported the news on *Today*, quickly switching to a video feed of the twin towers.

Meanwhile, President George W. Bush arrived at an elementary school in Florida to help promote the importance of education.

At our retreat, I was just making my way back toward my seat so the morning's main agenda could begin. As I sat down, I felt Tom nudging my shoulder. He handed me a note to pass to Michelle. I gave it to the first lady.

She looked at the contents—and suddenly looked somber.

A phone was handed to her. Gov. Engler, her husband, was on the line. Michelle immediately stood up.

I turned to Tom. "What's this about?"

"Terrorists attacked in New York," he said.

I wanted to talk to Gov. Engler while he was on the phone, already fearing that some self-proclaimed Muslim group might be involved. My gut was sounding an alarm.

But events were moving too fast. The call was over. I had no chance to talk with him. Someone had grabbed a TV from another room and carried the set to where we had been meeting. We had to find an outlet, plug in the set and turn it on.

The scene showed the twin towers, and that ghastly plume of smoke from the north tower.

9:03 a.m.

The five hijackers, who had taken control of the second flight from Logan, now crashed their plane—with 51 passengers and a flight crew of nine—into the south tower of the World Trade Center.

At our retreat center, we gasped. Someone whistled in shock.

Everyone was scrambling. Phones were ringing.

My eyes widened.

I saw a body plummet from one of the upper floors.

My mouth opened.

We looked at each other in disbelief: The scene was beyond comprehension. New York City's great landmark was engulfed in smoke. The upper floors were ablaze. Someone already had jumped!

Then another jumped! People actually were leaping from the upper floors!

Everyone at the retreat center fell silent.

We simply watched as the network began to loop the video, so we saw these horrors again—and again—and again.

9:37 a.m.

American Airlines Flight 77 from Dulles crashed into the western side of the Pentagon, setting off a massive fire. The flight crew of six, 53 travelers and five hijackers were killed, along with 125 Pentagon personnel.

TV networks almost immediately reported an explosion at the Pentagon, but little was known about the details. Confusion was rising. One TV network initially told viewers about an unconfirmed report of a fire raging at the Pentagon—but with no mention of a plane crash.

Time passed as TV crews shifted their locations to report firsthand.

I was sick to my stomach.

Yet I was paralyzed like everyone else, staring at these ghastly scenes.

The sheer magnitude of this attack was unthinkable. I wished I had been able to talk with Gov. Engler for just a moment—to somehow express my horror.

Each of us wanted to express the agony we felt watching our landmarks burn and real people jumping to their deaths, but none of us could find words to express the feelings coursing through us.

9:52 a.m.

National security officials had been monitoring Osama Bin Laden's network in Asia and picked up chatter among associates of his group—already calling each other on cell phones to celebrate the attacks. That information somehow became public. Broadcasters on FOX, CBS, NBC and CNN began citing Osama Bin Laden as a possible suspect.

If that speculation was true—if so-called Muslims had perpetrated this heinous act—the consequences would cascade in unthinkable ways.

I felt powerless, angry and numb.

We all were anxious; fearful.

The first lady had been escorted from the retreat site and was gone.

9:59 a.m.

The south tower of the World Trade Center collapsed in front of us—on our screen at the retreat center—and on TV screens in the living rooms and schools and offices of millions of Americans.

At first, a dense, gray cloud blinded everyone, making the great roar we were hearing all the more terrifying. Even the TV crews were overwhelmed.

What was happening? Another explosion? Another crash? That blinding dust was so all-encompassing that it took a while for reporters to even comprehend that the tower had fallen.

Then, the dust began to settle. The sky cleared.

The truth hit us.

In an instant, New York's skyline had forever changed.

The tower was gone!

Gone!

10:03 a.m.

United Airlines Flight 93 from Newark crashed in a field about 80 miles southwest of Pittsburgh: Those four hijackers had been overwhelmed by some of the flight's passengers and crew. At the retreat center, we had no idea that this fourth crash had occurred. Associated Press would not carry that story for more than half an hour.

10:28 a.m.

The north tower collapsed.

We could not stop watching. The world was changing before our eyes.

We were not alone. Billions around the world were watching.

There was no relief from the panic. We had been watching these attacks in real time for more than an hour. The staccato effect of the looped videos was a drumbeat of unthinkable carnage.

We did not know the scale that morning, but people already were comparing this to Pearl Harbor.

This was certainly the deadliest terrorist attack in world history.

I thought of the Quran's famous admonition to save innocent lives—and its condemnation of killing innocents. Taking one innocent life was like killing "all humankind."

This must be close to what "all humankind" looked like. Untold numbers were dead. Giant landmarks were falling. The whole world was traumatized.

We were witnessing mass murder in real-time.

As we silently made our way out of the retreat center to our cars, we had no way of even guessing that the final toll would be 2,996 killed and 6,000 others injured.

Noon

Officials across the U.S. and Canada were clearing the skies of all air-craft—the first time such a mass grounding had occurred across North America. Even before President Bush addressed the nation, U.S. Sens. Orrin Hatch and John McCain were telling the world that this was an act of war and Osama Bin Laden was the likely perpetrator.

I was making my way home along I-94—normally just a couple of hours—but I found myself driving slower that day.

Then my cell phone rang. Jeff Werner, the Bloomfield Township police chief, was calling. "Victor, we've stationed two police cars by your mosque."

I could barely summon a response, but I thought a chief of police might know more than reporters. I asked him: "Who's responsible for this?"

"It's obviously a terrorist act," he said. The crashing of four planes in one morning certainly was no accident.

I thanked him sincerely for his immediate instinct to protect our com-munity, but I said, "Chief, please don't waste your resources." I explained that we were in the midst of a major remodeling, and portions of our center had been demolished; I wasn't too worried about vandals. Then, I realized that our telephone connection had cut out. Overloaded commu-nications networks were a problem for everyone around the world that day.

Jeff's call had jolted me out of my stunned silence at the carnage we had witnessed. This was a time for action, and I felt proud to be an American—part of a country where law enforcement agencies were proactively concerned about minorities even in the midst of a national emergency. As I drove, I thought of a long list of deadly rampages against vulnerable minorities after major tragedies. In many parts of the world, attacking minorities was the automatic, convenient response in national emergencies. And, in many of those countries, police forces would simply stand aside and let innocents reap the fury of the mobs. I was so thankful that we were Americans.

There was little traffic on that long freeway spanning southern Michigan. As I drove, I kept praying: "Oh God, let this not be the work of Muslims!"

At that point, Osama Bin Laden's name had popped up on nearly every network—but only as a possible culprit. I didn't even recall his name being mentioned that morning, among the many possibilities. I kept praying: "Please, not Muslims."

Despite those pleas, I could feel my own dreams crumbling. Within hours that day, I had been honored by Gov. Engler's decree at a gathering of some of Michigan's brightest and best leaders—and I had been looking forward to an upcoming reception at the White House with other Muslim leaders that autumn. My eight years on Engler's commission had ended. Ahead of me were so many opportunities to help my community contribute to a stronger America.

Then, that same morning, followers of an evil extremist in a cave halfway around the world had pulled off unbelievably sophisticated, concerted terrorist attacks in history.

My calendar was circled with upcoming dates that I had thought held a bright destiny for all of us. This tiny circle of zealots had ripped that calendar to pieces.

1:04 p.m.

The radio began carrying a taped message from President Bush:

"Freedom itself was attacked this morning by a faceless coward. And freedom will be defended. I want to reassure the American people that the full resources of the federal government are working to assist local authorities to save lives and to help the victims of these attacks. Make no mistake. The United States will hunt down and punish those responsible for these cowardly acts."

By the time I got home and pulled into the parking lot of the mosque, local police already were responding. I immediately spotted a white van that I didn't recognize, and pulled up alongside it. A man was simply sitting there, behind the wheel. I didn't know him.

I wasn't thinking about my own appearance. Early that morning, a Michigan State Police trooper at the retreat had presented me a special gift: a blue cap with a Michigan State Police logo on the front. As I left the retreat, I had simply worn it all the way home. When I lowered my car window to talk to the man, the driver began to yell at me, then abruptly took off. It must have been that cap! That was troubling, so I jotted down his license plate number.

A police car was parked farther back in our parking lot. I drove over to that officer and reported the plate number. The driver of the white van lived in the subdivision behind our property. Within five minutes, a police cruiser was at his door. As it turned out, he was acting on anger and adrenaline that afternoon, but had committed no crime.

The next day, he returned to the mosque and apologized. I'll never forget what he said: "I was overwhelmed with emotions. I'm sorry for my behavior."

I was moved by his example and have often told that story over the years. I could tell from talking with him that he was a good, sincere man. He simply was overcome by the horrific events of 9/11. His first instinct was to lash out. But, what he did after that initial impulse was exactly what Islam teaches. We repent. We reconcile. I wish we all behaved like that man in the white van.

Overall, Americans went out of their way to bless with kindness their Muslim friends, colleagues and neighbors after 9/11. After all, Muslims had lost friends and family in these terrorist attacks, as well. It would take a while for many of those stories to emerge. Among the most famous was Mohammad Salman Hamdani, a Pakistani-American police cadet and EMT specialist who rushed to the site of the attacks to help the injured. When he was reported missing by his family, law enforcement officials initially investigated him as a possible collaborator. Later, his body and his medical bag were found in the rubble. Congress officially named him as a heroic Muslim first responder. His name now appears on scholarships, honoring his example of selfless service that day. Dozens of other innocent Muslims were counted in the death toll that day.

8:30 p.m.

Senior White House officials told Congress and reporters that Osama Bin Laden almost certainly was guilty of these crimes, but President Bush did not mention his name in a nationwide address from the Oval Office. He talked about how many lives had been snuffed out that day: "Moms and dads. Friends and neighbors. Thousands of lives were suddenly ended by evil, despicable acts of terror."

He said: "Terrorist attacks can shake the foundations of our biggest buildings, but they cannot touch the foundation of America. ... Today, our nation saw evil, the very worst of human nature, and we responded with the best of America, with the daring of our rescue workers, with the caring for strangers and neighbors who came to give blood and help in any way they could."

That was my hope for America, too.

Wednesday, September 12, 2001

Once again, I turned to the power of the pen.

Our home had become a clearinghouse for reporters, politicians, law enforcement officials and community leaders, calling at all hours as they tried to chart a course through the chaos. While most Americans were remarkable in their compassion for Muslims whom they knew, the nation now was furious with our new enemy. American anger was turning on a dime, with a laser focus on Bin Laden and his terrorist followers—just as American fury had turned toward Japan after Pearl Harbor.

I knew that we needed to encourage prominent displays of interfaith solidarity. We also needed to get our collective American-Muslim voice into the major news media. Here in Michigan, religious leaders met on the day after September 11 to plan an interfaith service. Such interreligious services were in the works coast to coast, including one at the Washington National Cathedral—where President Bush was in attendance, along with congressional leadership.

I spent days talking with everyone who sought my support and advice. I wrote an op-ed column for one of the statewide newspapers. I agreed to interviews. This was a time to speak and write clearly and openly. I was inspired, in turn, by all of the religious and political leaders who felt the same.

Monday, September 17, 2001

American presidents have rarely visited mosques. It was always considered such a provocative act that only President Eisenhower, in his second term in office, was bold enough to pay a visit to the Islamic Center of Washington with his wife, Mamie. I have to credit President Bush with making a return visit to that mosque, just six days after the 9/11 attacks. That took courage—and it also put an end to rampant rumors that Bush might follow the example of President Roosevelt after the attack on Pearl Harbor. Roosevelt had ordered the mass internment of Japanese Americans. Would Bush do the same? I never suspected he would. Rumors to that effect were unfounded. But I was thankful that Bush firmly put them to rest with his address at the mosque.

He called American Muslims "friends" and "taxpaying citizens."

He made it clear to everyone: "These acts of violence against innocents violate the fundamental tenets of the Islamic faith. And it's important for my fellow Americans to understand that." He paraphrased the Quran's basic principle, 30:10, condemning violence against innocents: "In the long run, evil in the extreme will be the end of those who do evil."

He even went off script to emphasize this point. "The face of terror is not the true faith of Islam," he said. "That's not what Islam is all about. Islam is peace. These terrorists don't represent peace. They represent evil and war."

In the same week that Bush was visiting the mosque, the state-wide Catholic newspaper in Michigan covered Muslim reaction to the September 11 attacks—from the perspective of our family.

The paper's longtime correspondent, Robert Delaney, reported the story, headlined "Shocked by Sept. 11." Here is what he wrote:

> *Victor and Shahina Begg, and their children, are still mystified how people claiming to be devout Muslims could have committed the terrorist events of Sept. 11.*
>
> *"Muslim-Americans also died Sept. 11 …" Victor Begg points out, adding that the reports that some of the terrorists spent the previous evening in a nude bar don't jibe with the idea they were fervent Muslims.*
>
> *Shahina Begg calls the Taliban, Afghanistan's former rulers, "a cult" that has mixed cultural beliefs with religion to produce a distorted form of Islam. The Taliban's notorious strictures on women are especially strange, considering that the Prophet Muhammad's own wife was a businesswoman, she adds.*
>
> *Recalling her reaction and that of other Muslim students at Bloomfield Hills Lahser High School on Sept. 11, Sofia Begg says, "There was just disbelief. You couldn't understand why, because you know your religion and you know what God would think.*

You wonder how somebody could claim this to be a righteous act, why somebody would even do this."

She appreciates attending a small high school, with a diverse enrollment, where most students know each other. "People weren't mean, but they had a lot of questions," Sofia says of her fellow students.

Her brother, Sami Begg, 23, a senior at GMI Institute in Flint, says, "At first, I didn't believe a Muslim did it. Then, when they came out with the news that it was, I was pretty upset. But the actions of that group of people don't reflect the point of view of all Muslims. These were not the actions of persons who were living the way they should; it's not part of the religion," he says.

Yusuf Begg, 17, a senior at the same school where his sister is a junior, has a similar recollection of his feelings: "I was just shocked, but I go back to a saying, 'Never judge a religion by its people; judge a religion by its scripture.' If these extremists did it, it doesn't cancel out the whole Muslim people."

Friday, September 21, 2001

The biennial Mackinac Republican Leadership Conference was still scheduled for September 21-23. I was torn about making that long trip: Each day, I went back and forth about whether or not we should go. Perhaps a prominent Muslim couple would not be welcomed at such a conservative event so soon after 9/11.

At that time, the Republican Party was still in the hands of moderates and several people reached out to encourage us. "It's important for you to participate, Victor—especially now," one friend told me.

So Shahina and I drove to the northern tip of Michigan's mitten and took the ferry across the strait to the historic island. The ride was bracing. The water was rough. The autumn winds were chilly. I kept thinking about the reception we would receive—and what I would say to the colleagues I would meet again in this new calendar that was unfolding for all of us.

We rode the horse-drawn taxi to the Grand Hotel that overlooks the waters connecting two Great Lakes, Huron and Michigan. I remember settling into a rocking chair on the hotel's famous "world's longest front porch." I looked out at the five-mile-long Mackinac Bridge, the longest suspension bridge in the Western Hemisphere. Although David B. Steinman is usually mentioned as the bridge's overall designer, the historical record says that Steinman turned over most of that design work to his top civil engineer, Abdul Hasnat. I was sitting on the front porch of an iconic symbol of Americana, looking at a stunning steel expanse that is vital to international connections every day. I thought: That's the genius of Muslim contributions to the fabric of American life. That bridge is a shining symbol of the daily contributions of Muslims, working at all levels of our life together. This is what we hope to do as Americans. Whether our contributions are tiny or as grand as that bridge—at our best, each day, we make connections that help strengthen the whole world.

What a tragedy that Shahina and I—and all Americans—had to face this moment of grief and anger over what a handful of deadly zealots had done in the name of Islam.

I thought of all the times I had told people, with such confidence, that Islamic values align with American values—that there wasn't a better place in the world to be a Muslim. I wasn't alone in that confidence. All the way back to Mohammed Webb in the 19th century, American Muslim leaders have shared this dream. In fact, I believe that to this day. But that afternoon, on the porch of the Grand Hotel, I wondered: What will happen now?

As that conference opened, our old friends greeted us with open arms. Shahina and I were so glad we made the trip. There was so much emotion that, when Shahina shook hands with Gov. Engler, tears started to flow down her cheeks.

The governor comforted her.

I will never forget that moment.

In my pocket, I carried a prayer that I had written with Syed Salman. I never shared the prayer with anyone else, but I carried these words with me as my hope for God's guidance as we all stepped into this new world:

> *O God Almighty—we have gathered here at a point when we can turn to none but you. And we have gathered here as one humanity, all servants of you, our Lord, in great sorrow and affliction that has fallen on our nation.*

O protector of the isolated and the weak—we ask for your protection and your mercy at this moment of great tragedy.

We ask you to have mercy on those who have departed from us in this tragedy and for solace, comfort and strength to their families and friends. We ask you for help for those that are helping the victims in this tragedy, the service men and women. And, we ask you to guide and help our leaders who you have appointed to guide our nation in making the right decisions.

We ask for your mercy and grace for all of us who have gathered here and all the people across our nation and all the people of the world.

O Almighty—turn this tragedy into an opportunity to bring about peace in the world. Strengthen us in our faiths, and strengthen our resolve to establish justice, truth and peace in all your lands.

Amen.

CHAPTER 11

'We Must Do More Than Pray'

Help one another in goodness and God-consciousness.
Quran 5:2

We believe in God,
and that which has been revealed to us,
and revealed to Abraham and Ishmael, Isaac and Jacob,
and to Moses and Jesus, and the Prophets.
We make no division between any of them,
and to God we surrender.
Quran 3:84

Americans came together in the aftermath of 9/11 as never before. In overwhelming numbers, Americans joined hands across lines of creed, class and color. Millions of us were instinctively united in our heartache and our compassion. That is not a universal response to tragedy in our world today. In some parts of our world, tensions between groups are a tinderbox—so, any such attack can spark deadly violence targeting minorities as scapegoats. After 9/11, we did have to struggle mightily against a rising tide of bigotry—but one brave soul after another volunteered to help in the effort to calm fears and bust myths. One reason I take such pride in being an American is that, for most of us, our first instinct after a tragedy is to come together and respond in compassionate ways. We saw that kind of response unfold across Michigan in the days after 9/11.

This was a huge challenge, because most of us initially felt numb as we watched the events unfold—even as an overwhelming anxiety took hold. That certainly was what I felt: a mingling of sorrow, sickness and fear, combined with my anger at those who committed these crimes. My heart was heavy. I was in pain. So, it certainly was inspiring to see the immediate actions of many neighbors. Some of the professional first-responders from this region packed up their equipment and drove to New York City to help with the catastrophe—among them was Ali Taqi, a medical student and a volunteer firefighter from our mosque. Thousands of other men and women reached out closer to home to support those who had lost relatives and friends. As the casualty list was compiled, the death toll repeatedly struck close to home. We discovered that two former residents of Bloomfield Hills had been in the towers when they collapsed. Another woman, who lived in nearby Oakland Township, had traveled to New York City for an important business meeting at the World Trade Center on the morning of the attacks. One of the flight attendants and some airline passengers killed on 9/11 were from Michigan. In all, the *Detroit Free Press* reported, 16 men and women with "significant ties" to our state were killed. That number actually was much larger when we listed all of the victims who had connections through friends and family in our state.

In the immediate wake of 9/11, everyone Shahina and I knew seemed to be in motion.

September 12 dawned as a strange new world. No one had any idea, at that point, whether or not to brace for additional attacks. The TV and radio coverage never stopped. Reporters kept repeating tragic details from the three crash sites, over and over again. Nationwide, America was on high alert. That morning in southeast Michigan, the sun rose in a clear, blue sky. Yet as we walked outside on September 12, we sensed something unusual in the air around us. It took a while to discern the differences, but we realized that southeast Michigan's normally busy skies were absolutely empty. There were no feathery white contrails crisscrossing the deep blue above us, because all flights were grounded. No industrial clouds rose from factories; they were closed. The white noise of daily life in our industrial metropolis was stilled.

Three epicenters of interfaith activity on September 12 were Detroit; Oakland County (where I lived); and Dearborn, the home of thousands of Muslim families. I became involved in all three.

In downtown Detroit, the rallying point was Fort Street Presbyterian, a soaring Gothic Revival church that was founded in 1849 and is on the National Register of Historic Places. The Rev. Mark Keely, Fort Street's pastor at that time, had been involved in our interfaith work before the attacks. Mark's reputation across religious lines, the active support of his congregation and the church's landmark status near the Detroit waterfront made Fort Street a natural gathering place. Church officials met on September 12 and authorized a public announcement that they would open their doors every day to welcome anyone who needed a moment of solace in the heart of the city. Officials also agreed that they would turn over their upcoming Sunday morning hour of worship to an interfaith service, with an invitation to Jews and Muslims to join Christians. The church had an annual tradition of displaying flags from around the world on World Communion Sunday, and those flags were brought out to surround the interior of the church, as a sign of global solidarity.

That first Sunday interfaith service at Fort Street, on September 16, was freighted with emotion, anxiety and hope (in part because the Jewish community would be celebrating Rosh Hashana, their new year holiday, at sunset on September 17). Despite the convergence with their busy High Holidays, our Jewish friends showed up and spoke in concert with Muslim leaders. Everyone hoped to calm the emotional backlash from these attacks. Rabbi Norman Roman came to Fort Street from Temple Kol Ami, located near our congregation in Oakland County. Roman told the crowd, "This, my friends, is not the time to prejudge and to form opinions before facts are known; to blame any group for the acts of crazed individuals." To emphasize his point, he blew a loud blast on a ram's horn, a defining symbol of the Jewish new year. He told people that this was a call to harmony and peace—and a rejection of the temptation toward reprisals. At his side in that September 16 service was Imam Hassan Qazwini, the leader of the Islamic Center of America. Qazwini echoed Roman's call for calm and urged people to remember that their Muslim neighbors are fellow Americans.

That Sunday morning gathering turned out to be a prelude to an epic demonstration of interfaith solidary on the following Sunday, September 23, at Fort Street. Once again, flags from around the world lined the church (which was packed beyond the 1,200-seat capacity of its wooden pews). For two hours that afternoon, men and women prayed, chanted, sang and called for peace from the perspective of many religious traditions. A city-wide choir sang, "Open the eyes of my heart, Lord! I want to see you!" The emotion of that anthem touched so many people that journalists, in their newspaper and TV reports, described the tears they saw glistening on many faces. Even though, at that point, 12 days had passed since 9/11, everyone still was grief-stricken, confused and searching for clarity. At this service, Christians were represented by the most influential Catholic leader in Michigan, Cardinal Adam Maida, who made a point of distinguishing between justice and vindictiveness in American responses to the attacks. This was not a time for vengeance, Maida declared. Already, anxiety over the likelihood that the U.S. would declare war was rising. Maida went out of his way in those terrifying first days to express his solidarity with Muslims. Beyond taking part at Fort Street, Maida also made time for a personal visit to a Dearborn mosque—with reporters in tow—to make the point that interfaith cooperation was alive and well in southeast Michigan.

Gale-force winds of anger were in the air, as well, and this was far more than a moment when we should simply withstand bigotry with a thick skin. Hate crimes against Muslims, as reported by the FBI, rose after 9/11 to several hundred reported incidents nationwide—ranging from assaults to intimidation. Cases of assaults, the most serious of these crimes, totaled 93 by the time that year ended. The balance of the crimes listed by the FBI ranged from vandalism to verbal and written abuse. These were the flash points we all anticipated after 9/11—and were hoping to keep to a bare minimum.

Americans were asserting their patriotism from coast to coast, and we wanted to generate a public awareness that patriotism should inspire us to unite—not divide. We needed a visible outpouring of interfaith solidarity to make it clear to potential perpetrators that violence was not an acceptable response.

When compared with the rest of the nation in the weeks after 9/11, southeast Michigan was unusual in its scale of interfaith activity: more than 50 religious leaders from across the region headed to Dearborn to talk on September 12. I was surprised by the new alliances that were forming all around us. Among the strong allies who showed up for that first discussion were some of Dearborn's Christian clergy. They already had local Muslim friends and understood the high stakes we were facing. I also was surprised by the strength of the support from Jewish friends.

During this time I was reminded that my Jewish friends had been dealing with bigotry for decades—especially in southeast Michigan. Many Jewish leaders were as pragmatic as I was about the ways in which we needed to respond; they knew exactly what would happen otherwise. Even as anti-Muslim crimes rose in the months after 9/11, there also were twice as many incidents aimed at Jews during that same period, the FBI reported. In fact, my Jewish friends pointed out to me that this has always been the pattern: Each year, American Jews bear the brunt of the largest portion of religion-related hate crimes as documented by the FBI. Our Jewish and Muslim communities are both in the crosshairs of hate groups. We were in this together after 9/11—and we are to this day.

My friend Sharona Shapiro was the Michigan area director of the American Jewish Committee on 9/11. "I was horrified as I watched the towers come down on the TV in my office here in Michigan," she said. "Among everything else, I was experiencing all the personal fears of a mother whose child was in harm's way! My son had just arrived in New York a few weeks earlier for orientation at Columbia University. So, I was dealing with all kinds of emotions—as well as the threats that showed up right away here in southeast Michigan."

Michigan's Jewish leaders were some of the first in our religious community to spring into real action as peacemakers. First, they faced a geographic crisis. On 9/11, David Gad-Harf was the executive director of the Jewish Community Council of Metropolitan Detroit and was stuck in Israel by the worldwide grounding of flights. David had been part of a long-planned visit to Israel by American Jewish leaders and, after 9/11, it took him nearly a week to find his way back to Michigan. As a result, Sharona was in charge of the immediate Jewish response in Michigan, and I worked with her in those early days.

Sharona said, "We talked by phone, and David and I agreed to divide up what we have to do. In his role, David works with the other religious leaders—the bishops, the imams and all the others. But he's caught in Israel, and I am here, on the ground. I had to get working right away to deal with the absolutely ridiculous myths that popped up."

Incendiary anti-Semitic myths snowballed alongside anti-Muslim myths. As Sharona recalled: "Close to home, we had two myths about Muslims that people kept spreading right after 9/11: One involved a local restaurant and the other one was about a gas station where people from the Middle East worked. These ridiculous stories popped up about how Middle Eastern men at these two places were seen laughing and partying during the attacks. It wasn't true, but I spent a lot of time—and I talked to a whole lot of people—to help put that to rest. Those first few days were very difficult."

Anti-Semitic conspiracy theories quickly followed. One of the most outlandish was a claim that 4,000 Israelis who worked for a company in the World Trade Center had all known the attack was coming and stayed home from work on 9/11. That, too, was total fiction. There was no such company. Many Jews who worked in the twin towers died in the attacks, along with Muslims and Christians.

"The stuff we heard after 9/11 was so wild and hateful," Sharona noted. "I can't count the angry phone calls I took. A lot of people said threatening things. Some just hung up. So I had to deal with these problems right here, in our communities, in those first few days when David was trying to get home from Israel to help."

Working together in southeast Michigan, our religious communities had a significant advantage because of a long, shared history of interfaith responses to major crises. To put it simply: Interfaith support is in the DNA of Detroit's culture.

Throughout the 20th century, Detroit ranked with Chicago, New York, Washington, D.C., London and Rome as global hubs of interfaith innovation. Among these major urban centers, the Motor City gained a reputation for its very practical responses to hatred. Our religious leaders certainly had seen their share of it! Naturally, I was drawn to their pragmatic style, because my family was steeped in India's multicultural history. I had grown up understanding that there was nothing like solid friendships to overcome suspicions of each other and forge new bonds. This had been true in Hyderabad, and it certainly was true in Detroit, as well. People like Sharona and me understood that our Motor City was really a giant crucible into which immigrants of all races, ethnicities and creeds had poured, in search of industrial jobs. Clashes involving minorities had broken out repeatedly in southeast Michigan across the 20th century.

My own awareness of the danger we now faced—and the need for an active response—is what drove me to fully embrace my role as a peace activist. This wasn't a path I had consciously chosen. I was an entrepreneur, busy with all the demands of a large-scale retail operation. I wasn't an ordained clergyman. I wasn't an expert at working with religious coalitions or some of the clergy who soon responded to our calls to action. But, as a businessman, I knew one very important thing: If I was going to accept this challenge, I had to make it clear to my colleagues that peace "activists" must, first and foremost, *act*. As important as prayer is in all of our religious traditions, we had to envision ways of working together that went beyond interfaith prayer.

Today, as I see old friends who I worked with back in 2001, the one thing they remember most often about the days after 9/11 is this: "Victor, you challenged us to do more than pray." I'm proud of that. Like Sharona, a prompt action was demanded of me. There was no time to lose.

We had Detroit's interfaith DNA on which we could draw. We were able to point out giants whose examples we could follow, stretching back to the early years of the 20th century. One reason interfaith cooperation sprang up in Detroit in the 1920s was the toxic, anti-Semitic campaigns of Henry Ford. Later, Ford's son and grandson repudiated his bigotry, but the historical record shows that Henry Ford was a relentless anti-Semite who promoted his hatred internationally. That's not my opinion; it's the historical record. Historians credit Henry Ford with valuable insights as an industrial pioneer, but his focus was narrow. Ford only had a basic education, and he showed little personal interest in studying world history or learning about other cultures. The most humiliating public display of Ford's lack of education came in a libel suit he filed against the *Chicago Tribune*, which had provoked his wrath by calling him "an Anarchist," "ignorant," and "incapable of thought." The lawsuit he filed against the *Chicago Tribune* turned out to be a mistake on Ford's part, allowing the newspaper's attorney to grill Ford in a courtroom for most of a week about his general knowledge of the world. This led to an embarrassing series of revelations. In one widely reported example, Ford thought the American Revolution took place in 1812. After witnessing all of his gaffes in the courtroom, the *Chicago Tribune* concluded that Ford was "virtually illiterate."

While that court case was fodder for lampooning Ford in the popular press, there was a far darker side to his dangerous mixture of ignorance and vast wealth. Many of Ford's friends and associates had heard him privately promote anti-Semitic myths, including a belief that World War I had been caused by Jews for their own benefit. Ford was not secretive about these claims: He made them privately, and then began to talk about them publicly. Eventually, Ford bought his own newspaper, *The Dearborn Independent*, and began publishing his own anti-Semitic diatribes. Ford transformed that little, local paper into a national publication by distributing copies through his Ford dealerships across the U.S. The newspaper's long-running anti-Semitic attacks included material from the notorious *Protocols of the Elders of Zion*. This was vicious propaganda originally created in the Russian Empire—prior to the Russian Revolution, in 1917—that had been used to justify imperial pogroms against Jewish villages. Ford invested heavily in reprinting English translations of the *Protocols of the Elders of Zion*, and ensured that as many as 500,000 copies were distributed. Even after the protocols were conclusively exposed as fraudulent propaganda, in 1921, Henry Ford never stopped promoting that message.

In this history, I clearly see the parallels with the Trump era, when outrageous claims are spread through social media—the equivalent of Ford's newspaper in his day. The claims are ridiculous! Former President Barack Obama is a Muslim. He wasn't born in America. Large crowd of Muslims in New Jersey celebrating the September 11th attacks. Muslims are plotting to implement Sharia law around the world. Each claim has been proven to be false over and over again, and yet these myths keep spreading through the grassroots like wildfire.

That's what happened in Detroit in the mid-1920s. With the spread of this homegrown hatred and Ford fanning the flames of anti-Semitism, we saw the Ku Klux Klan arise again and seek political power. The anti-Catholic, anti-black, anti-Jewish Klan was promoted from the pulpits of some of Detroit's most prominent evangelical churches. In the 1925 city election, a Klan candidate had a good chance of capturing the mayor's office. From one church's pulpit, women voters were warned that any white woman who did not support the Klan candidate should be tarred and feathered.

The danger of a Klan takeover was so great that the *Detroit Free Press* fostered the first major interfaith demonstration in the city's history. As that 1925 election approached, the *Detroit Free Press* used its front page to publish dire warnings from the city's most famous Jewish leader, Rabbi

Leo Franklin of Temple Beth El, and a local Protestant pastor (who would soon become internationally famous), the Rev. Reinhold Niebuhr. Both men urged voters to reject the Klan's appeals and myths. Both men said that the basic values in their religious traditions condemned such hatred. On Election Day, the Klan candidate lost. Interfaith activists won that battle.

The real irony was that, at that time, Rabbi Franklin and Henry Ford were next-door neighbors in the city's posh Boston-Edison neighborhood. The Motor City's tooth-and-nail cross-cultural clashes were nothing if not deeply personal. These were conflicts between neighbors. Even as Ford was becoming one of the world's most prolific publishers of anti-Semitic material, he was making an annual gift of a new Ford automobile to his Jewish neighbor, the rabbi. When Franklin returned the car in 1920, in protest, Ford seemed unaware that he had offended his Jewish neighbor! Ford's folksy view of friendship was that Franklin would somehow over-look his global anti-Semitic campaign.

By the time of the Pearl Harbor attack in December of 1941, Detroit had become a world-class exporter of anti-Semitism. Historians have documented Ford's fondness for Hitler in the 1930s and, in turn, Hitler's high regard for the automaker. Nazis promoted Ford's anti-Jewish pub-lications in Europe—and, of course, created a tidal wave of their own hate-filled propaganda. But Ford was not singing a solo in Detroit. One of the nation's most popular radio commentators was the Rev. Charles Coughlin, who chimed in with his own anti-Semitic warnings that were broadcast via radio to a vast nationwide audience. Once again, there are direct parallels with today's far-right commentators attacking Muslims on our airwaves.

As had happened in the 1920s, Coughlin's new wave of anti-Jewish pro-paganda finally led to another milestone in Detroit's interfaith activism; once again, Rabbi Franklin was the spearhead. The National Conference of Christians and Jews had existed since 1927, co-founded by the famous social worker Jane Addams and two men who became U.S. Supreme Court Justices: Charles Evans Hughes and Benjamin Cardozo, who was the Jewish co-founder in that trio. In the mid-1930s, this group commis-sioned interfaith speakers to barnstorm from coast to coast with messages of cross-cultural cooperation. Based on that model, Rabbi Franklin and progressive Christian clergy founded Detroit's first real interfaith network in 1940. Once again, Franklin chose one of Detroit's nationally known pastors as his collaborator. This time it was the Rev. Henry Hitt Crane of Central Methodist Church. Crane was already a prominent, outspoken pacifist and an opponent of both fascism and anti-Semitism. They called their new group the Detroit Council of Catholics, Jews and Protestants; eventually, they changed that name to the Detroit Round Table of Catholics, Jews and Protestants. They were aiming specifically at the anti-Semitic hatemongers of the 1930s and "the growth of totalitarianism abroad and divisions within the Detroit community inflamed by such preachers ... as Father Coughlin. The aim of the roundtable was to foster religious and racial brotherhood and to counter those who would divide the community on religious or racial lines."

No one seems to have noticed that Muslims were not invited to the table. We did not have the presence in the community that we have today.

Even though Coughlin had been the most famous Catholic voice from Michigan before World War II, Detroit Catholic leaders—under pressure from the White House after the attack on Pearl Harbor—finally silenced the radio priest in May 1942. Perhaps emboldened by that step, Catholic leaders doubled down on their interfaith outreach after World War II. In the early 1960s, Detroit Cardinal John Dearden became known around the world as a champion of progressive change in the Catholic Church. He was a leading light in the Second Vatican Council that allowed Catholics to celebrate the Mass in their own native languages rather than the traditional Latin. Dearden was especially influential in backing the 1965 approval of *Nostre Aetate*, the most important interfaith declaration of the 20th century. Its final name in English was translated as "In Our Time," but its original draft was called "Decree on the Jews." The document's main focus was officially condemning the anti-Semitic teachings that had been part of the church for centuries. This change in Catholic teaching was so important that it took the bishops and cardinals four years to hammer out its final version! As Catholic leaders worked on that text at the Vatican, someone noticed that language about Islam was missing. So, they added: "The Church regards Muslims with esteem. They adore the one God, living and enduring, the all-powerful Creator of heaven and earth who has spoken to people; they strive to obey wholeheartedly His inscrutable decrees, just as Abraham did, to whose faith they happily link their own." That short passage about our faith was lumped under a heading that, in English, was: "Declaration on the Relation of the Church with Non-Christian Religions."

I look back on that turbulent era with the bittersweet realization that, as a Muslim community in southeast Michigan, we missed both the worst and the best. Somehow, we escaped the fury of the anti-Semites. Neither Henry Ford nor Rev. Coughlin bothered to fire their long-range flame-throwers in our direction. But, at the same time, we also were ignored by the heavy-hitters in the religious world as they organized their new interfaith councils. Through all those years, we were the world's second largest faith, yet most of these interreligious pioneers did not even have us on their radar.

As Muslims, should we be thankful? Or should we look at this period as a slight toward Islam? Ultimately, I think, all we can do now is learn from that earlier era. We have roles to play in confronting Islamophobia and averting a resurgence of virulent anti-Semitism.

What I understood so clearly after 9/11 were three simple words: Interfaith activists act!

I had an iron-clad case, based on our shared history. At their best, religious leaders in southeast Michigan had acted in the 1920s and 1940s and 1960s. Over and over again, action had made the difference. Henry Ford's bigotry, years ago, remains an embarrassing chapter in the company's history, but fortunately, his son and grandson rejected his anti-Semitism and committed themselves to multicultural programs. By the 1980s, the Ford Motor Company welcomed what the company today calls Employee Resource Groups—organizations of employees whom the company says "share similar characteristics or life experiences." These ongoing groups are supposed to use their personal and social connections to build a better working environment. Among the first of these to be recognized were the Ford Chinese Association, the Ford-employees African-Ancestry Network and the Ford Asian Indian Association. They proved to be both popular and good for business. Then, in 2001, the Ford Interfaith Network was established, and its members became staunch supporters of interreligious projects both within the company and in the larger community.

I brought that same kind of pragmatic strategy to the first gathering of religious leaders in Dearborn on September 12, 2001. That's why I talked in blunt terms that day. That's why people still recall what I said—and what I did as a result. Before I went to the meeting, I braced myself for what was about to unfold. I knew I would have to exercise my thick skin. I grew even more concerned when I realized that most of the clergy who walked through that door on September 12 were faces I had never seen. They were not used to my kind of thinking.

"To put it simply: Victor shocked people that day," says the Rev. Daniel Appleyard, an Episcopalian priest who became my dear friend and ally. The clergy—like Dan, who lived and worked in Dearborn—all had well-established working relationships with Muslim leaders and they had immediately called each other on 9/11. Before the sun went down on 9/11, they had held their own local prayer service at Dan's church, Christ Episcopal Church, Dearborn, where they were joined by dozens of their Muslim neighbors, including Eide Alawan (Chuck's brother) and Rafael Narbaez. They were way ahead of us in planning other local responses, as well. In one particularly poignant demonstration of solidarity, Dan, Eide, Rafael and the Rev. Daniel Buttry of First Baptist Church of Dearborn also invited local men and women to gather for prayer outside the Henry Ford Museum in Dearborn.

On that morning of September 12, Dearborn clergy had arranged for our meeting space inside a local mosque. More than 50 shocked and grief-stricken religious leaders from across southeast Michigan walked into the room that day, obviously struggling to sort out what to do next. As the room filled to capacity, I hoped that this would be the start of a whole new kind of coalition. But none of us knew what to expect and, at first, there was a lot of talk about organizing a prayer service.

"This was a whole new cross-section of people for most of us. And, I was pleased to see that people from all the major religious groups showed up," Dan Appleyard recalls. "I can still remember them: Jewish represen-tatives were there; representatives of some of the bishops were there; a good number of African-American leaders were there. Most of these people weren't used to working together, certainly not in the middle of a crisis like this. And the focus of the conversation really revolved around planning the upcoming prayer service together. That's the main thing we thought we could achieve.

"Then, in the middle of that planning, Victor stood up and said: 'I'm not sure we need another 'kumbaya' moment. Unless we start actually working together, even on the difficult issues that divide us, none of this conversation today is going to make any difference.'"

Dan speaks of the scene as vividly as I do. I will never forget that moment when I dared to stand up among all of those esteemed religious leaders. I also remember the unsettling feeling that rose in me as I watched the responses on the faces looking back at me. They were not ready to hear what I was saying. But I felt so strongly that I just kept going. I said, "Do you realize that this is the first day of a new calendar? Simply holding hands and praying is not enough. Prayers are needed, but we must do more."

The room went silent.

Truth be told, I offended some people. In Dan's words: "I'm proud to say that I was the first one to talk after Victor said his piece. My response was, 'Victor, I couldn't agree with you more.' Then I tried to show that there was more than one pathway that we could follow. I could see the room was divided and I wanted to pull people back together again. I turned to Victor and I said, 'Victor, we do need to work together, but we also need to pray together.' That helped us to move ahead. The planning continued for the upcoming interfaith service."

Also in the room with us was the other Dan from Dearborn: the Rev. Dan Buttry. His career as a peacemaker eventually would take him out of his local Baptist congregation and send him around the world full-time as the Global Consultant for Peace and Justice for American Baptist Churches. Dan Buttry recounts: "At that September 12 meeting, the main challenge was that a lot of people arrived whom we didn't know; who didn't know each other. At that point, for instance, I didn't know Victor. But from my own years of peace work, I certainly came to that meeting with an awareness that we had to get much more engaged in working both locally and globally if we hoped to make any difference. Right away, I understood what Victor was saying. We weren't surprised that, after that meeting on September 12, Victor asked both of us to come to another, smaller meeting on his boat down at a Detroit riverfront marina."

Dan's right about that. As the meeting went on, I took note of those who agreed with the need to focus on taking action. That's why I asked the two Dans and some others to a meeting on my boat. I literally wanted to pull these men on board. I wanted to get underway. I wanted something tangible to come from all the talk. So, stepping onto my boat later that week were three Muslims—myself, plus a Hispanic-Muslim leader, Rafael Narbaez, and an African-American Muslim scholar, Sherman Abd al-Hakim Jackson. In addition, there were three Christians—the two Dans, and also the Rev. Felix Lorenz, who had served in several Christian denominations and was very active in interfaith work.

I took the boat out a short way to Lake St. Clair, where I anchored and let the wake of passing vessels rock us gently as we talked. The cool breeze and sunny skies temporarily helped us forget the trauma that had shaken not just our nation, but the whole world. That day on those waters between the U.S. and Canada, we arrived at a consensus to build a strong interfaith coalition that could act in concert. The time had come. We fondly remember that little group, to this day, as "the boat people."

Of course, we knew that we had to rapidly expand our circle. Because my own Muslim community had been largely ignored in interfaith coalitions for most of the past century, I was acutely aware of the many people who we tended to exclude for one reason or another. We needed to enlarge the list of people we would include in our work.

That expanded vision started with including women. The majority of clergy were men, but some of the strongest and most active allies from the start of this effort were women. Very early in the morning on September 11—even before the first plane struck in New York—one of my neighbors in Oakland County, Brenda Rosenberg, already was engaged in interfaith work. She had an early phone meeting with a colleague in an existing national peace initiative. Even before the 9/11 attacks, Brenda had been involved in diversity education to combat bigotry. So, after her early-morning phone meeting, she turned on the TV—and saw the attacks beginning in New York. Brenda was horrified, like everyone else, but she immediately sprang into action. Like me, Brenda understood that activists act. Like me, she wasn't an ordained clergyperson. Like me, she had worked in retailing for many years. The pinnacle of Brenda's career had been as senior vice president for fashion merchandizing and marketing for Federated Allied

Department Stores. She traveled the world, making decisions about the latest trends that would show up in high-end American stores. She had always been a passionate supporter of the Jewish community, and like me, she found that the events in her life kept pushing her relentlessly toward interfaith activism.

On September 11, as I was making my own plans to meet with religious leaders in Dearborn, Brenda was dialing through her own list of friends, asking each one: "Who works with Muslims around here? I need to talk to someone who can make an introduction."

"I was so frightened that day," Brenda recalls. "I knew what was coming. This wasn't the first time someone had tried to bring down the World Trade Center. In the earlier 1993 bombing attack, the perpetrators had cited the U.S. support for Israel as one motive. I knew right away that we were going to be blamed again. I told people, 'Our heads are in the sand if we don't take this seriously and begin planning our response. There's going to be a backlash. Yes, it's going to be aimed at Muslims—but it's also going to be aimed at Jews.'

"So I just got on the phone and kept calling people, asking over and over, 'Who knows Muslims we can work with?' The answer kept coming back: Sharona Shapiro. And that's how I wound up getting very involved with Sharona and the American Jewish Committee. The very next day, Sharona and I showed up at Victor's front door to meet him and start talking. We hit it off immediately. In those early months of our work together, Victor and I got this reputation. It makes me laugh to say it now, but it was true. They started calling us 'The Bulldozers.'"

I love the way Brenda puts it: "That didn't surprise Victor or me. We both came out of retail. We both understood the big picture of what it took to really grab hold of public attention—and to really do something powerful that would change perceptions. We clearly understood we must plan something very visible, very vivid, very memorable. And, that's how we came up with the idea of literally mingling our blood. We would organize an interfaith blood donation program. While Victor was doing his things, like organizing 'the boat people,' I was involved in so many other things. I was there at the big Fort Street worship service when Cardinal Maida spoke. And, together—Sharona and Victor and another Jewish friend, Sheri Schiff—we were all working on organizing this big interfaith blood drive."

To this day, Brenda remains a dear friend. Because she promptly came to our house and met my family, she soon found ways for my entire family to get involved in our interfaith work. My wife, Shahina, turned out to be the public face of our blood drive—and certainly was in the media reports that followed. We got the Red Cross on board and we reserved space at a public high school on October 14. While I was still trying to coax the Detroit-area religious leaders into some kind of active coalition, this alliance with Sharona and Brenda quickly was producing fruit. We called the event "Remembering the Victims of the Sept. 11 Tragedy and Rebuilding Community." From the beginning, we did our best to attract reporters. The news media was a powerful platform for changing public opinion. So, we were thrilled when reporters and photographers actually showed up. In particular, we were pleased that the *Detroit Jewish News* devoted a two-page spread with five photos and a lengthy story, including a big photo of Shahina next to a Jewish woman with the headline "Coming Together." The *Detroit Jewish News* reporter described how the Red Cross had set up its donation center next to tables that offered helpful literature on Islam and Judaism—plus tasty platters of Middle Eastern food donated from local restaurants. We even had a Toys R Us-sponsored area where children could color a paper American flag for a $1 donation to the Red Cross. We tried our best to send the message that patriotism called all of us together.

The *Detroit Jewish News* story opened: "The gymnasium at Andover High School in Bloomfield Hills has seen many opposing teams vie for victory. On Sunday, Oct. 14, Detroit-area Jews and Muslims came together for a very different purpose: unity, communication and the mutual desire to find and celebrate their common ground."

We were making a difference—at least, in our small corner of southeast Michigan. In one month, we had shifted the regional focus, however briefly, from ground zero to "common ground." That was the kind of shift in public perceptions we needed to replicate as rapidly as possible. We all could see that the number of hate crimes against Muslims and Jews was spiraling upward that year. We knew that we had to build our own countermomentum. Beyond one-time events like the blood drive, we knew that we needed a solid infrastructure—a new organization to continue building awareness that what we, as Americans of different faiths, share far more than what might divide us.

One problem we had to confront was that, throughout the 20th century, religious leaders often were content to form two-way partnerships. We faced that same temptation after 9/11. In the Dearborn working group, Christian and Muslim leaders were daring to build new bridges. In the Oakland County working group, Muslim and Jewish neighbors were planning pioneering projects.

I knew that we had to expand from our half-dozen Muslim and Christian "boat people" to a far larger circle that would span all the groups across southeast Michigan. To begin that process, we needed room to work. I called in a favor from Sam Yono, an Iraqi Christian who owned a Ramada Inn just north of Detroit, in Southfield. Sam donated a meeting space and even provided coffee and cookies. We adopted the name Ramada Ramblers.

"Thanks to Victor's efforts, we started meeting regularly at the Ramada Inn," Dan Buttry recalls. "But, for quite a while, we didn't address the problem that we were mostly Christian and Muslim men meeting and trying to form a new interfaith organization. We had reached the point, in early 2002, of trying to get a grant to fund some of our ongoing work—and that's when we finally had to address our limitations. If we really were going to expand in a sincere way, we realized that we had to stop our planning and go back to square one, and include Jews in our planning circle. We couldn't do this as a Christian-Muslim project, and we couldn't simply invite a few Jews to join us as a kind of 'add-on,' with our plans already underway. We decided, after months of meeting already, that we had to re-start our planning process with new Jewish partners joining us at the table. And that's what we did. And we got it right, this time."

Buttry was always a crucial leader in our group and, of course, I knew he was right about broadening the circle. The Ramada Inn where we were meeting was located in Oakland County, where the majority of our Jewish community resided. I had convinced David Gad-Harf, who was the public face of the Jewish community at that time, to attend our first meeting at the Ramada. Yet, over the months, we had not seen as much involvement from Jews as we saw from Christians and Muslims. I also wanted Brenda to get involved in this circle.

Brenda laughs as she recalls her debut at the Ramada Inn. "You can imagine the surprise when I walked into the room—this high-energy Jewish woman taking a seat with all the men," she recalls. "I mean, I had no problem walking into a room full of professional men—I'd been doing that for years in my retail career. But it was a little bit of a surprise when I sat down."

As we added to our Jewish membership, we began calling ourselves Interfaith Partners. Helping to guide all of this expansion was the other major pillar in our new organization: a third Dan, the Rev. Daniel Krichbaum. As we began working together in late 2001, we all respected Krichbaum and regarded him as one of Michigan's most talented interfaith strategists. Like Dan Buttry, Krichbaum had started his career as a local pastor and then moved on to larger challenges. By 2001, Krichbaum was head of the main Detroit-area interfaith council, a group that is known today as the Detroit Roundtable for Diversity and Inclusion. Krichbaum's work was so effective that, before his death in 2015, he became Gov. Granholm's chief operating officer and, later, the director of the Michigan Department of Civil Rights. No question, our "third Dan" was able to help us move mountains. Among other major contributions, Krichbaum also brought on board his chief assistant, Steve Spreitzer, to help us. Today, Spreitzer is CEO of the Michigan Roundtable.

I was elected the first chairperson of Interfaith Partners, as we officially became an arm of the Michigan Roundtable under Krichbaum's guidance. He suggested that we broaden our mission from building relationships among religious leaders to actively engaging entire congregations. He suggested that we invite synagogues, churches and mosques to buy into our work by adding their spiritual and financial support. Our goal was to extend the benefits of interfaith relationships to the grassroots—and to raise enough revenue for the Michigan Roundtable to continue to provide staff assistance to our programs.

Krichbaum also helped us secure our first grant, from the Andrus Family Fund. Much of that effort was spearheaded by Dan Buttry, who coordinated our draft proposals and negotiations with Andrus. Our grant proposal described the situation in blunt terms: "The terrorist attacks of September 11th marked the end of business as usual. Though this was a profound and shaking experience for the entire nation, with our large

Arab and Muslim community, Detroit experienced September 11th with an added intensity. Detroit became the focus for some of the FBI investigations. Muslims experienced harassment and vandalism, and some community members have been detained without charges. Many Arab Muslims rushed to show their patriotism in the face of these provocations. The religious and political communities reacted almost immediately to show solidarity, build trust and maintain community peace.

On Nov. 4, 2002, Andrus awarded us our first $32,000 to kick off a six-month planning process in which we could work with groups across the region to "develop a two-year action agenda" that would build "a more cohesive Detroit metropolitan faith-based community." In the world of nonprofit development—which often takes years to achieve a first significant grant—we were moving at the speed of light. Eventually, through Andrus and other support, we were able to hire part-time congregational organizers. The first staff person we brought on board was the Rev. Sharon Buttry—Dan Buttry's wife, who was a long-time peace activist herself.

In 2004, Sharon was perfectly poised to play a major role in defusing what became internationally known in headlines as "Detroit's call to prayer crisis." These events unfolded in the city of Hamtramck, a Detroit enclave. Dan and Sharon lived in Hamtramck, which enabled Sharon to respond promptly and decisively to the crisis. The flashpoint was news that a mosque was planning to install large speakers to broadcast daily calls to prayer from its roof. That was a reasonable decision by the mosque's perspective, because so many regular attendees lived in the neighborhood. Around the world, the *adhan,* or call to prayer, is a welcome part of many cities' soundscapes. In densely populated neighborhoods, the *adhan* has a practical purpose: It helps the faithful remember their prayers.

Many Hamtramck residents still nostalgically thought of their little city as a Polish-Catholic neighborhood. In recent decades, the city had become far more diverse, but this new sound threatened fond memories of older Catholic families in a particularly poignant way. Some residents felt so strongly about banning the *adhan* that angry words were spoken at the local city council. Picketers showed up on the sidewalk outside the mosque. Media reports of that local opposition soon drew protesters from across Michigan. Then that news went viral. Eventually, we saw extremists—including skinheads and other white supremacists—who drove cross-country to protest in the streets. TV news crews from as far away as Europe and Asia were landing in Detroit to cover the confrontation. I remember talking to news crews from Switzerland and Japan!

Sharon was able to work with her Hamtramck neighbors behind the scenes, bringing together Muslim and Catholic leaders. She brought me in to help reassure the many recent Muslim immigrants that we all were working in their best interest. A major breakthrough came when Sharon got the public support of local Catholic clergy, who pointed out that the *adhan* was similar to their own ringing of bells to mark the traditional Catholic times for worship and prayer. In the end, lots of the Interfaith Partners members got involved and enough public support was generated that the Hamtramck City Council voted unanimously to allow the mosque to proceed. In fact, that incident later was transformed into an annual interfaith Thanksgiving dinner, along with other ongoing service projects in that community. We came through an explosive confrontation without physical injuries or property damage. We ushered in a new era of interfaith cooperation. And this was because we were poised to act appropriately.

Meanwhile, up in Oakland County, Brenda Rosenberg was inspired by her work with Muslim leaders—especially Imam El Amin in Detroit—to begin working, in 2004, on the creation of a play about Abraham (the patriarch revered by Christians, Jews and Muslims). This was another example of the truly visionary nature of our work in southeast Michigan. The idea to create this play had come to Brenda in a dream one night, after an inspiring conversation with Detroit's Imam Abdullah El Amin. Over a lunch together, they were bemoaning the continuing religious divisions in our world. El Amin pointed out to Brenda that Abraham's sons, Isaac and Ishmael, also are revered by Jews and Muslims around the world. As they talked about the sometimes-stormy history between these two branches of Abraham's family, El Amin said that conflict does not have to define our family relationships. He talked about what must have happened when these two sons inevitably came together again, after Abraham's death. That image—of a family coming together—touched off Brenda's vivid dream that night, inspiring Brenda to coordinate a full-scale theatrical production that became known as *Reuniting the Children of Abraham*. Brenda worked with Rick Sperling, founder of Detroit's acclaimed Mosaic Youth

Theatre, to develop a script. A group of Christian, Muslim and Jewish teenagers was recruited to provide authentic voices and experiences. These teenagers would meet regularly with the writer and talk about their lives, their religious experiences and their hopes for the future. Their real-life stories would be incorporated into the final production. Sofi, our daughter, was very involved in creating that script. The play was produced at a Detroit theater, and prompted the Fetzer Institute to provide a grant that would turn the whole process into a peacemaking toolkit. Brenda led that effort, as well, developing a complete curriculum to encourage other groups to recreate our process of bringing people together from all three faiths to tell their stories. Eventually, the project became a CBS-TV documentary that was broadcast nationally.

The theatrical production was so deeply stirring that Shahina left a 2006 performance and began talking with Jewish and Christian women about forming their own organization, aimed at empowering women from diverse faith traditions to work together. They called themselves Women's Interfaith Solutions for Dialogue and Outreach in Metro Detroit—or, WISDOM, for short. Along with Shahina, the prime movers were Gail Katz, a well-known educator and active volunteer in the Jewish community, and Trish Harris, a Catholic and a master community organizer. These women took a page from our playbook that emphasized: Activists act! Their first big project was a women's Interfaith Build with Habitat for Humanity, which brought together 55 Muslim, Catholic, Protestant, Jewish and Baha'i women to put up siding, windows and doors on two homes in Pontiac.

All of these efforts resonated from coast to coast. Brenda's play and peacemaking program was viewed by CBS's nationwide audience. WISDOM began sending teams of women on the road in a very popular program called Five Women, Five Journeys, which is a program that continues to this day. Five Women, Five Journeys is an evening of conversation with a panel of five women about the real-life experiences of families in different faith traditions.

Then books began to be published, reaching readers across North America and beyond. Daniel Buttry published four books that have been used by groups around the world, including *Interfaith Heroes* and *Blessed Are the Peacemakers*, collections of inspiring stories about men and women who crossed religious boundaries in pursuit of peace. Brenda distilled many of the principles she had learned into *Harnessing the Power of Tension*, a guidebook for bringing people together in the midst of conflict. Shahina and the WISDOM team published more than 50 real-life stories of women who dared to form friendships across religious lines in a book called *Friendship & Faith*.

By 2010, our Interfaith Partners group had branched off from the Michigan Roundtable to establish the nonprofit InterFaith Leadership Council of Metropolitan Detroit (IFLC). That group was led for years by businessman and University of Detroit religion professor Bob Bruttell. Like Krichbaum before him, Bruttell was adept at strategic thinking. Noticing my aggressive approach to encouraging change, he stamped me as "a natural-born disrupter"—a badge of honor for one who believes change rarely happens organically. Activists act! Working under the banner of the IFLC, we soon sparked national headlines when we took action against an incendiary demonstration in Michigan by anti-Muslim activist Terry Jones, who had come all the way from Florida with the intention of burning a Quran outside our largest mosque, the Islamic Center of America. In an event called "Vigil for the Beloved Community," the IFLC brought together 1,500 faith leaders from across southeast Michigan to support the Islamic Center and to defuse the attention brought on by Jones's protest. We overwhelmed Jones's message in the news media: we avoided violence and we reminded everyone that religious diversity is part of what makes America a great place to live.

That's what brought *Time* magazine's Joe Klein to my house on the eve of 9/11 that year. He was making an election-year road trip around the country, reporting on his adventures for *Time's* readership. Joe told me that he wanted to see how interfaith relationships were affecting the mood of the nation. There was no better place to take such a litmus test than southeast Michigan, Joe said.

When Joe showed up at our home, he joined me for dinner with family and some friends. I told him, "We want to build this country; not destroy it. Our real statement is going to be tomorrow in Detroit: You're going to see dozens of Muslims joining as many Jews and Christians in an interfaith community service effort in Clark Park tomorrow." I invited him to accompany us, to see how we were commemorating the 9/11 anniversary. Working with WISDOM's Gail Katz and a host of other partners, a diverse religious cross-section of volunteers had been invited to flood the south side of Detroit for a day of community-wide cleaning and repairs. Surrounding Clark Park are neighborhoods filled with thousands of Hispanic, black and Arab families. Christians and Muslims are neighbors: they work and shop together. Their children attend the same public schools.

What Gail had not anticipated was that a conservative, evangelical church in northwest Michigan was responding to the open invitation. A bus full of kids from the church, along with adult chaperones, was on its way to Clark Park, in the hopes of experiencing an interracial event. Michigan is both overwhelmingly white and evangelical; the pastors in that church had not imagined that we would welcome volunteers of all faiths. Only when their bus unloaded, in Clark Park, did they discover that Muslims were involved. One of these evangelicals began to express his concern that an imam was scheduled to participate in an interfaith kickoff supplication. That wasn't something they, as Christians, could accept, they told Gail.

Joe Klein and his colleagues witnessed the incident. Joe wrote: "Victor was upset. A leader of one of the Christian groups had complained to the organizers about having a Muslim deliver a prayer at the opening ceremony. The complaint ran precisely counter to the spirit of the morning."

Joe quoted Gail as saying, "We really wanted to make a statement on 9/11—an interfaith statement that, in Detroit, we're about working together to better the community. I mean, if you can do it in Detroit, you should be able to do it anywhere, right? But, we've had this happen—and, yes, the leader of the youth group mentioned that he didn't want the imam to deliver a prayer. And now, with all the time and energy we put into getting this organized, if there's a negative spin on this, it's going to break my heart."

Joe concluded his column for *Time* this way:

> *I hear you, Gail! All too often we media types focus on the kerfuffle and forget about the good works. And there were significant good works going on in Detroit on this 9/11. We drove past several parks where City Year volunteers, Muslims, Christians and a scattering of Jews—who'll join in greater strength tomorrow,*

after the Sabbath and Rosh Hashana have ended—were cleaning, painting, laughing and talking.

Together.

But the act of ignorance happened, too. And, it's one small example of the sort of injustices that solid citizens like Victor Begg, and several million other Muslims, are experiencing in this country right now.

The Clark Park experience wasn't surprising to me. For years, I had been a very active Republican and knew lots of conservative Christians. What caused me to become less active in those political circles was my growing awareness that many Christian conservatives believe that religious freedom means they are free to impose their faith on the rest of us. These theocrats don't understand that religious diversity makes America stronger; it makes our nation a beacon to the rest of the world. We have no choice but to cooperate, if we hope for a peaceful future. Generational change is slowly moving the culture toward acceptance. The portion of evangelicals in America continues to shrink every year, according to Pew Research. A sure sign of Americans' weariness with religious conflict is the fact that, now, 1 in 4 Americans refuses to give pollsters an answer when asked to name a religious affiliation. As of 2019, a growing number of popular Christian preachers are publicly giving up the label "evangelical" as it is becoming politically toxic. They are calling for inclusion.

Contrary to claims that the whole world is moving toward secularism, religion is not vanishing in America. "The U.S. remains a robustly religious country and the most devout of all the rich Western democracies," Pew Research reported in July 2018. "In fact, Americans pray more often, are more likely to attend weekly religious services and ascribe higher importance to faith in their lives than adults in other wealthy, Western democracies, such as Canada, Australia and most European states."

Religion remains a potent force for good—or for political conflict. Community by community, we must decide which path we will take. The good news is that the interfaith movement has become a burgeoning cottage industry. Many public meetings now include interfaith invocations. That's startling to me, as one of the pioneers who ushered in this movement.

Today, we see advertisements for interfaith comedy shows, interfaith art shows, interfaith concerts and interfaith Habitat for Humanity builds.

The bad news is that, while we may have won many cultural contests, we haven't won the broader campaign to reach a consensus in this country that interfaith diversity is a positive American value. The FBI's tracking of hate crimes after 9/11 showed a dramatic reduction by 2002, to one-third of the rate of assaults and intimidation that we saw in 2001. The most serious category—actual assaults—dropped by two-thirds, from 93 in 2001 to 34 the next year. I believe that that was due to the efforts of like-minded men and women, working for inclusion. I am deeply troubled that the rate of violence began to rise again in 2015, with the new openness to anti-Muslim voices that burgeoned during the Trump campaign and other efforts from the far right. According to the FBI, religion-fueled hate crimes surpassed 2001 rates in 2016. Once again, the long list of minority victims shows how much we, as Muslims, share with so many other groups. Even a sampling from the FBI report conveys the larger picture.

- In 2016 (the last full year of data analysis as of mid-2018), there were 4,426 victims of race-, ethnicity- or ancestry-motivated hate crimes. Of those, 50.2 percent were victims of anti-black bias.

- There were 1,255 victims targeted due to sexual-orientation bias. Of those, 62.7 percent were victims of crimes motivated by anti-gay, male bias.

- There were 1,584 victims of anti-religious hate crimes. Of those, 54.4 percent were victims of crimes motivated by anti-Jewish bias; 24.5 percent were victims of anti-Muslim bias; and 4.1 percent were victims of anti-Catholic bias.

"We have to agree to disagree in a civil way—and remain friends afterward." That's a bit of wisdom I will never forget from David Gad-Harf, the public face of southeast Michigan's Jewish community right after 9/11.

During one particular flare-up in Middle East conflict, *The Detroit News* interviewed both David and me as spokesmen for our respective communities. Just as I expected, David warned me that we would be pulling no punches. "Victor, sometimes our community-relations goals conflict with our respective advocacy needs," David told me. We expressed our clashing viewpoints eloquently enough that *The Detroit News* published the story on its front page.

Then, David and I talked. His first words were, "Victor, I'm hoping we didn't sound like enemies in the *News*." That was my hope, too. At the time, we had strong bonds both personally and professionally in ongoing programs. As much as I disagreed with the points David had made in our interview with *The Detroit News*, I appreciated his honesty about the viewpoints within his community. Strong leaders know that we must be prepared to withstand both public controversy and the inevitable waves of discontent within our own communities. As long as he served his community in that role, I trusted David to be honest and civil in both our cooperative work and our public debates.

When I think of all of the dear friends like David—and the battle scars we have accumulated together—I still can confidently affirm: We must not respond to crises by pulling back from whoever currently might be "the other." We must not demonize the minorities living among us. That's not the true teaching of Islam, nor is it the true teaching of Christianity.

Muslims around the world were pleased when a bishop from Argentina became pope in 2013 and named himself Pope Francis—the first pope in 2,000 years to choose that name. We welcomed the signal he was sending around the world. We all know the story about the original St. Francis's courage in 1219, when Crusader armies from Europe were facing the sultan of Egypt near the mouth of the Nile. Fearing death, Francis nevertheless crossed enemy lines. Instead of violence, Francis was met with hospitality, and he spent several days living in the sultan's household. In their discussions, neither man convinced the other to change his religious perspective. In the end, Francis was peacefully escorted back to the Crusader camp. The Catholic Franciscan order celebrates St. Francis's courage and says that, by 2019, their priests will have been involved in forging interfaith relationships for 800 years. The story inspires people to this day. One of the most popular interfaith programs moving around the country features a showing of the 2016 film *The Sultan and the Saint*, which originally aired on PBS. The film was produced by Michael Wolfe and directed by his co-founder at Unity Productions, Alex Kronemer. I helped to organize such a showing at the Community Church of Vero Beach, in Florida.

I think of the great Sufi mystic Jalal ad-Din Muhammad Rumi, whom *The New York Times* points out is the best-selling poet in the United States. That may be startling, but it is true. Of course, most Americans think of Rumi as a poet of love. His books fly off the shelves into the hands of lovers young and old, who like to borrow some of his best lines. Rumi certainly was deeply focused on the meaning of love, but his love was far larger than romance. Rumi often wrote about the all-embracing love that flows from Islam. He lived and wrote his poetry in the same era as St. Francis, although the two men never met. I sometimes wonder what might have happened had they encountered each other. Just imagine how they might have collaborated!

I often reflect on Rumi's famous verse about calling people together, no matter what their faith might be. He lists groups that often were considered enemies of one another in the turbulent 13th century. In English, his words are:

> *Whoever you may be—come!*
> *Even though you may be*
> *An infidel, a pagan, or a fire-worshipper—come!*
> *Ours is not a brotherhood of despair.*
> *Even though you have broken*
> *Your vows of repentance a hundred times—*
> *Come!*

Whatever our individual religious traditions may be, consider the fact that the most universal greeting in our world today is still this: "Peace." Jesus is "Prince of Peace." One of the 99 names of God, in the Quran, is "Peace." We may pronounce that word differently: Hindus say *shanti*; Jews say *shalom*; Muslims say *salam*. At the root of who we are, as humans, all of us hope to come together, one day, in peace. We all dream of finding harmony and wholeness.

CHAPTER 12

I Am a Sushi

Among those who have divided their religion and become
factions, each party rejoicing in that which it has.

Quran 30:32

On December 30, 2006, Iraq's deposed leader Saddam Hussein was exe-
cuted by hanging. Conflicting reports quickly circled the planet about his
treatment and his final words. Prominent in those reports was a claim
that, just before he died, Saddam had a brief verbal dispute with a guard
about a Shia cleric. (Saddam was Sunni.) The guard shouted praise for a
Shia cleric during the execution, to taunt Saddam; Saddam scoffed at the
cleric's name. Then Saddam died.

This touched off a wave of angry responses, stemming from Sunni-
Shia tensions to other political issues. One source of anger among many
Muslims was the timing of Saddam's execution—it occurred during the
Islamic celebration of Eid al-Adha, which seemed inappropriate. (That
would be like scheduling a major American execution for Easter morning.) Other troubling issues involved Saddam's treatment at the hands
of his guards—which included that final Sunni-Shia confrontation on
the gallows. Extremists among Saddam's supporters lashed out in various
ways.

Does that sound like an obscure bit of historical trivia? Perhaps it is for
most Americans, but in my community, it struck close to home.

My phone rang. A reporter told me, "Iraq's sectarian violence may be
coming to Dearborn. This foreign Sunni-Shia feud could be playing out
in American neighborhoods like on the streets of Baghdad." News media

in Michigan wanted to localize the international story and this looked like a hot lead.

"I don't see that happening," I responded, trying my best to downplay the idea. But this wasn't the only reporter pursuing that story.

Fueling the rumors was some vandalism—stones thrown through the windows of a couple of local buildings and graffiti spray on a Shia mosque. Oddly enough, no two news reports had the same details. In some, the graffiti was sprayed on an abandoned building; in others, the rocks were thrown through the windows of businesses, not mosques. Whatever had actually happened, reporters were sure they had caught the scent of a news story and weren't going to let it go.

The reporters persisted: "What about the graffiti? Could this be the first sign of local sectarian conflict?" And: "What about the broken windows?"

"It's probably just vandalism. Maybe a disgruntled individual did it. There's no sign of any big conflict," I insisted. I was doing my best to fend off callers who simply wanted to fuel these divisive rumors. Although I have appeared in countless news reports over the decades, I have also declined my share of invitations from reporters whom, I suspect, were trying to feed off anti-Muslim anxieties. This was a time to turn down most interview requests, I thought. Spreading these rumors would not help anyone.

Sometimes, I found myself on thin ice with my Muslim friends. That was the case when a Chicago-based TV news producer called me to ask about Sunni-Shia relationships in Michigan. Even in Chicago, Ruth Ravve had heard about the graffiti and wanted to do a story about the potential for sectarian conflict. This call from Ruth came years before Trump was elected and Fox News became more politically polarized. But, even in early 2007, the Fox News staff was widely regarded as anti-Muslim among my friends.

"No one with a sane mind would agree to talk to Fox," one friend said, warning me that I should not even think about accepting Ruth's invitation.

Still, if Fox was going to do a national story on this provocative Sunni-Shia issue, then I wanted to ensure that the report was as balanced as possible.

So, what is this potentially explosive Sunni-Shia division between Muslims? The roots of the split extend back to the year 632, when the

Prophet Muhammad died, and the remaining Muslim leaders disagreed about who should succeed him as their leader. That dispute was the origin of the Sunni and Shia movements.

I like to downplay that history. I tell people, "I am a Sushi. Yes, I understand those tragedies and passions that unfolded more than 1,300 years ago, but I have always worked toward intrafaith relationships within our community."

Thanks to years of work on building bonds, this split has not turned into a serious flashpoint in southeast Michigan. In spite of that, though, no public spokesperson for Islam can avoid this perennial question. Whenever I talk about Islam at schools, conferences or community gatherings, I close my session with questions from the audience. One of the first questions is always: "What's the difference between Sunnis and Shias?"

Answering this question involves a history as long and complex as the answer to the question, "Among Christians, what's the difference between Protestants and Catholics?" In short, I could say something like this: "This political and theological conflict goes back many centuries. It is like trying to explain all the complicated reasons that Catholics and Protestants fought each other in Ireland for so many years. Do you really want me to explain all the historical details? We'll be here a while."

One reason I downplay this question is that the Sunni-Shia split is not an urgent issue in most of the world. When the question comes up, I answer accurately: "Well, there aren't as many issues separating the two branches of Islam as there are separating Catholics and Protestants." That always surprises my American audiences—most of whom are Christian— but it's true. On the basics of Islam, Sunnis and Shias agree on all of the so-called five pillars: We profess that there is only one God; we practice five daily prayers; we expect to make charitable gifts, called *zakat*; we fast each year; and we try to make a pilgrimage to Mecca. There are bigger differences remaining between Catholics and Protestants. For example, those two branches of Christianity agree on the same Ten Commandments, but they insist on numbering them differently. Catholics and Protestants also disagree on what should be included in the Bible. Catholic Bibles contain 73 books; Protestants only accept 66 of those books. In contrast, Sunnis and Shias share the exact same Quran. Every Muslim in the world agrees that the Quran has 114 *surahs*.

If an audience seems interested in more background, I usually say something like this: "What's the beef between Sunnis and Shias? It's about succession and politics. Upon the passing of Prophet Muhammad, one group wanted his young son-in-law, Ali, to inherit leadership; another group, which held a majority, elected the man they felt was most qualified: Muhammad's companion and confidant, Abu Bakr. The first caliph, then, was Abu Bakr. The word "Shia" is usually translated as "partisan" in English. More than a millennium later, these "partisans of Ali" continue to mourn the injustices suffered long ago by Ali and his family. In contrast, the word "Sunni" refers to the followers of the "practices" of the Prophet Muhammad. This quickly gets confusing, because Shias also follow the Prophet's practices. The history gets even more complex, because Ali later was chosen to be a caliph, after all!"

There's much more to the ancient story, of course. Once each year, members of predominantly Shia mosques recall, as if it was yesterday, a tragic battle at Karbala in central Iraq, where members of Ali's family were killed. On the 10th of the Islamic month of Muharram, in a sacred observance known as Ashura, these deaths are recalled with fresh eulogies and tears. Within the Shia community, men who can recount the details of the battle in dramatic fashion are highly sought after to perform their recitations at Ashura services. Sunnis also remember these sorrowful events, but don't engage in ceremonial mourning like the Shia. Sunnis mark the occasion with fasting, but are not focused on the battle at Karbala. Sunnis are following a tradition that says the Prophet Muhammad himself observed a fast on Ashura, which he believed was the day Moses saved the Israelites from the pharaoh.

How could I hope to explain even part of that in a 15-second video clip on Fox-TV?

What I wanted to tell the Fox reporter was that I have grown tired of attempts to exploit these divisions. Asking me to explain all of this is like asking an American clergyman to explain the long history of Catholic-Protestant divisions. These disputes aren't relevant to daily life in American communities. As I see Islam growing around the world, I am convinced that more and more Muslims are embracing a non-denominational approach to the faith.

That's how the Prophet Muhammad saw the world. During his lifetime,

Muslims were a single community. Yet they also were living in one small corner of the world. Today, most Americans are surprised to learn that Muslims live on all five inhabited continents. According to Pew Research's global study of Islam, "More than 60 percent of the global Muslim population is in Asia and about 20 percent is in the Middle East and North Africa. ... India, for example, has the third-largest population of Muslims worldwide. China has more Muslims than Syria, while Russia is home to more Muslims than Jordan and Libya combined."

There are many other urgent human rights issues and conflicts that Muslims are facing around the world, and I wish we could increase awareness about some of those more important global issues. However, if Americans know anything about Islam, they know about the Sunni-Shia division. What most Americans don't know is that this conflict is limited to a few corners of the world today. "Of the total Muslim population, 10-13 percent are Shia Muslims and 87-90 percent are Sunni Muslims. Most Shias live in just four countries: Iran, Pakistan, India and Iraq," Pew reports.

That kind of answer wouldn't satisfy a television reporter. Even if a news crew taped me explaining all of that background, I knew that that section of video would wind up on the cutting-room floor. That lack of interest in historical context is not a problem exclusively with Fox: that's how news reporters work. Journalists know that conflict drives ratings. Portraying our Muslim-American neighbors as divided and violent guarantees that a story will move to the top of the nightly news.

I had been warned against accepting the Fox News invitation. I certainly was clear-eyed about journalism after years of talking with media professionals, but I also understood the value of engaging in this difficult dialogue. I also felt that, when the opportunity was offered, we had to speak to the Fox viewers. In my long experience, most journalists are seeking the truth. So, I agreed to talk with Ruth. She had an impressive background, including time spent working in Pakistan, Afghanistan and Jordan. As we discussed the arrangements on the phone, Ruth seemed fair to me.

Her request was reasonable. "I'd like to visit a mosque in your area," she said.

Cautiously, I said, "Our Muslim Unity Center is a good place to visit.

We built the place with resources from both Sunnis and Shias, so that's a good reason to come see us." I knew that it was a unique hook for a national news story. One way to guarantee the success of a media report is to pierce a popular myth, and if other reporters were stoking the idea of a simmering Sunni-Shia conflict, then Ruth's reporting at the Muslim Unity Center could help bust that myth. This could be a positive experience for all of us.

Before we finished, however, I was clear in my warning: "Ruth, our community is wary of Fox-TV. Keep that in mind, please."

As soon as we finished the call, my spirits sank. I began to worry. Would Ruth's crew try to single out individual men and women at the mosque for interviews, and then select just the most provocative things people might inadvertently say on camera? How might they try to spin this story? I knew that I already was on thin ice, because I had ignored the warnings of friends in setting up this visit.

First, I made sure that this visit began at our home. I wanted time to talk over the issues before we got to the mosque. Shahina and I welcomed the Fox crew informally, with food and beverages. All of us sat in our family room and talked. To make sure they could successfully get a myth-busting story about Sunni-Shia friendship, I invited a Shia friend to join us. Eide Alawan is the brother of my old mentor, the late Chuck Alawan. Both Eid and I are comfortable talking with non-Muslims, and we are veterans of many interviews with reporters. Eid also was happy to adopt my new term for crossing this historic divide: Sushi.

Together, we sat on a couch that faced Ruth and her cameraman. We used our best line: "We are Sushi." That particular clip didn't make the cut for the final Fox report, but we had made our point.

"We are Muslims first; Shia or Sunni second," Eid said.

"We're a single community of believers," I said.

They didn't use any of those lines, but they did quote Eid when he said, "We're coming together like Muslims aren't doing in the rest of the world—and the reason for it is that we have an opportunity to feel part of this country and feel that we have a future—and it's not a one-sided situation where Shiites are in control or Sunnis are in control."

After the interview at my house, we drove to the Muslim Unity Center and arrived just in time for midday prayers. As the TV cameras rolled, the muezzin's *adhan* melodiously echoed under the high ceiling. Sunni and Shia Muslims lined up, shoulder to shoulder, faced Mecca and prayed to one God.

Ruth's Fox-TV report turned out to be balanced. Overall, it was a very positive portrait of our community. The headline on her report was: "Sunni and Shiite Muslims in the U.S. come together in life and prayer." I sighed in relief at the opening lines: "The call to prayer at the Unity Center mosque in suburban Detroit is unique, not because of what's being said, but because of who answers the call: Both Sunni and Shiite Muslims."

To help spread this news, I wrote a column for the *Detroit Free Press* and headlined my essay bluntly: "There is no Shia-Sunni strife in USA." I wrote: "Incidents of vandalism at a mosque frequented by Shia Muslims in metro-Detroit have prompted media speculation that the sectarian disease plaguing Iraq might be spreading to American soil. But the disease isn't contagious. Factional violence between Sunnis and Shias is not another thing Americans need to add to their list of things to be afraid of. Shia and Sunni Muslims have lived in peace in Iraq for centuries, just as Catholics and Protestants live together peacefully in America."

Even as all of this was unfolding in early 2007, I knew that my own activism had to focus as much on building healthy intrafaith relationships as fostering interfaith connections between the major religions. I knew that Muslim leaders had to come to terms with the rising tide of new immigrants, because many of these families carried with them raw wounds from conflict zones in the Middle East. Some of them had even lost loved ones to sectarian violence. Muslim leaders tend to focus on their spiritual duties and on the management of local mosques. Most of them have little time to proactively address larger, community-wide issues.

As a community builder, if I was going to address the potential of such tension, I had to begin by looking for allies. I wasn't alone in recognizing that, while we had avoided violence so far, our community was experiencing signs of friction. My late friend Syed Salman and the well-known African-American Imam Abdullah El-Amin had worked with me for years in establishing friendly relationships among imams.

By the time we were ready to take practical steps, we had an inspiring example from southern California that we could hold up, to move our own community forward. Parallel to our work in the Detroit area, the national Muslim Public Affairs Council (MPAC) had been working on improving relations between Sunni and Shia leaders in other parts of the country. In April 2007, MPAC made national headlines by hosting a ceremonial signing of the Intra-Faith Code of Honor between Sunni and Shia leaders in southern California. Following their example, I was determined that southeast Michigan would be the second region in the nation to forge such a public pledge of unity. I approached my friend Sherman Abd al-Hakim Jackson to moderate our discussions, and I was thankful that he agreed to help. Everyone respected his scholarship, as already, he had published several books on Islam with Oxford University Press. He held three appointments at the University of Michigan, teaching in near-Eastern studies, law and Afro-American studies. Eventually, he was recruited by the University of Southern California to accept an endowed chair that let him pursue his research in religion and American culture. With Jackson facilitating the dialogue, we were able to hammer out our own Sunni-Shia manifesto that was acceptable to all parties. Like MPAC, we also called our document a code of honor. After a good deal of discussion spanning the entire Detroit area, a Shia mosque was selected as our signing venue.

I sent out a press release on official letterhead of the Council of Islamic Organizations of Michigan (CIOM) that began with a respectful, *"In the name of God, the All-Merciful."* We announced that our signing ceremony would be on May 10, 2007, as "a demonstration by Shia and Sunni Detroit-area Muslim leaders of their commitment to speak out against communal divisions and all forms of sectarian division and violence."

The heart of the new agreement was as follows:

> *As Muslim Americans who live and struggle for a dignified existence for Islam and Muslims in a spirit of peaceful coexistence and respect for all, we believe that the practical challenges of the future supersede the ideological differences of the past. In recognition of our communal duty to promote goodness and peace, we remain eager to offer any help we can and to join hands with all those who wish well for the Family of Believers (Ummah) in stopping the senseless, inhumane violence in Iraq and elsewhere in the world.*

In our view, we must begin by preventing such tragic sectarianism from spilling over into our Muslim communities in the United States. As a first step toward this goal, we agree to live in peace and respect each other in accordance with a 'Muslim Code of Honor.' We remain committed to this Muslim Code of Honor not only during times of agreement and ease but, more importantly, when faced with contentious issues and in times of mutual disagreement.

Toward the end of the proclamation, we inscribed verses from the Quran 3:103-105, that the leaders all agreed should guide us:

"And hold fast, all together, to the rope of God, and be not divided among yourselves. And remember with gratitude God's favor upon you, when you were enemies and He joined your hearts in love. Thus, by His grace you became brethren. And you were on the brink of the Fire, and He saved you from it. Thus, does God make His Signs clear to you, that you may be guided. So, let there arise out of you a band of people inviting to all that is good, enjoining what is right and forbidding what is wrong. They are the ones to attain felicity. And be not like those who are divided amongst themselves and fall into disputations after receiving clear signs. For them is a dreadful penalty."

I was thrilled at the outpouring of support from Muslim leaders! Among the prominent signers were: Imam Steve Elturk (Islamic Organization of North America); Imam Mohammad Ali Elahi (Islamic House of Wisdom); Imam Hassan Al-Qazwini (Islamic Center of America); Imam Muhammad Musa (Muslim Unity Center); Imam Husham Al-Husainy (Karbala Islamic Educational Center); Imam Abdullah Bey El-Amin (Muslim Center of Detroit); Imam Abdul Latif Berry (Islamic Institute of Knowledge); Sheikh Ali Suleiman Ali (Muslim Community of the Western Suburbs); and Hajj Dawud Walid (Council on American-Islamic Relations, Michigan chapter).

Many of the signers framed this document and displayed it in their mosques. It's still on the walls of Muslim centers. Each time I see a copy of that Code of Honor, I am impressed—especially at the names we unexpectedly added at the bottom of the page. This demonstration of unity turned out to be so popular that, on the day of the signing, we were

supported by even more Muslim leaders than we had anticipated. Some
came from other Michigan cities, including Lansing. We wound up with
28 signers, squeezing in the final names at the bottom of the page.

Everyone regarded this signing as such a solemn occasion that I decided
to have 35 copies made. I asked the imams to personally sign these copies,
so that they all would be historical documents suitable for framing and
public display.

Reporters had set up cameras at the signing event; the news went
out nationally. After our accomplishment, Michigan Governor Jennifer
Granholm praised what we had achieved. She said, "All religious leaders
should jointly sign on to a message of cooperation like this." Later that
year, the Islamic Society of North America (ISNA) followed up with a
similar proclamation at their annual Labor Day convention in Chicago.
I'm proud that they chose our Michigan text as their guide as they developed their own statement.

While this was an inspiring milestone for our community, I knew
that the Code of Honor was also a whip that we would need to crack in
the future if overseas divisions began to creep back into our community.
When conflicts blow up in the Middle East, American imams sometimes
forget past pledges. When new immigrants arrive with fresh wounds, new
attention must be paid to soothing the inevitable sectarian friction.

Such an occasion came around the following year, due to more violence in the Middle East. Rumors began circulating once again. Signs
of friction were apparent. We had approved this Code of Honor and we
had hung it on our walls, but did that piece of paper really mean anything? Raising such a provocative question amounted to using the whip.
The imams knew, of course, that we could not let our community slide
into conflict. In July 2008, imams from across southeast Michigan recon-
vened and revisited their earlier commitment. When they met, the imams
proposed practical steps to implement the code. Before they closed their
meeting, they adapted a new resolution:

1. To abide by the Code of Honor, it is essential that we establish
   good working relationships among the Shia and Sunni
   communities, led by the imams. Follow up on the Code of
   Honor, signed by the imams of southeast Michigan so that the

Muslims (Shia and Sunni) live together peacefully in America, regardless of our fundamental differences.

2. Adhering to the Code of Honor, to encourage respectful language in our institutions and discourage speech or material that engages in rhetoric of *takfir* (disrespect of other Muslims).

3. To be aware of those promoting *fitna* (discord). We must not allow such individuals or groups to distract us from our struggle for a dignified, peaceful and respectful coexistence.

4. To cooperate and work with all Muslims on issues that affect all of us regardless of any differences amongst us.

5. To have the Council of Islamic Organizations of Michigan as the medium to facilitate communication between Sunnis and Shias.

6. To have a regular forum of the Muslim imams/scholars/ community leaders, to deal with issues that affect both Sunnis and Shia within their own communities.

7. To encourage our national organizations, through the example of our brotherly cooperation, to also honor the terms of the Code of Honor we signed in Michigan.

Despite that major public milestone, our work was not finished. Our community had grown so large and diverse over the years that we had to address our divisions on multiple levels. The bullet points in the imams' 2008 resolution pointed to the CIOM as a crucial bridge between Sunnis and Shia. However, we still had to address another chasm that had formed in southeast Michigan. That chasm had opened even before the incidents of vandalism drew reporters' interest in our divisions. In 2005, the Islamic Shura Council of Michigan (ISCOM) had been established by Sunni imams to support community service projects among the Sunni mosques. When I first heard that news, I was disappointed: the CIOM was supposed to be the unifying organization. Nevertheless, ISCOM began doing good work in the community and took on a life of its own. Then, after the tensions of 2006 through 2008, Muslim leaders realized that it was not in their best interest to have even the appearance of competing councils.

For years, I had promoted CIOM, even stepping in more than once to help shore up its leadership and programming when the council's energy seemed to be fading. We could not let our community's growth be an excuse to let sects divide our leadership, so I renewed my efforts to expand CIOM for a few years. Among other things, I tried to learn all I could from similar councils across the country. I often picked up fresh ideas, especially a project that was proving to be popular in California: an annual statewide mosque open house. This was a great marketing opportunity. Mosques would open their doors and welcome neighbors with special hospitality, hosts to explain Islamic traditions and helpful literature. This could be produced with shared costs for printing brochures and promoting the event through news media.

I expanded on this idea by asking Governor Jennifer Granholm's office to recognize the date of the open house as "Muslim Day." We received our proclamation from Lansing, which we enlarged into posters and placed at the front entrance of participating mosques. The big day was a smash hit! Mosques from every corner of southeast Michigan participated. Media coverage was huge, and it seemed that everyone turned out to look inside our mosques. The feedback was encouraging. Our non-Muslim neighbors went home happy, having made new friends and enjoyed terrific ethnic food.

Still, the rift between the two councils had to be closed—and I knew I was not the statesman to achieve such a major goal. I was too associated with CIOM and I had ruffled too many feathers with my activism, over the years, to even think about leading such an effort.

Fortunately, we had talented young blood rising to the call of unity. At that time, Syed Muhammad Mohiuddin—the son of one of my high school classmates—was finishing more than a decade of studies at the University of Michigan, Boston University and Michigan State University. He emerged as both a physician and an expert in program design and strategic planning. Today, he has moved on to work in Washington, D.C., but at the time we needed him, he was still living in Michigan and was getting involved in various nonprofits, including United Way for Southeastern Michigan. Like most young professional Muslims today, Mohiuddin understood the value of unity. He shouldered the major responsibility for coordinating what turned into two years of joint retreats and professionally facilitated community conversations. Finally, everyone agreed on a common mission. While I was stepping toward the sidelines, I was reassured to see Mohiuddin and his cutting-edge level of resources moving into leadership. Of course, he was not alone: He is part of a whole vanguard of young Muslim leaders.

The bottom line was that, by January 2011, a community-wide meeting had endorsed a merger of the existing councils. By 2012, CIOM and ISCOM formally merged, to form the Michigan Muslim Community Council (MMCC). New bylaws were adopted through consensus, thereby changing the structure of the organization from membership to directorship. A new logo was designed for the MMCC, which displayed a map of Michigan and the words "Serving the Community Since 1988." The mission statement read: "Unifying communities, promoting the best Islamic and American values, and pursuing social justice in America."

That's why, today, I prefer to tell people—simply—"I'm a Sushi." Shahina and I continue to follow Sunni traditions, while Eide Alawan follows his family's Shia traditions. There are small differences in the ways we practice prayer and mark observances throughout the Islamic year, but we all are Muslims and we believe that nothing should separate us as brothers and sisters in the faith.

The idea of maintaining this sectarian division has never made much sense to me. When I first was trying to come to America, my Shia friend Mujahid Hussain helped me secure my student visa. Then, we lived as roommates. Throughout my entire life, I've worked and shared fellowship with Muslims from both movements.

I want to tell friends in other parts of the world: "Learn from us! In America, Shia and Sunni families live in mixed communities. When differences arise, we apply the best practices of conflict resolution and resolve our differences."

Wherever Shahina and I travel across this country, I meet like-minded Muslims. During the month of Muharram, one year, we visited a mall and noticed a shop selling specialty teas. Neatly displayed on a table at the entrance was a flask of hot tea, with little cups so people strolling through the mall could have a taste. Shahina and I both love tea, so we wound up exploring the shop.

The owner noticed Shahina's hijab and greeted us with a warm greeting: "*Salaam alaikum!*"

"*Wa'alakium salam*," I replied. We began to talk. His family originally was from Iran, a largely Shia nation. Of course, I was aware that this was the month of the most emotionally charged observance in the Shia calendar. "You must be getting ready to observe Ashura," I said.

He smirked. "Somebody killed somebody a long time ago! So what?"

"Sorry to mention it," I said.

He waved his hand, dismissing my concern. "Why should we live in the past?"

That's a very American response to history. For centuries, America has been the one country where people come with the hope of reinventing themselves—of becoming something new. Although many of us seem to have lost sight of this core value in the age of Trump, the American Dream has always been that this is a land where everyone has an even start on making a new life.

The owner of that tea shop was repeating one of America's most popular slogans: Why should we live in the past?

I thought back to that Fox-TV report by Ruth Ravve—the one that had caused me so much anxiety. In her final report, I was quoted as saying, "We are Muslims—that's all that is important. Americans are a beacon to the rest of the world in terms of the pluralistic society that we have created here. We have lived together for a long time, and we want to make sure that that message goes out to the rest of the world."

For the Shia perspective, Ruth quoted my friend Eide Alawan: "I'm convinced the kids of our future generations are going to be building a better country for us, a better community and a better understanding of one another in the Islamic tradition."

In the end, Ruth Ravve's lengthy report was a truly American story. As she edited her final report, she made exactly the choices I had expected her to make. In choosing what was most important to show her Fox News audience in the precious moments of airtime she was given, Ruth never devoted a single moment to explaining the Sunni-Shia history. She completely ignored it. Quite simply, she knew that history doesn't matter much to most Americans.

That's my prayer for our Muslim-American community: May we all one day become Sushis.

CHAPTER 13

A Blue Mosque

To God belong the East and the West;
wherever you turn, there is the Face of God;
God is All-embracing, All-knowing.

Quran 2:115

"The Muslim Unity Center should look like the Blue Mosque!"

That was the enthusiastic recommendation from the king of Bloomfield Township—at least, that's how Shahina and I came to think of Fred Korzon. In 1999 he had left his office as township supervisor, after 18 years, but he remained an influential force.

When we visited the Korzons' summer home on Lake Michigan, near Traverse City, Fred eagerly talked about a recent tour of Turkey. He was so inspired by the beautiful, 17th-century Blue Mosque in Istanbul that he began visualizing what the Muslim Unity Center could become.

That was quite a transformation. When we first launched our proposals for the Muslim Unity Center, our initial meetings with township officials had been cordial—but the whole process of winning acceptance had been challenging. As a result, I had built strong friendships with many men and women who were serving our community over the years, including police officers and firefighters. For example, whenever I had access to a suite at the Palace of Auburn Hills or at Joe Louis Arena in Detroit, I invited some of these friends to watch the Pistons or the Red Wings. The Muslim Unity Center also hosted open houses, so that neighbors could become more familiar with us. Our building was designated as an official polling place, as well, and is where Shahina and I went to cast our ballots (along with our neighbors). We liked to welcome township programs in our building.

Now Fred saw the center as a vital part of his community, and he wanted our building to look as impressive as the mosques he had seen in his world travels. He wasn't alone. A member of the Square Lake Neighborhood Association, Brian Palmer, had expressed his opinion in blunt terms: "Your mosque shouldn't look like a storefront." I did not take offense at that. As people drove past our building, I knew that its appearance was still defined by the lines of the old classroom wing. It was a well-kept building, but it was not an impressive landmark.

When even our neighbors were recommending an upgrade, I was convinced that we should expand. There were practical concerns, as well: we needed to attract new Muslim families, so that they could choose our center as their congregation. Remodeling and expanding the center made a lot of sense.

Mosque leadership was cheerfully receptive to the idea, but I needed photos to help planners catch this vision. Photos of the so-called Blue Mosque—actually, the Sultan Ahmed Mosque—are widely available online, but its grandiose design was beyond our capability. That vast landmark has a capacity of 10,000 people, with a dome that soars 141 feet into the city's skyline. The last time we tried to win local approvals, we were burned for sketching a proposal that was too grand for the neighbors to accept. This time, I needed to show people something reasonable. On a business trip to Cincinnati, I caught sight of a beautiful mosque with an impressive—yet more modestly sized—dome and minarets. I also learned that this mosque, the Islamic Center of Greater Cincinnati, emphasized cultural diversity and outreach—values I hoped would continue to define the Muslim Unity Center. On the Ohio mosque's website, the congregation's mission statement made it clear that these people were committed to "a high-caliber, multi-faceted and inclusive Islamic institution, serving as a resource for the community." They pledged to "promote cooperation, religious understanding and community harmony through outreach, education on Islam, and collective work countering ignorance, prejudice and bigotry." The more I thought about this Ohio mosque, the more I realized something: That was the kind of design—and the example—that could inspire our supporters. On my return to Michigan, I turned off of I-75 and bought an instant camera from a drugstore. I spent a long time walking around the mosque, snapping photos that I would bring home with me.

I was fully on board, eager to tackle this major campaign. Next, I began to talk with experts about what was possible. In 1999, Shahina and I had remodeled our residence. We had chosen Young & Young, a Michigan firm that had built or remodeled some of the most impressive homes in our area. We commissioned these architects to transform our colonial home into a Mediterranean villa. I like to describe what they developed as "Islamic architecture," because it reminded me of Moorish designs I had seen in Spain. When the project was done, we had large front pillars, a red-tile roof and a stucco-looking exterior. The builder was Usztan LLC, a company that had been around since 1975 and had established a solid reputation. We had to survive a year of inconveniences during construction, but the result was stunning. Our home did not look like a remodel; the design and construction were so artful that the house looked like it had always been a villa.

When I initially discussed the mosque expansion with professionals at Young & Young and Usztan, they recommended that we construct a new prayer area. The classrooms and gym could remain, but be remodeled in keeping with the new design. The architects recommended custom, precast, burnished block paneling that could be applied to the façade. Large domes with skylights would be added to the entrance and the main sanctuary. The old sidewalk to the front door would be replaced with a pillared walkway. The building's old chimney, which stood above the boiler room, could be converted into a minaret. The initial cost estimate was several million dollars, and the overall plan included a new waterline, an expanded septic field, bathrooms, wiring for a new speaker system with TV monitors, internet and security systems with exterior cameras, a children's play area, an imam's apartment, new wooden flooring in the gym, kitchen upgrades and a funeral facility.

This was exciting! I was ready to rock 'n roll.

Then, from these high-flying visions of our future, I faced the first of many questions: How would we finance this project? How would we get a building permit for such a major expansion after having made compromises with our neighbors when we first started? Many neighbors had become good friends and encouraged our plans—but others clearly recalled that our initial agreement involved a promise that we would not expand. Even as we were tackling the thorny issues of funding and approvals, I spent a lot of time trying to get neighbors excited about the new vision. This time, I was relieved to discover that most neighbors liked the idea of having a more attractive building in the neighborhood.

Donors were generous, as well. We were blessed to see two major donors, Ismael Basha and Jamal Elhout, stepping forward right away. I joined them in putting substantial money into the project. First Federal Bank was an important ally, as well, in providing a new mortgage. I knew one of the senior executives, Chip Miller, and we both served on the board of the Michigan Roundtable. Township Clerk Wilma Cotton helped us begin the process of clearing the hurdles for township approval.

One of the most inspiring gifts was $5,000 from Gary Grewal, a successful Sikh businessman and a good friend. One day, as I was opening my mail, I found Gary's check—and was so impressed to find this non-Muslim sharing our goal of promoting unity, even beyond the boundaries of Islam. As I looked at his check, memories of Hyderabad's diversity flooded over me. Perhaps, I thought, we could achieve our own golden era of interfaith cooperation.

With much fanfare, we announced our plans and set a date for breaking ground. A large billboard was planted in front of the Muslim Unity Center, proudly displaying a picture of the new mosque.

This was the dawn of a new age for our congregation. It also was when I learned—the hard way—that launching a new community is different than sustaining its development over time. At the time of the Muslim Community Center's origin, I had been a one-man band: I welcomed lots of supporters—most of whom already were close friends—and as we opened our doors and our membership grew, I still kept my hand firmly on the center's helm. Soon, other major donors, board members and lots of program volunteers enthusiastically shouldered a major share of the ongoing operation. As we launched this expansion, though, I finally realized that I had reached the limit of my ability to supervise everything. I learned much of this lesson through a series of painful confrontations, and in retrospect, I realize that this was the inevitable transformation from a founder's vision to a community consensus.

In Oakland County, all I had to do was look around me to see evidence of other, similar religious and philanthropic visionaries who had preceded me. The architectural masterpiece that now is known as Kirk in the Hills Presbyterian Church originally was a pet project of Col. Edwin S. George. He earned his fortune in Michigan's fur trade and, quite literally, started building an enormous church on his personal estate. Not far from George's project was Christ Church Cranbrook, now a part of the Episcopal Church, which was built by newspaper baron George Booth and his wife, Ellen, on their 175-acre farm. Both of those churches successfully made it through the transition—from their founders' control, and into the hands of church members. They remain strong and draw visitors from around the world, offering architectural beauty as well as inspiring worship services. At the Muslim Unity Center, I began to realize that it was now my turn to go through the sometimes-rocky process that the Georges and the Booths had experienced before me.

The first painful lesson came with our construction committee's decision—over my strong objections—to turn over management of the building contract to a member who claimed expertise. The committee was eager to save the money this fellow promised he could trim from the budget. I could see that this was a mistake, but the committee's majority did not heed my advice. Before the vote, I faced the uncomfortable question: "Brother Begg, why wouldn't you trust our judgment?" The majority ruled. All too soon, however, everyone could see that I had been right. We suffered substantial financial losses and had to replace this man with a qualified contractor. Together, we had made the decision; together, we suffered the consequences; and together, we moved ahead with the construction.

This transition was full of costly lessons, both financially and psychologically. At one point, a dispute arose when some Muslim zealots got a good look at our new prayer hall. Suddenly, I began to hear: "Brother, your new mosque doesn't face Mecca."

I was stunned. Of course we were facing Mecca! Irving Elementary School had been constructed in a northeastern direction, due to the curvature of Square Lake Road. Upon acquisition in 1993 and until our expansion in 2000, we had heard no objections to the direction of our prayers. Anyone can search Google, these days, and find that northeast is the proper direction from our location—the shortest distance to Mecca, given the curvature of the planet. What these zealots were raising was a level of precision in the direction that seemed outlandish to me. My anger at what I regarded as their divisive nitpicking led me to respond in an outspoken way. Once again, I would learn that this center was no longer my show to run. Some of the confrontations got nasty. I was stung to hear these critics tell me, "You're dealing with Allah!" As if I wasn't a true Muslim! They were openly insulting me, and that only made me madder.

Calming myself, I decided that I would not respond in kind. Piling insult upon insult would not help anyone. Instead, I summoned a substantial body of information on this issue. I found that the most important factor, in our case, was a prohibition against second-guessing after a mosque is substantially complete. That's the point we had reached in our construction. If a new mosque is designed in good faith, then the mosque should stand united. Muslims should not spark discord by debating the direction of prayer. On this point I was reassured by Sheikh Hamza Yusuf, a man whom both *The Guardian* and *The New Yorker* describe as "the West's most influential Islamic scholar." Among his many other accomplishments around the world, Yusuf co-founded Zaytuna College in Berkeley, California. In answering my question, Yusuf looked deep into Islamic traditions, concluding that "once a mosque is constructed, the direction of prayer cannot be changed at a later time using new technology like a GPS or even a modern compass." The underlying issue is that, even if someone might pay to tear down the mosque and build a new one with this kind of fine-tuned adjustment, such a proposal would violate the core principle that prevented Muslims from destroying a mosque. Bottom line: Once a mosque is finished, the faithful should unite in prayer and quick bickering.

I went even further in developing my case, consulting as many Muslim scholars as I could reach with this question. Among Muslims, a single scholar may be discounted by supporters of other traditional schools in Islamic jurisprudence. For example, Yusuf had drawn from traditions handed down in the Maliki school. Sheikh Ali Suleiman Ali of the Canton Mosque added a perspective to my case from the Hanafi school. He advised that "there is a 90-degree allowance from long distance, per Imam Hanifa." The basic idea was that, given the wide latitude of direction, a Muslim could be sure that at least one shoulder was correctly facing

Mecca. Another friend, Imam Musa, responded from the Shafi'i tradition, pointing out that devout Muslims may disagree partly because Prophet Muhammad himself displayed some differences throughout his life in various matters of daily life. In other words, Musa was saying that the zealots should stop complaining because Islam is broad enough for some disagreement among Muslims.

There was a general theme running through all of the responses: Carrying on a disruptive debate about the issue was a bigger problem than the precise direction. As usual, my old friend Sherman Abd al-Hakim Jackson got right to the point in no-nonsense terms: "I'm sorry to hear that an educated community, living in a well-to-do suburb, is wasting their energies on a trivial issue like this one."

I even paid for a directional study by an engineering firm, which determined that we were off by just a few degrees. Fired up and armed with a thick file of theological and engineering expertise, I called for a meeting to resolve the matter. I walked into the meeting convinced that I had the answers. No one could disagree after considering all of this evidence.

Anticipating a quick consensus on my exhaustive report, I also had a proposal for an addition to our design: We should inscribe on the wall of our new sanctuary—in the direction of our prayers—the verse from the Quran 2:115, "To God belong the East and the West; wherever you turn, there is the Face of God; God is All-embracing, All-knowing."

Instead of consensus, I was met with a stubborn refusal to accept what I regarded as Islamic common sense. Not only did the critics refuse to give up their complaints, but my proposal for the Quranic inscription was shot down in flames.

This was turning into a lesson I had to learn the hard way, and it was officially time to turn over even more control to the mosque's leadership. The property was still owned by I-Comp, the original LLC that I had set up with the first supporters and which had allowed the Muslim Unity Center to use the property on a token long-term lease. Now we had reached the point in our timeline when those first investors were expected to donate their shares to the Muslim Unity Center. New members of the congregation were clamoring for this step to be taken, and while there was some initial reluctance in our founders' group, we agreed to donate our shares per our original intention. The bylaws were rewritten to set up a two-tier system: Any of the original group members who wanted to continue serving would become the founding trustees, and an elected board of directors would run the mosque, through a full-time administrator. The first directors would be appointed by a vote of the trustees with staggered terms for reelection.

The Muslim Unity Center was changing rapidly, and I realized that it soon would be beyond the power of any one individual to control. At least I could codify our founding principles so that coming generations would remember our high hopes for a 21st-century American-Muslim mosque. To develop such a text, I called on my friend and writer Rafael Narbaez, a Texas-born, Hispanic convert who had been on a nationwide speaking tour. I also was helped by the late Omar Khalidi, an eminent Islamic scholar at the Massachusetts Institute of Technology and a Hyderabad native. The following statement emerged:

> *Religious functions: The mosque is the center of the religious and life-cycle functions of the community.*

> *Melting pot: This is where diverse cultures forge a new American Islamic identity.*

> *New solutions: We need to derive authentic Islamic solutions to conditions in American culture.*

> *Safe harbor: We are a spiritual home for all Muslims sailing modern life, who may be lacking the family-social network.*

> *Building the next generation: Weekend, a part-time religious school, summer programs and recreation activities should be provided for the youth. Gen X and millennials hold the future of the community. Open the leadership door for them.*

> *A beacon of light: We should invite others to the true faith.*

> *Post 9-11 existence of the Muslim community: We will serve as a united, inclusive, participatory and involved leadership, protecting the homeland and countering the forces of radicalism and Islamophobia.*

Starting from that vision, I worked with Rafael on a larger statement. He was an ideal partner in this effort, both because of his wide experience as a speaker and because he came to Islam by choice. He had traveled widely, visited many Muslim communities and had a keen eye for the best practices in mosque operations. He had completed the Hajj at an unusually young age. In fact, I wanted to nominate Rafael as our executive director—but that was one more of my ideas shot down by the new board. At least Rafael and I finished our concept paper.

The Concept of Worship at the Unity Center

All variations among the major schools of thought in regards to religious affairs must be respected. The Muslim Unity Center is neither a Shia nor a Sunni mosque, with the criteria of being a Muslim member being:

- Adherence to the basic pillars of Islam: acceptance of the unity of God and Muhammad as his messenger, daily obligatory prayers, zakat or mandated charity, fasting in Ramadan and Hajj.

- Acceptance of the Quran and its guidance as the final authentic divine revelation, preserved in its entirety as the true word of God Almighty.

- Recognition of a second source of guidance being the *hadith*, authentic and universally accepted sayings and traditions of Prophet Muhammad—may God's peace be upon him, and the *seerah*, the historical record of the life of the holy Prophet.

English is the official language of the center. Prayers, recitation of the Holy Quran and religious services are naturally conducted in Arabic. The lectures and the sermons are delivered in English.

Bi-annual Eid celebrations. Eids are to be celebrated based on the moon sighting by the North American Fiqh council, a body of Muslim scholars that works with the Islamic Society of North America. The center will not object to celebrating other internationally accepted events, such as the birthday of Prophet Muhammad.

Women must participate equally. Muslim Unity Center bylaws require that women are to be part of the board of directors and the board of trustees.

A dress code must be observed. All sexes must abide by modesty in dress when coming to the mosque. Head covering is encouraged but not mandatory, with one exception: Women participating in congregational prayers will cover their hair and wear loose clothing as is customary when performing prayers. This exception is applied during performance of prayers only and when in the main prayer room.

Social norms will be respected. Prayer areas are designated for men and women in the sanctuary. To maintain efficiency of space and to respect feminine needs, the women's prayer area is reserved on the second-floor mezzanine of the sanctuary with women's bathrooms. During social and educational events in the gym or social hall, seating will be designated for the family as well as in separate areas for women and men, but only if they so desire.

On outreach & civic engagement. The Muslim Unity Center, as one of its important goals, maintains a policy of reaching out to other faiths, neighbors, local government and law enforcement. The goal is to build bridges of understanding, learn about others and participate in the larger community. The mosque, being part of the tri-county Muslim community, will maintain membership in the regional Muslim Community Council, supporting collective efforts to build unity in the Muslim community and to counter growing Islamophobia.

Even though I was working overtime, at that point, to cast my founding vision into the future, I faced further reversals at the hands of the mosque's new leaders. It became obvious that our original construction budget was off due to mistakes by the first builder, and the red ink was making everyone anxious. I could not simply write a check of that size, as my furniture business was declining and I already had made large donations that maxed out my capacity to give. My friend Ismael Basha suggested expanding the base of trustees, conditional on major donations. Approval for this idea was an uphill battle and I began to feel more and more isolated in arguing this case. When we finally got Basha's idea approved, another issue arose. The first wave of responses came from several Syrian doctors who wanted to support the center. Once again, I had to object. As generous as these physicians were, accepting them as a group would mean that more than half of our board was from a single ethnic background. Once again, I was a vocal minority. I lost the vote. These new donors were good people, but they also were moving the center—at least symbolically—toward their ethnic identity.

As our leadership evolved, the collective memory of our early struggles began to fade. I began to feel like a man who, while stranded on a deserted island with friends, wakes up one morning to find that everyone else stole away on a raft in the night. Even as I was completing the documentation of the center's founding principles, I felt that our distance from those early goals was growing with each passing month.

Perhaps I failed the test of a founder by not adapting to the growth of the community I had launched. I sometimes wish I could go back in time and meet others, like Col. George or the Booths, who lived through this kind of transition. I do know that the Quran's 3:159 is a reminder to the Prophet Muhammad that he would inevitably face difficulties in interpersonal relations: "So by Mercy from God, (O Muhammad), you were lenient with them. And if you had been rude and harsh in heart, they would have disbanded from about you. So, pardon them and ask forgiveness from them."

I know that I was not at my best at times, as I found myself repeatedly in the minority. By the time our construction project reached its final stages, in late 2002, I also was balancing big family commitments. Our eldest son, Sami, was getting married, and we had a house full of relatives from across the country.

In the midst of our family celebration, I resolved to make a break with the center. The final document I prepared was drafted with help from my cousin, Abdul Samad, who was a brilliant construction engineer in California. We wrote a detailed report, outlining milestones, the status of the construction project and highlighting items that still had to be completed. I handed over my resignation from the board of trustees on December 27, 2002—nine years after receiving the occupancy permit.

There was little objection. Soon afterward, Syed Salman passed away (may God bless his soul). Salman was instrumental in supporting me during the early days. Tootla, Siddqui and Ismael Basha—those active in helping with the project—also left after some time. Syed Khalid Baghdadi and Zubair Rathur, too, completed their terms and found that there was no support to extend their tenure. Eventually, the entire board of trustees was comprised of Syrian Americans. We had come full circle, and the Muslim Unity Center was run by one ethnic group.

I continued to attend the center's religious services, because the mosque was just a few minutes' drive from our home. Then we moved to Florida. Occasionally, we still visit the center when we are back in Michigan. Shahina and I are both happy to see that the center is well-kept and well-managed. Looking at the congregation now, from our new distance, we can see that those now managing the center are wonderful people, opening their doors to all who are seeking spiritual refuge. We are very pleased to see a wide range of services offered, including weekend school, summer programs, outreach efforts, a lecture series, civic engagement and other forms of community service. At the top of the center's website is a hospitable greeting: "Where faith, family and fun come together." That certainly reflects our original dream. In fact, the center's Statement of Principles echoes many of the themes in the concept paper I drafted with Rafael.

From my vantage point, the Muslim Unity Center is on the track the founders envisioned. A dynamic new Yemeni-American imam leads the congregation. Today's board of trustees is still dominated by one ethnic group, but the board of directors is an ethnically diverse group of four women and three men.

I am especially proud to see the mission statement emphasize that the center "affirms the principles of the social order established by the Prophet Muhammad (Peace Be Upon Him), including the establishment of a thriving and vibrant community free of ethnic, racial, cultural or national divisions."

That's a vision we share.

CHAPTER 14

A Muslim Republican in the Age of Trump

Our civil rights have no dependence on our religious opinions
any more than our opinions in physics or geometry.

Thomas Jefferson, in his text for the Virginia
Statute of Religious Freedom, 1786

"Real Americans aren't Muslim."

No, I'm not quoting one of the extremists who have flocked to Donald Trump's banner, although many partisans on Trump's fringe have said such things in the past few years. This was something I heard close to home, in a conversation with my barber. While our community in Florida was building a new mosque, we rented space for prayers in a shopping center. This woman's shop was near our prayer hall and, as an entrepreneur myself, I always try to support local businesses.

At first, I thought we were establishing a warm relationship. She told me that she liked to see Muslim customers. "They're very hospitable," she said. That's true, of course. Hospitality is a cultural hallmark of Islam.

She also told me about a friendly Muslim restaurant owner, next door. "He's so nice. He sometimes gives me a free meal."

I assumed she would like to learn more about Islam, so I tried to drop some helpful information into our conversations as she cut my hair. I said, "Did you know that as many as 30 percent of the African slaves brought to this country were Muslim? And, today, 28 percent of Muslim Americans are black."

She shook her head, puzzled at what I had just told her. At length, she said, "Sir, I do not think that is true. It cannot be."

"Sure it is," I said confidently. "You can Google it, and you'll find lots of historical sources. There's an exhibit about this at the Smithsonian in Washington, D.C. One of the most famous Muslim slaves got here half a century before the Revolutionary War. He wrote a whole book about his experiences."

"No, sir. I find this hard to believe," she insisted. Then, after a pause, she explained why this did not seem possible to her. "Sir, African Americans are regular Americans. Real Americans aren't Muslim."

I was shocked. She was so polite in her insistence in defending this myth! I guessed that she was regularly listening to some bigoted preacher or politician and had swallowed their bias in its entirety. When she saw my surprise at her words, she tried to reassure me. "We Americans like the way we are, sir," she said.

I realized that this woman needed someone to open her eyes. I thought we might talk again when I returned, so I wanted her to remember me. I pulled out a business card with my photo on it. As I handed over the card, she smiled at the photo. In that picture, I am wearing aviator sunglasses and a baseball cap that reads, "Old Guys Rule."

She grinned as she accepted my card, tapping her finger on my photo. "Now you look American!" she said.

Where do we even begin to address such basic ignorance about our status as Americans? I wished that my friend Chuck Alawan had lived to see this era. I would have invited him to Florida and taken him with me to the barbershop; Chuck was an Army veteran who could have been the long-lost twin of country singer Kenny Rogers. Or I could have introduced my barber to Imam Suhaib Webb, who was born William Webb—the blond, blue-eyed grandson of a preacher. Webb converted to Islam and, today, is a widely respected Muslim leader.

Webb once told me, "Whenever I'm in a waiting room, I tell the staff at the front desk that my first name is Muhammad. They have trouble pronouncing my first name, Suhaib, anyway. Then, when it's my turn and they call out that name I gave them—'Muhammad!'—I watch the reaction in the room. People are always surprised when I stand up."

For decades after I came to America, I never heard the word "Islamophobia." Just after World War I, a few religion scholars began using the word in obscure journals, but most Americans never heard anyone use the term. In fact, almost no one used the word until a prominent British think tank, the Runnymeade Trust, published a report that promoted racial and cultural harmony, in the late 1990s. One of the hurdles we should learn to overcome, the Trust advised, is the growing grassroots fear called "Islamophobia." After that, the term jumped into the public square—and it skyrocketed around the world after the attacks on 9/11.

By 2004, UN Secretary-General Kofi Annan told a conference in New York, "When the world is compelled to coin a new term to take account of increasingly widespread bigotry, that is a sad and troubling development. Such is the case with Islamophobia."

One major reason why this fear has mushroomed is because of a shadowy, multi-million-dollar industry produced by anti-Muslim fearmongers who finance websites, events, publications and videos. This isn't paranoia on my part: The nonprofit Center for American Progress (CAP) has been tracking the small but influential group of Islamophobes who have poured millions of dollars into terrifying disinformation about Muslims. This nonprofit, CAP, is often described as a "progressive" organization, but its major funders include the Ford Foundation, the Bill and Melinda Gates Foundation and the foundation set up by the family of Sam Walton. As a result, CAP is about as solidly middle-American as the Walton family's Walmart stores. CAP has issued two lengthy reports about these fearmongers, both titled *Fear, Inc.*—one in 2011, and then an updated version, called *2.0*, in 2015.

According to CAP reports: "This disturbing campaign of misinformation and demonization bears resemblance to some of history's darkest chapters. The roots of Islamophobia—ignorance, disinformation and sweeping generalizations—bring to mind despicable anti-Semitism and the struggles of other minorities for equal rights in the United States. Millions of law-abiding Muslims in America today face day-to-day discrimination, unlawful surveillance and profiling simply because of their religious beliefs. The Founding Fathers enshrined the free practice of religious beliefs in the Constitution; Thomas Jefferson specifically had the protection of Muslims in mind when drafting the First Amendment."

The 2015 report traced eight donors who gave $57 million to fuel Islamophobic projects between 2001 and 2012. "A small group of foundations and wealthy donors serve as the lifeblood of the Islamophobic network in the United States," the report stated. "They fund right-wing think tanks and misinformation experts who peddle hate and fear of Muslims and Islam in the form of books, video, reports and websites. A dedicated group of anti-Islam grassroots organizations and right-wing religious groups then use this propaganda to feed their constituency."

What does that constituency's impact look like in everyday life?

On the morning of Nov. 9, 2016—the day after Trump won the election—I was scheduled to present a cultural-competency training course requested by a local police department. This would be my first experience in leading such a program. A young attorney, Somera, had worked with me to prepare this joint presentation. We had carefully outlined our roles: She would begin by presenting an Islam 101 overview, then I would be there to debunk myths. I was serving as an expert in describing how our Muslim neighbors typically live their lives throughout the year. By explaining some of the family customs and seasonal practices police officers might encounter on a call, we reasoned, these officers should be more comfortable serving our community. Since the police department had proposed this program, we were eager to accept their invitation and wanted to make it a memorable occasion for everyone. Shahina had even made samosas from scratch and Somera was going to bring an assortment of pastries.

This was a new experience for me, and the date certainly was not ideal. I had been up very late watching the election updates and digesting the results. I had slept little and was awake early to prepare for the day. I was already dressed in my suit, sipping a final cup of coffee, when the phone rang.

"Oh, Uncle!" Even though Somera was greeting me with her usual, affectionate term of respect, I was shocked by the frantic tone in her voice.

"What is it?" I asked.

"Oh, Uncle, I cannot come today."

"Somera, we're doing this as a team today—and you can't come?" I then realized that she was very upset, and that my own anxiety was misplaced. "What happened to you, Somera? Why can't you come?"

"My front door has been spray-painted with Islamophobic graffiti and someone threw eggs on my front windows!"

I was furious. Trump had just been elected on an anti-Muslim platform and I assumed that one of his supporters thought that such attacks were now the wave of the future.

It was heartbreaking. Somera had to devote her day to making a police report and dealing with the damage to her home. Meanwhile, I packed up my laptop, our informational handouts and Shahina's samosas. I made the presentation alone, to a group of officers who were as shaken as I was at the overnight attack. My presentation that day wasn't the best that could have been presented, but the relevance of what we were discussing couldn't have been more powerfully felt by everyone in the room.

With fearmongers from the fringe constantly pumping misinformation to Americans through the internet and other media, the danger keeps growing each year. Hateful claims about Muslims are no longer limited to the cowardly vandals, such as those who attacked Somera's home under the cover of night. Even before Trump's election, we had heard leading Americans advance dangerous anti-Muslim myths.

In the past, I have proudly supported the Republican Party—and I was horrified, in that summer of 2016, to hear former U.S. House Speaker Newt Gingrich lash out at Muslims on Fox News. At the time, Gingrich was jockeying for a high post in Washington if a Republican won in November. He wanted to demonstrate that he was as tough on Islam as other right-wing activists. When Trump's friend Sean Hannity asked Gingrich to respond, on his Fox-TV show, to a deadly terrorist attack in Nice, France, Gingrich jumped at the chance. On national TV, Gingrich referred to the myth that American Muslims are trying to take over the country and replace the U.S. Constitution with Sharia, Islam's traditional code of behavior. This idea is laughable and has been debunked by every responsible news media organization, but somehow, Gingrich had bought the myth and spewed it on Fox.

"Western civilization is in a war," Gingrich told Hannity. "We should frankly test every person here who is of a Muslim background—and if they believe in Sharia, they should be deported.

"Sharia is incompatible with Western civilization," Gingrich continued. "Modern Muslims who have given up Sharia—I'm glad to have them as citizens. Perfectly happy to have them next door." But, he said, this attack in France was the "fault of Western elites who lack the guts to do what is right, to do what is necessary."

This wasn't a casual offhand remark. Gingrich barreled along, demanding a Big-Brother approach to watching all Muslims—an idea straight out of George Orwell's *1984*. "Look, the first step is you have to ask them the questions," said Gingrich. "The second step is you have to monitor what they're doing on the internet. The third step is—let me be very clear—you have to monitor the mosques. I mean, if you're not prepared to monitor the mosques, this whole thing is a joke."

In reporting what happened, *The Washington Post* bluntly told its readers that this was a crazy idea. The newspaper stated, "Gingrich's proposal, which made no distinction between U.S. citizens and noncitizens, would violate scores of First and Fourteenth Amendment-based Supreme Court rulings and laws that, together, bar discriminating on the basis of religion, favoring one religion over another by the government and restricting freedom of expression and belief."

Of course, I knew that already. This was personally offensive to me, especially because I had once respected Gingrich as one of the major leaders in my political party. Not only did he make those outlandish claims to Hannity, but the next day, Gingrich doubled-down on what he had said in response to the widespread backlash from mainstream Americans. He insisted that there was nothing wrong with trying to root out potential killers living among us. That made matters even worse. I thought: If he couldn't apologize, why couldn't he at least shut up?

You might think that such an incident is trivial—just another in a long series of disputes over "political correctness," in the fury of a political campaign. The problem with outbursts by people of Gingrich's stature is that they foster even greater outrage in people in small communities all over the country.

In Michigan, Muslims witnessed one of the most extreme diatribes from a businessman who served as president of the village of Kalkaska, a little town in the northwest Lower Peninsula. Until 2017, most Americans only knew of the town as the setting for Ernest Hemingway's short story, *The Battler*. Then, in the summer of 2017, international headlines described the town's president, Jeff Sieting, as posting a rant on social media, titled "Kill Them All." His post compared Islam to "flesh-eating bacteria," a "death cult" and "the crown jewel in Satan's design to destroy all humanity." The Facebook text called for nuclear bombs to be dropped on Mecca and

Medina, as well as the 10 largest Muslim-majority cities. Sieting got the basic material for this post from a North Carolina extremist—but Sieting defended these claims when other community leaders and reporters asked him about the rant.

Sieting was well known for playing with political fire. He also was involved in a long-running dispute over an enormous pro-Trump banner that he hung over a hotel in downtown Kalkaska. He was so defiant about his political activism, in fact, that he drove around town in a Chevy truck with a decal on the back that read, "Neighborhood Bully." In his Facebook bio, he described himself as "a White Christian Conservative American that strongly believes in the Constitution as it was written." He openly enjoyed his notoriety, defending his right to rant and to display his Trump banner in the middle of the town.

Finally, in May 2018, the village's voters recalled him—but the final tally was close: 215 voted for Sieting and 326 voted to replace him with his opponent, Harley Wales. Sieting was forced out of office and lost his official soapbox as the elected head of the village. I hope that that is the last we will hear from Jeff Sieting, but those 215 voters who supported him continue to haunt me. Just like Hemingway fell in love with the woods and waters around Kalkaska in 1916, tourists still flock to that region every year. Can you imagine the courage it would take for a young Muslim couple, enjoying a tour through Michigan, to stay the night in Kalkaska's hotel? I'm sure lots of local residents would welcome them with open arms, but Jeff Sieting is still hanging around the woods up there— and so are his 215 supporters.

As I look back, I regret that such fearmongering fringe dwellers gained a foothold in the Republican Party. That's my party! That's the party of Thomas Jefferson and Abraham Lincoln! Before 9/11, I always thought we had a good shot at convincing a majority of American Muslims to become loyal supporters of the GOP. My analysis was sound: Muslims generally cling to conservative social values; we believe in strong families; many of us either own a business or have relatives who run businesses, so we tend to favor lessening government regulations. As I envisioned the political possibilities in the 1990s, Muslims fit a typical Republican profile. We could have become an influential force within the GOP.

Our collective experiences since 2001, however, have pushed most

Muslims toward Democratic candidates. Pew's latest research on these issues, conducted in 2017, reports, "Muslim Americans have strongly favored the Democratic Party for at least a decade. Two-thirds of Muslims, 66 percent, now identify with or lean toward the Democrats." This is becoming a deeply entrenched attitude. "About three-quarters of Muslim Americans, 74 percent, say President Donald Trump is unfriendly toward them," Pew states. "And they are no fans of Trump's: Just 19 percent say they approve of the job Trump is doing as president."

There's no love lost on either side. White House officials have gone out of their way to distance themselves from American Muslim leaders. For our part, we are not eager to accept invitations as long as Trump and his colleagues continue to spew anti-Muslim rhetoric.

Ibrahim Hooper, from the Council on American-Islamic Relations, summed it up for *The New York Times*: "There is absolutely zero engagement with the Muslim American community. Not good, not bad, not indifferent. Zero." Trump's words and actions have had, he said, "a tremendously negative impact on Muslim Americans."

The missed opportunities still haunt me. At the 2016 Republican National Convention in Cleveland, I wanted to hear proposals that would strengthen our country and our founding principles—not more attacks on vulnerable minorities, including Muslims. As the convention ended, I wrote an op-ed column for our local Florida newspaper, headlined: "As a Muslim Republican, I see my party missing opportunities."

I wrote, in part:

> *The Republican National Convention should have planned a workshop on Sharia, led by a qualified scholar, to counter ignorance about Islam. Wise and sensible policies can be designed only with a proper knowledge base. … Sharia, in many ways, is analogous to Jewish law, or Halakha. Both terms primarily mean 'a pathway' to live a spiritual life according to one's religious beliefs. Sharia is overwhelmingly concerned with personal religious practices like obligatory daily prayers, fasting in Ramadan, charity, food choices, marriage and divorce—a path to religious discourse. And there is no consensus among Muslims regarding the rules, as there are multiple schools of*

thought, ranging from strict to liberal observances. Asking Muslims to abandon Sharia is like asking Jews not to follow Jewish law or Catholics to distance themselves from their canon law. An important aspect of Sharia is to obey the law of the land, which is the U.S. Constitution for American Muslims.

Knowing the facts will help pursue the right goals, especially when it comes to fighting the scourge of ISIS in partnership with Muslims. Muslims are leading the charge against ISIS by countering their ideology. Many Muslim-American scholars and leaders are on the ISIS hit list because they vehemently oppose the terror group, its practices and its claim to religious legitimacy.

I wish Muslim Republican leaders were given a chance to send that message from the Republican Convention.

Once, Republican presidents saw the value in building healthy relationships with Muslims both within the U.S. and abroad. *Foreign Affairs* magazine recently wrote about the urgency in filling a position created under President George W. Bush. The magazine cast this appeal to the Trump team in pointed terms, headlining the article: "Why the U.S. Needs its Envoys—Particularly at the Organisation of Islamic Cooperation (OIC)." The article went on to explain the role of this envoy, which once was a symbol to the world of America's efforts to cooperate in peaceful development and conflict resolution. The magazine stated, "Since 2008, the special envoy to the OIC, which was created at the tail end of President George W. Bush's administration, has represented the United States at the OIC, a 57-member international organization made up of states with substantial Muslim populations. Its membership spans the globe and includes some of the United States' closest allies, such as NATO members Albania and Turkey, and half of its major non-NATO allies—Afghanistan, Bahrain, Egypt, Jordan, Kuwait, Morocco, Pakistan and Tunisia. The OIC actively engages with the United States on a wide variety of issues, such as conflict resolution, countering extremism, humanitarian affairs, human rights, and economic development."

This is such an obvious first step for Trump's team—fill the position and get on with this important outreach that Bush started. The OIC is the world's second-largest intergovernmental body after the United Nations. But throughout 2018, the Department of State's website for the envoy's office stated, simply: "This position is currently vacant."

Another missed opportunity is the White House Office of Public Engagement, which was formalized under President Gerald Ford as a public sign of a new openness to dialogue with ordinary Americans after the dark days of the Nixon administration. As it gained popularity under both Republican and Democratic presidents, the office became known as "the front door of the White House." During the Obama years, the office was active in welcoming Muslim leaders from across the U.S. When Trump took over, my name was on the list of candidates to serve as a Muslim-American liaison in that office. So far, however, the Trump team's main step has been renaming the office: it is now termed "public liaison," which sounds a lot less proactive than "public engagement." One bureaucrat briefly held that liaison post in 2017, but it was then left vacant for nearly a year. If someone from the White House ever contacts me, I am not sure I would accept unless I perceived that the administration was truly receptive to our voice.

One of the most visible breaks with Muslim leaders was the Trump team's cancelation of the annual White House Eid banquet, an event in which earlier presidents would invite Muslims to celebrate the end of the fasting month of Ramadan. It was a chance to build a rapport with grassroots leaders and, recognizing the long-term interest in that bridge-building, the Obama staff made a point of inviting younger men and women. Our son-in-law, Farhan (a Harvard graduate) was among the young Muslim leaders Obama met with over the Eid banquet one year.

After presidents Bill Clinton, George W. Bush and Barack Obama had established this as a valuable tradition, the Trump team canceled the banquet in 2017. In the summer of 2018, when Trump resumed the practice, *The New York Times* reported:

"The White House's guest list for President Trump's first dinner celebrating the Muslim holy month of Ramadan included a Who's Who of diplomats from the Middle East. But the event turned out to be more notable for who was not there: representatives from Muslim-American groups. ... Mr. Trump has seemingly made little attempt to repair his fractured relationship with Muslim Americans—even those in his own party."

Perhaps the only way to restore the balance in the Republican Party is to do what Shahina and I have done in recent years: reacquaint ourselves with America's Founding Fathers.

The architects of our Constitution anticipated a religiously diverse America. Historians continue to debate the exact nature of the religious beliefs of the men who signed the Declaration of Independence and later approved the Constitution: Some insist they were Christian, but other historians argue that many, including Jefferson, believed in more of a universal divine spirit. For example, Jefferson famously went through a great deal of trouble in using a razor to slice out all passages from his Bible that describe Jesus's miracles and supernatural nature. He preferred to keep only those passages focused on Jesus's life, teachings and his moral code. The Smithsonian Institution keeps a facsimile edition of Jefferson's condensed Bible in print, to this day. I am amazed to find that Jefferson's view of Jesus seems to have been close to our Muslim view of Jesus, who is revered in the Quran as a great prophet and moral teacher.

Whatever the Founding Fathers' exact beliefs may have been, they recognized that religious values were good—and that people of all religious faiths should work together to build up America. Unity in diversity was their core belief. In 1782, six years before the Constitution was ratified, they settled on our national motto: "*E pluribus unum*," or "Out of many, one."

Three years after the Constitution was ratified, the Bill of Rights was added to ensure that the Founding Fathers' vision of a welcoming nation was forever guaranteed. Americans are free to follow the path of our individual religious beliefs. I still wholeheartedly believe in that American promise. That's a commitment we must preserve and renew so that we can sit comfortably, as equals, at the community table. I still believe that that vision can be a reality, even though Islam has been besieged by Islamophobic mania. In earlier eras of American history, Catholics bore the brunt of such hatred; so did Jews and members of the Church of Jesus Christ of Latter-day Saints, among other persecuted religious minorities. Those religious groups survived these scourges, and so will Muslims.

An especially enlightening trip, meant to reacquaint ourselves with America's roots, was a tour Shahina and I took of Virginia's historic triangle: Williamsburg, Jamestown and Yorktown. We wanted to immerse ourselves in the life and legacy of the principal author of the Declaration of Independence, Thomas Jefferson. I was impressed to find the William & Mary College bookstore selling copies of historian Denise Spellberg's fascinating book, *Thomas Jefferson's Quran: Islam and the Founders*. The first sentence in her book sums up Jefferson's vision: "At a time when most Americans were uninformed, misinformed or simply afraid of Islam, Thomas Jefferson imagined Muslims as future citizens of his new nation."

When I read those words, I thought: Boy, do Americans need to hear from Jefferson today! Spellberg explains that Jefferson was so interested in Islam that, as a young man, he bought a Quran and kept it as a reference book throughout his life. His Quran is now in the Library of Congress. When Jefferson became president, he understood the customs of Ramadan. In 1805, he hosted a Tunisian envoy and scheduled the start of the White House dinner after sunset, to accommodate the envoy's fasting.

Years before the Constitution's Bill of Rights was written, Jefferson had helped to enshrine religious freedom in the laws of Virginia. To do so, he drafted the first major law focusing on religious freedom in America: the 1786 Virginia Statute for Religious Freedom. I wish that document was required reading for all Republicans today, because Jefferson certainly got it right. In the preamble to that statute, he pointedly protested against "the impious presumption of legislators and rulers, civil as well as ecclesiastical, who, being themselves but fallible and uninspired men, have assumed dominion over the faith of others, setting up their own opinions and modes of thinking as the only true and infallible." Jefferson so strongly opposed that kind of faith-baiting in politics that he called politicians "criminal" if they stooped to such bigotry.

His 1786 statute went on to declare:

> *That our civil rights have no dependence on our religious opinions any more than our opinions in physics or geometry,*
>
> *That therefore the proscribing any citizen as unworthy of the public confidence, by laying upon him an incapacity of being called to offices of trust and emolument, unless he profess or renounce this or that religious opinion, is depriving him injuriously of those privileges and advantages, to which, in common with his fellow citizens, he has a natural right …*

Be it enacted by General Assembly that no man shall be compelled to frequent or support any religious worship, place, or ministry whatsoever, nor shall be enforced, restrained, molested, or burdened in his body or goods, nor shall otherwise suffer on account of his religious opinions or belief, but that all men shall be free to profess, and by argument to maintain, their opinions in matters of religion, and that the same shall in no wise diminish, enlarge or affect their civil capacities.

Even more inspiring was our visit the next year, in 2015, to Mount Vernon. The more I learn about Washington, the more I cherish his leadership. He was a forward-looking innovator who, like Jefferson, had the foresight to envision America's religious pluralism blossoming. Washington quoted from the ancient Hebrew prophet Micah, in a Bible passage that states:

"They shall beat their swords into plowshares,

and their spears into pruning hooks;

nation shall not lift up sword against nation,

neither shall they learn war anymore;

but they shall all sit under their own vines and under their own fig trees,

and no one shall make them afraid."

During his first term as president, Washington received a warm letter of encouragement from Moses Seixas, the head of the Touro Synagogue, in New Port, Rhode Island. On August 18, 1790, Washington reciprocated the gesture in a letter that is now read aloud each year, on the anniversary of that date. The Touro building is the last surviving synagogue from the American colonial period, and dignitaries, including Supreme Court justices, have taken part in the annual ceremony.

The famous passage of the letter says:

Happily, the government of the United States, which gives to bigotry no sanction, to persecution no assistance, requires only that they who live under its protection should demean themselves as good citizens in giving it on all occasions their effectual support. ... May the children of the stock of Abraham who dwell in this land continue to merit and enjoy the good will of the other inhabitants—while everyone shall sit in safety under his own vine and fig tree and there shall be none to make him afraid. May the father of all mercies scatter light, and not darkness, upon our paths, and make us all in our several vocations useful here, and in his own due time and way everlastingly happy.

And, to that, all I can add is: Amen!

Chapter 15

'Let It Not Be a Muslim!'

We shall test you with something of fear, hunger,
loss of wealth, lives and fruits (of labor)—
but give glad tidings to those who patiently persevere.

Quran 2:155

"Oh, God, let it not be a Muslim!"

That's a new prayer American Muslims have learned to pray any time headlines pop up about an explosion or mass shooting since the first attack on the World Trade Center on February 26, 1993.

Two years later, we were hit with a tidal wave of hatred. Just after 9 a.m. on April 19, 1995, someone blew up the Alfred P. Murrah Federal Building in Oklahoma City. The attack, which killed 168 people and injured more than 680 others, was so unexpected and devastating that police had no immediate idea who could have pulled off such an attack. Stone, steel and nearby vehicles were shredded in the smoky mass of rubble.

Watching events unfold on TV that morning, I saw the news crews arriving and the details rolling in from reporters: "It's a terrorist attack." "There has been a huge loss of life, and rescue crews still are rescuing survivors." "Dust is everywhere." "… a massive bomb, perhaps a car bomb."

I watched on live network television as a fireman carried a child with a bloodied face. For hours, first responders continued to remove bodies from the rubble. The details from that morning were a foreshadowing of images we all would see on 9/11.

My heart sank as I watched. I prayed: "Oh, God, let it not be a Muslim!"

Most Americans are horrified by such deadly devastation, as millions experience shock, anger and sickness at the mournful loss of life. We all should focus our prayers on the victims and their families, as well as the brave police officers and firefighters on the scene. Instead, I also have to worry about the backlash that I know will wash over my non-Muslim neighbors.

During the first 24 hours after the Oklahoma bombing, no one had solid information about what had happened. Yet that did not stop the Islamophobic fringe from leaping into panic mode and broadcasting wild stories across the airwaves. Claims quickly spread far beyond the fringe, as some extremists made it onto mainstream radio and TV news shows and were identified as "terrorism experts." Conservative talk-radio host Bob Grant went on the air from the WABC studios in New York City, ranting about how he wanted to personally gun down Muslim terrorists. Grant told his audience that the problem was Islam itself: the religion promotes violence, he claimed. "It is violent. It is violent," he said. "They preach violence, for heaven's sake!"

Things got even worse when the normally first-rate, balanced journalists chimed in—echoing and amplifying the bias! On the day of the attack, *Nightline*'s Ted Koppel solemnly told the world that police were searching for "two Middle Eastern men." CBS News's Connie Chung said, "U.S. government sources told CBS News that it has Middle East terrorism written all over it." *The Wall Street Journal* called it a "Beirut-style car bombing."

The next morning, *The New York Times* drew a direct link to the 1993 attack, reporting, "Some experts focused on the possibility that the attack had been the work of Islamic militants, like those who bombed the World Trade Center in February 1993. ... Several news organizations, including CNN, reported that investigators were seeking to question several men, described as being Middle Eastern in appearance, who had driven away from the building shortly before the blast."

What a shock when everyone realized that the conspirators were home-grown, U.S. Army veterans Timothy McVeigh and Terry Nichols! These guys hated government officials because of the way federal agents handled the siege in Waco, Texas, in 1993. They timed their attack to coincide with the anniversary of the fiery conclusion of that standoff with the Branch Davidians. As he started up his truck that morning, McVeigh even chose to wear a T-shirt proclaiming "*Sic Semper tyrannis.*" That's the phrase John

Wilkes Boothe shouted when assassinating President Lincoln—"Thus always to tyrants." This attack was planned by pure, white-bread, right-wing extremists who felt they were acting on deep roots in American history. They had nothing whatsoever to do with Islam.

In fact, these guys had ties to lots of other Midwestern, church-going, gun-loving, anti-government activists. Yet when the true identities of the bombers and their buddies were revealed, not one news source referred to them as "Christian terrorists"; that would have been far too close for comfort, wrote Richard Goldstein in *The Village Voice*. Goldstein sarcastically summed up this frenzy to find a Muslim scapegoat: "We have met the enemy—and he is anyone but us!"

At the time, I did what I could. This was the era when I was in Michigan and coordinating the Muslim American Alliance, a forum that had been pulled together to respond quickly to public issues. That day, I didn't even take the time to write a formal press release. I simply typed up a brief announcement of a press conference, then faxed that page to Detroit-area newsrooms. We did not have our own building, so I reserved a room in the Southfield Westin Hotel for the afternoon event. I was still new to crisis management. I remembered that someone had told me that "blue looks good on TV," so I picked out a light-blue shirt, a dark tie and a blue suit.

I distilled my message to three points:

1. Muslims condemn terrorism—period. That has become such an often-repeated mantra that, now, all American-Muslim leaders know it by heart. Every American-Muslim website I have seen devotes space to such a condemnation.

2. All Americans are horrified and saddened at the loss of life. I emphasized that Muslims are Americans, too.

3. We hope that journalists will show some restraint until we know more about the attackers. Fearful rumors do real damage to our neighbors.

Reporters from major newspapers, radio and TV stations showed up, eager to hear from Muslims.

"Thank you all for coming," I said, as TV lights glared, cameras whirred and reporters scribbled on notepads. I went over that first point, which I would be forced to repeat many times over the years: "We condemn such terrorist acts." Then, I sincerely tried to put into words my own heartbreak at the massive loss of life. "All Americans are horrified," I told the reporters. "We all are searching for answers. We all want to catch the guys who did this."

Then, I said, "But, please: Remember that no one knows who is responsible for this violence right now. Don't jump to conclusions."

The press conference was effective. I showed up in the next day's newspaper reports and my voice resonated across the airwaves. We helped to calm some of the fears in southeast Michigan.

Only later did we learn that McVeigh had been arrested shortly after the bombing by an Oklahoma state trooper who had spotted him driving a car without license plates. When the officer stopped McVeigh and saw that he was carrying a gun, McVeigh quickly wound up in jail. That's where McVeigh was sitting when federal investigators finally connected all of the evidence. They started with a vehicle identification number on a rear axle from the truck that was found at the scene; that led to the rental agency that owned the truck. McVeigh had not used his real name to pick up the truck, but a sketch of the suspect was made. Within several days, reporters had McVeigh's name as the likely bomber—and discovered that he already was in custody.

Unfortunately for American-Muslim families, this has become a pattern over the years. Disaster strikes! An explosion or mass shooting erupts in the news media. Headlines flood across millions of smartphones. We, as American Muslims, start our prayers—for the victims, of course, and for ourselves.

One of the worst crises occurred on the morning of April 16, 2007, when Seung-Hui Cho, a South Korean-born student, began his shooting spree at Virginia Tech. The carnage went on for more than two hours before Cho finally committed suicide. Right away, news reports initially described an "Asian-looking" man, and Islamophobic bloggers leaped to the conclusion that he likely was a Pakistani Muslim.

That was another day I prayed, "Oh, God, let it not be a Muslim!"

Even after Cho's name was surfacing in the news media, one blogger refused to apologize, adding: "If it does *not* turn out that the shooter is Muslim, this still is a demonstration to Muslim jihadists all over that it is extremely easy to shoot and kill multiple American college students."

As a voice of the Muslim community, I became a kind of first responder myself, trying to calm fears even as we shared in the collective sorrow after such senseless attacks.

Nevertheless, I felt as if I was caught in the eye of a hurricane when Omar Mateen, a 29-year-old Florida security guard, opened fire at the Pulse nightclub in Orlando. At 2 a.m. on July 12, 2016, Mateen began shooting and eventually killed 49 and wounded 53 men and women. We soon learned that he was a local man.

Shahina and I had moved to Florida's Treasure Coast to retire. The region is named for a Spanish fleet of treasure ships lost in a storm in a 1715 hurricane. We are situated just north of the Gold Coast, the region of Miami and Fort Lauderdale. Treasure Coast is comprised of Indian River, St. Lucie and Martin counties. Mateen's Afghan-American family had moved to this area in 1991, when Mateen was 5. He went to school in St. Lucie and Martin and, as an adult, co-owned a home in Port St. Lucie. His family had ties to our Muslim community.

Once again, I found myself back at the center of a national tragedy. Our area of Florida is conservative, majority-Republican country, and while we know that many of our neighbors are Trump supporters, we had never experienced incidents of Islamophobia. My neighbors know who I am, because I often write for the Treasure Coast newspapers. If I hear any response to my columns, they are words of encouragement. One neighbor likes to tell me, "I'm glad you speak up."

Suddenly, an army of reporters invaded our corner of Florida, wanting to talk to anyone who had ever known Mateen. The whole community felt a responsibility. Soon, I was using my years of experience to connect with Christians, Jews, Hindus and the LGBTQ community in organizing an interfaith memorial service at the Community Church in Vero Beach, Florida. We followed the service with a candlelight vigil in a public park by Indian River.

The most emotional moment of the evening was when Sana Shareef, a Muslim teenager, played the Christian hymn *Amazing Grace* on her clarinet before reading, in Arabic, from the Quran. I will never forget a gay man who was on stage with me that evening, so overcome by the experience that he reached out and hugged me. Resting his head on my shoulder, he cried.

I looked out across a sea of a mourners, all of them stone-silent in respect for the victims and their families. Many wept. I was the last speaker on the roster, representing the Islamic Center. I wondered how I would be received, as a Muslim speaking in the wake of this catastrophic crime. When I was introduced, I nervously got to my feet.

I felt the rising applause and stood at the microphone, with Shahina at my side, each of us holding a candle.

"God intended for a colorful world—black, white, brown, yellow and red," I said. "Yes. He made us male and female, and also gay." Thunderous applause erupted.

This was Ramadan and the sun had set, so Shahina and I had agreed that we would break our daylong fast as a public act of sharing peace and the blessings of our faith. Each of us took a traditional bite of a date and a sip of water.

Then, Shahina stepped down into the crowd and offered a bowl of dates. One woman with tearful eyes accepted this symbolic gift, lifted a date toward her lips, and said, "I'll save the seed to remember this day."

Our human connection that night came from the depth of our souls. The spiritual message I delivered as a practitioner of my faith helped bring unity to a crowd that was desperately seeking some sign that peace was possible.

Specifically, Shahina and I live on Hutchinson Island, which we tell people is "what all of Florida once was." There are large tracts of preserved land, parks and quiet beaches. Other than the wildlife refuges, the big draw is the National Navy UDT-SEAL Museum. This is where the Navy set up a base in 1943 to train amphibious teams to overcome obstacles on enemy-held beaches during World War II. The historic Little Jim Bait & Tackle still sits near the end of one of the two long bridges that connect the island to the mainland. On a large, open deck by the store, boaters and other customers enjoy drinks and what the limited menu offers, sitting at the outdoor tables under colorful umbrellas. Sometimes there is live music.

Our condo overlooks the Atlantic Ocean, which lies 200 feet away and beyond the dunes. From our rear balcony, we see the Indian River Lagoon, a part of the intracostal waterway. A cool sea breeze relieves some of the humidity when it gets into the upper 90s in summer. We see ocean sunrises and incredible sunsets behind the wide river. In our garage, I keep a kacanoe, my hybrid term for a kayak that seats two, like a canoe. At the rear of our property, we have a dock with access to the river and its canals, enabling us to paddle our little craft to several small, scattered islands. We enjoy herons, anhinga, pelicans, manatees and dolphins. Fish regularly jump out of the water with a welcome splash, breaking the serenity and adding to the charm.

Residents in our high-rise building are mostly retired, though not all. Many spend their winter months here, then head north for the summer. We decided to make Florida's Treasure Coast our permanent residence upon retirement, after being snowbirds for many years. Like many of our neighbors, we welcome children and grandchildren during the holidays. We've come to know the families of our neighbors and they've come to know ours. We often break bread together and we look after each other's property when we travel.

We are the only Muslim couple among 90 residents of the 19-story condo building. Since Muslims constitute 1-2 percent of the U.S. population, we thus mirror the national average as a minority among our neighbors. My wife wears hijab, so everyone knows our religious identity. Any fear of Islamophobia quickly melted away when we attended our first gathering of neighbors. We were welcomed warmly.

We have the friendliest neighbors imaginable. In fact, they have even become proactive about our customs. Once or twice a month, the social committee holds a potluck. We bring a dish to pass, like everyone else. When all the food is assembled, our friends point out any pork in the dishes, knowing that we are Muslim and will want to avoid those. Shahina, in her colorful hijab, is now on the condo welcoming committee and plays canasta with the ladies on Wednesdays. When we take long walks along the beach, we pass beachcombers who always nod and smile. I go fishing with one of our neighbors, "big" George. His wife, Barbara, is one of Shahina's walking companions.

The neighboring Fort Pierce has a quaint little downtown with cafes and eateries lining the streets, a renovated marina and a promenade along the river. The Manatee Observation and Education Center is popular with visitors. Music is in the air on the weekends. Kids feed the birds. In the park stands the statue of CeeCee Ross Lyles, a local hero of United Airlines Flight 93, which crashed in a Pennsylvania field on 9/11.

Weekends offer many festivities. On Saturdays, artists market their work and farmers sell fresh fruits, plants and vegetables at a local fair. We've become friends with some of these vendors, too: Gary, who sells hand-carved Native American flutes, taught me to play that instrument; Sandra, originally from Nicaragua, sells Indian clothing, and her Italian husband, Steve, sells jewelry. Shahina volunteers on Mondays at the public library, which is located in the growing downtown. The friendly staff there provided her with a spot in the building to lay out her prayer rug, for the afternoon prayers. Waterfront homes along the river and on the barrier island—like the one we live on, across the bridge—are primarily white and wealthy areas; west of downtown are racially mixed, middle- and lower-income neighborhoods.

The little mosque in town wound up in the national news because of two violent young men. Even before Omar Mateen's shooting spree, a young man who grew up in this area—Moner Mohammad Abu Salha— became the first American suicide bomber known to have killed himself in the Syrian conflict. He was just 22 years old in 2014, when he killed himself and several Syrian soldiers with a bomb. The FBI tried to track down how such an otherwise ordinary American kid had become rad- icalized enough to travel halfway around the world to join an obscure militia in the Syrian civil war, but they could find few clues as to what had transformed this basketball-loving teenager from an upscale family. Little was reported about him in American media, because agents could find little to say. His name resurfaced in the investigation surrounding Omar Mateen, but after another exhaustive inquiry, the FBI found no affiliation between the two terrorists nor did they find any close connection with the local mosque.

Perhaps I should say that this part of Florida has ties to several infa- mously violent men, because Timothy McVeigh also visited our area. As it turns out, his mother lived in Fort Pierce. It seems that every community, from coast to coast, has pockets of homegrown extremists. Some surface; some remain invisible. For a while, federal agents looked into possible connections between McVeigh and dangerous Florida militia groups. Finally, agents reported that they had found no links. McVeigh's visits to Fort Pierce apparently were simply to see his mother.

Trying to find geographic patterns in terrorism doesn't make a lot of sense in this era of internet connectivity, which brings the whole world into our smartphones. A kid in New York City is as likely as a kid in Los Angeles, or a kid in the mountains of Colorado, to stumble across an extremist website. Any of these restless, curious teens can get caught up in seductive appeals to violence. I am not a psychiatrist, nor do I claim to be a terrorism expert, but I do know that violence can erupt from any corner of the world, today.

I do know one thing: Shafiq Ur Rahman—the imam of the Fort Pierce mosque, where Omar Mateen once prayed—never preached radicalism. A heavyset, bearded Pashtun immigrant and medical professional, he once favored traditional garb but switched to ordinary pants and shirts in the aftermath of the violence. I am relatively new to the community, but longtime members of the mosque swear that no extremism has ever been heard in sermons preached at the mosque. If I have any objection to the sermons we hear, it's the kind of observation most Americans share with friends after a typical service: The sermons sometimes run a bit too long and don't address enough real-life issues.

After the shootings, the imam lamented the media attention on his mosque. "Did anyone ever interview a pastor where Timothy McVeigh went to church? After the Virginia Tech shootings, did anyone interview the pastor of the Chos' evangelical church?"

I was not as upset as the imam; I understood the need to ask questions. A proper investigation must probe all possible links to a terrorist. Perhaps because I have known lots of police officers over the years, I have a greater appreciation for their methods. What I discovered after the Mateen shootings was that the police knew him far better than the imam ever did. I have offered cultural-competence training at the Fort Pierce police department and learned that some of the current officers once went to school with Omar. At one point, he interviewed for a job with the police department.

On July 12, 2016, yet another terrorist struck in our corner of Florida. An anti-Muslim extremist burned the Fort Pierce mosque to the ground. The building was a total loss. The arsonist was arrested, pleaded guilty and, later that same year, was sentenced to 30 years in prison. Newspaper accounts called him deeply troubled and reported that he regretted what he had done, but investigators found a long list of anti-Muslim rants on his social media accounts. His rage was fueled by his hatred.

Once again, I was impressed by the community response. To show solidarity with the Muslim families who had lost their historic mosque, an interfaith prayer service was organized. The police chaplain joined in the candlelight service, along with other clergy. A crowdfunding campaign was started to help rebuild the mosque. Christians, Jews, Muslims and other community-minded people donated to the effort. The Fort Pierce House of the Believers was able to move to a new location and rebuild a prayer hall, plus an adjacent school. The outpouring of goodwill across this community was overwhelming.

We all know that extremists can burst through the cracks of our community without warning. Looking back, no one in the community would have guessed that this guy, who was posting angry messages about Muslims on his social media, would suddenly become an arsonist. He expressed extreme views, but who knew he would do something so violent? Even people who knew him were confounded and heartbroken at the devastation he caused to the whole community.

Here is where I focus my efforts, now: making a difference with the people I meet each and every day. That may sound naïve, but over time, it's a powerful approach to changing a community.

One day, David, a neighbor in our building, was at the outdoor pool. Sometimes I do laps, but this time I was headed to the adjacent hot tub to soothe my recently replaced knee. We exchanged a few pleasantries about our health. He wanted to know how I was doing with my new titanium joint.

"Hey, it's titanic!" I said, smiling.

After a moment, he asked, "Victor, aren't you a Muslim?"

"Yes," I nodded.

"If you don't mind, can I ask you something?"

"Sure." This kind of conversation is close to my heart. I settled into the water and moved my knee closer to the jets to help stimulate circulation. The water felt wonderful. I murmured a prayer of thanks to God.

David had summoned the courage to continue. He started by reassuring me that he appreciated my openness. "I had a Muslim coworker in Boston, but he never opened up to me."

"Happy to talk. What's your question?"

"Victor, what percentage of Muslims do you think are terrorists?"

There it was, a hot topic in a hot tub. He leaned toward me.

For years, I taught sales courses in furniture stores. I had spent more than three decades selling home furnishings. Step one was always asking customers about their needs and interests. I've answered the question he just asked so many times that I could have simply rattled off an answer. But I wanted him to sift the evidence, step by step, along with me. I asked, "David, how many do you think there are?"

He didn't have a guess, he admitted, but he was sincerely engaged in the conversation, now. So, I began with population data from the Pew Research Center, the CIA World Factbook, CNN experts and other authoritative sources. I did not lecture David; I chatted with him, step by step. I even suggested we overestimate the numbers from each source, "you know, just to be sure." Of course, I knew what the result would be. Terrorists are an infinitesimally small percentage of the world's Muslim population.

In David's case, I did not need to overcome some hardened Islamophobia he was harboring. We were neighbors. He was cordial, and we both enjoyed the conversation. I was pleased to have the opportunity to outline the facts for him, before some voice in the media could grab his attention and possibly substitute a hateful myth for the truth.

Like many of my neighbors in this part of Florida, David had been among the 62 percent of Americans who didn't know a Muslim personally. He had worked with Muslims, he told me, but had never gotten to know them. I was happy to help him cross the line and make a new Muslim friend.

Person by person, and friend by friend: good-hearted people can change the world.

CHAPTER 16

God Loves All Colors

Among God's wonders is the diversity of your tongues and colors!

Quran 30:22

An Arab has no superiority over a non-Arab …;
a white has no superiority over a black.

Prophet Muhammad, March 6, 632, in his farewell sermon

We must name racism and xenophobia as sins against our neighbors
and against the God who made us all in God's image.

Jim Wallis in *America's Original Sin*

As a Muslim raised in India, I had trouble wrapping my mind around America's collective culture of racism. Not long after I landed in America in 1970, I had an unforgettable encounter with racism while walking home from school in Detroit on a chilly September evening.

I use the phrase "America's collective culture of racism" because racism is not merely a matter of one person's opinion about another person; the problem is far larger and deeper than that. Our nation was built on the backs of slave labor, historians remind us. Our customs, laws and public institutions all rest on foundations of color-consciousness. Dig deep enough into the history of any long-standing American university, health care system, government department or cultural genre, and you'll find layers of racial bias. This is not a controversial comment—it's a fact. All we have to do is read recent news headlines to learn about people struggling with the legacy of racial injustice.

On the other hand, I am not holding up India as a multiracial utopia—and I am saddened by the deepening divisions there. Several years ago, Indian leaders were shocked by news reports based on the World Values Survey: In one question, the survey interviewers listed types of people who the respondents would not want as next-door neighbors, and in India, Jordan, Bangladesh and Hong Kong, more than 40 percent of people selected "people of a different race." Headlines soon circled the planet, naming these countries as "the world's most intolerant." Critics of the report questioned the methodology, but the results did not surprise me at all. India faces lots of problems with cultural, class and racial bias.

Where can we find the wisdom to overcome racism? People of faith can find it in scriptures. Muslims have been condemning racism since the dawn of Islam, and Jews, Christians and Muslims all share the sacred story that God created humanity from a single couple. The world—in all its colors—is one family. God loves all of us.

I credit my birth at a unique moment in British-Indian history, my many years of cross-cultural experiences and my Muslim faith for guiding me beyond the fatal traps of racism. However, I fell right into one of those traps on my walk home in 1970. The University of Detroit, as it was known at the time, is situated on Six Mile Road—two miles south of Detroit's northern border. Rapper Eminem made that racial and cultural divide world famous with his 2002 song and movie *8 Mile*. Living along that dividing line, Eminem is torn between the tensions within his impoverished, white family and his talent for a style of music that emerged from black culture. In the movie, he decides to leave behind the abusive relationships in his own home—but he is not sure that African-American artists will welcome him. In the title song, he resolves to take this daring cultural and racial leap, "and show these people what my level of skill's like—but I'm still white." Millions of people around the world saw the movie or heard the soundtrack, getting a vivid snapshot of racial tensions in that part of Detroit.

When I left campus that night, in 1970, I only worried about getting home quickly because the temperatures were dropping. I was cold the moment I stepped outside, and it was getting colder by the minute. I headed quickly across the four lanes of Livernois Avenue, intending to walk along Grove Street. As I turned toward Grove, I could see ahead of me a group of noisy black kids standing on the sidewalk.

Anyone from outstate Michigan reading this chapter is likely to think that they know where this story is headed, but here is what actually happened that night:

I had just arrived from India, and I had no idea what lay ahead of me that night. I saw no warning signs. All I knew was that I wanted to get home and warm up! My textbook and a notepad were tightly tucked under my left arm. Both my hands were in my coat pockets. My mind wasn't focused on the black kids in front of me; I was worrying about how I was going to pass my macroeconomics class. I didn't find the subject all that interesting, and my ears had not yet attuned themselves to American accents. Paying close attention in class was frustrating.

The kids grew louder as I approached. I had not yet developed my habit of greeting people I pass, like I do now, and I was walking silently and swiftly—a man on a mission. I got closer and closer. I walked right through their circle.

The revelation came when I walked through my front door and one of my roommates began to rant about my habit of walking alone after dark. "Victor, it's just not safe! You've got to be careful of black people on the street."

"What are you talking about?" I challenged him. "I just sailed through a group of them."

His jaw dropped. "What happened?"

"Nothing." I shrugged my shoulders. "I wasn't concerned—and nothing happened."

"I can't believe you just did that—and survived."

"Really?!" I couldn't believe what I was hearing. "What are you saying? We're supposed to avoid all black people? This is a city full of black people!"

My roommate caught his breath and began rattling off stories of muggings—and worse. In his mind, crossing a racial boundary and finding crime on the other side was the natural progression of life in Detroit. Here I was, just days into my new life in America and already getting a full-scale indoctrination into racism.

I'm proud to say that his warnings didn't stick. I'm stubborn, and this simply was not the way I saw the world. I went on to enjoy four years of living near the Detroit campus. I was never mugged nor had any other encounters with crime, except for a dumb decision one day to leave some large speakers I had rented for an event sitting in the backseat of my Chevy. I don't think I even locked the car's doors. Those speakers were just too tempting to someone who was passing. Other than one theft, for which I blamed myself more than anyone else, I experienced no crime in my neighborhood.

There were countless other lessons that people tried to teach me about race—either overtly, in words of warning and fearful tales they told, or through their actions.

When I took a job at a gas station to earn some extra money, I soon learned how to get along with Willy, the African-American manager. We finally hit it off when Willy saw that I was the most efficient pump jockey he had ever seen. Then, one day, a white district manager showed up while on an assignment to visit all of the stations in that chain.

I never learned exactly what he wanted. He got out of his car and immediately locked eyes on me. I wore a uniform with the company logo on my pocket. He smiled, extended his hand to me, and said, "Glad to meet you. I'm talking to our managers about …"

Standing beside me, Willy glared at the man.

When I corrected the mistaken identity, the district manager made things worse. He told me, "Oh, sorry! You just looked more managerial to me."

After that, Willy tore into him. He and the district manager had a roaring argument. I simply stood back in amusement, amazed at how foolish that white executive was about human relations. My amusement made Willy even angrier. Such were race relations in 1970s America.

At the university, suburban white students did not tend to fraternize with black students, nor were they too friendly with foreign students. A lot of the foreign students also kept a distance from black students. I was not a saint in this. Daily life seemed to be a never-ending pattern of small acts of avoidance—walking past one group of students to engage with another group, or deciding whom to sit with during the school day.

I received verbal coaching, too. I remember once saying something friendly to a black girl and then hearing from a friend, "Hey, you want to get beaten up?" Beaten up by whom? Why? I gave up asking those questions or challenging those attitudes.

Eventually, I fell into the trap of mainly courting friends among the foreign students. That did turn out to be a colorful cultural mix of men and women. Natural allies were other Muslims, which included a wide range of ethnicities, as well as Arab-Americans, including Christian Arabs. Events planned by the foreign student office brought together students from India, the Philippines, Europe, Japan, Africa and the Middle East. Thanks to that network, I saw what was possible when people dared to cross cultural, religious and racial lines.

The larger lesson that all of us on campus observed in those years was white flight. This mass move to the suburbs was emptying the city all around us. There were many contributing factors to these ongoing tensions and, through newspaper reports and campus conversations, we learned about those flashpoints—one right after the other. By the time I left the university, in 1974, I was immersed in the many layers of America's racial consciousness.

My own family defied the lines that people all around me were trying to draw. All I had to do was remember the faces around our dining room table: My father was darker than my mother, and my mother and two younger sisters were white as white can be. Today, the next generation in our family has a whole range of skin tones.

As I was growing up, my childhood heroes were a racial mix, as well. I was a huge fan of Muhammad Ali. As a kid, I didn't comprehend everything that had happened throughout his life, but I did know that he was a hero for raising international awareness about black Americans.

As a student, the one setting where I got to know some African-American friends was a makeshift prayer facility in a house in the Detroit enclave of Highland Park. As I gathered with other local Muslims for Friday prayers, I did not see any white Muslims for quite a while.

Five years before I set foot in America—and just after Malcolm X was assassinated, in 1965—Alex Haley had published *The Autobiography of Malcolm X*, based on a series of interviews with the Muslim leader. As I read that bestseller, I was fascinated by the man who was equal parts mystery and prophetic teacher. Malcolm started out in an American offshoot of Islam that emphasized racial divisions; he became disillusioned with the leaders in that group. In 1964, he made his hajj and his entire worldview changed. At that point, Malcolm switched his message to a glorious affirmation of racial diversity.

Now, when I talk to audiences about the hajj, I like to read from the letter Malcolm wrote in Mecca: "During the past 11 days, here in the Muslim world, I have eaten from the same plate, drunk from the same glass, and slept on the same rug—while praying to the same God—as fellow Muslims whose eyes were the bluest of blue, whose hair was the blondest of blond and whose skin was the whitest of white. And in the words and in the deeds of the white Muslims, I felt the same sincerity that I felt among the black African Muslims of Nigeria, Sudan and Ghana."

He planned to come home and preach the true Islam, he declared. "America needs to understand Islam, because this is the one religion that erases from its society the race problem. I have never before seen sincere and true brotherhood practiced by all colors together, irrespective of their color."

He wrote, "I am still travelling, trying to broaden my mind, for I've seen too much of the damage that narrow-mindedness can make of things, and when I return home to America, I will devote what energies I have to repairing the damage."

What a tragedy that his life was cut short! I agree with Malcolm's pleas. All of us must help to repair the damage of racism. Despite the lingering racial bias in America, I would rather live here than any other place on earth. This isn't a perfect country, so I want to make it better. This is a truly all-American Dream. We hope that America can serve as a beacon of light to the rest of the world.

That is why I spend so much time writing columns and talking to audiences. In addition to quoting from Malcolm during his hajj, I also relate a story I have adapted from the Quran about God's creation of the first couple. From an Islamic perspective, we are all part of this one, original family. Just as Jim Wallis described racism as "original sin" from his Christian perspective, Muslims regard racism as the first sin.

Here is the story, as I read it:

> *When God fashioned Adam from earthly clay, he asked the angels to "Bow down to Adam." (Quran 2:34). Angels usually don't ask questions—but they are intrigued, this one time, wanting to know: Why is God creating this being?*

> *The angels know that Adam's descendants will be endowed with the freedom of choice, which angels don't have. This ability to choose is sure to wind up shedding blood on the earth.*

> *God says to the angels, "You don't know what I know."*

That is the end of the conversation between the angels and God. Period. They obey and perform the prostration toward Adam, as instructed. Except Iblis—whom we know by his other name, the Satan (Shaitan, in Arabic). He refuses to bow down to this creature made out of lowly dust. Iblis disobeys God because he considers himself superior to Adam's earthly origins.

Satan had been a good guy until he confronted his racial bias. He was faced with an order to respect another creation—a lowly one, in his book. For disobeying God, Satan knew he'd be punished, but Satan asked God to give him respite until the Last Day so that he could mislead the children of Adam, whom he detested. Thus, racial prejudice was the first sin that we continue to fall prey to—if we listen to the whispering of Satan.

The lesson from this story: Racism is a quality of Satan. Both Adam and Eve were misled by Satan and ended up as losers. We must not fall into the same trap.

Adam and Eve and their children were created as the best of God's creation (95:4), but they can also become the "lowest of the low" by following in the footsteps of Satan.

In reading that story, I want to expose the ancient evil of racism. I then point out that the Prophet Muhammad confronted racism head-on through both his words and his example.

I like to tell the story of Bilal ibn Rabah, one of the most trusted of Muhammad's companions. He was born into slavery; his father was Arab and his mother was Ethiopian. All of the accounts of his life describe Bilal as tall and handsome with a dark complexion and an African appearance, taking after his mother. Bilal was known for having a beautiful voice, but he seemed to have no option other than slavery. Then, he heard of Muhammad's teachings and became one of the first converts to Islam. His biographers say that Bilal's owner was furious about this and subjected Bilal to a series of horrible tortures. Finally, Muhammad heard of Bilal's plight and made a deal for his freedom.

Accounts vary in regards to how the Prophet Muhammad developed the Muslim call to prayer, but writers agree that Bilal was the first man Muhammad asked to climb up the holy Kaaba and make the *adhan*. Through the years Muhammad had received a lot of criticism for his teachings about racial equality, and by inviting a dark-skinned, former slave to fulfill this high honor, Muhammad knew that he was making a revolutionary statement. Although Muslims disagree on some of the finer points about Bilal's life, all Muslims agree that Bilal should be revered as the model for all who followed in learning how to make the *adhan*.

In his farewell sermon, the Prophet Muhammad returned, once again, to his warnings against this first sin of racism. He told all of us:

> *O people!*
>
> *Your Lord is one Lord, and you all share the same father.*
>
> *There is no preference for Arabs over non-Arabs, nor for non-Arabs over Arabs. Neither is there preference for white people over black people, nor for black people over white people.*
>
> *Preference is only through righteousness.*

In Islam, the Prophet Muhammad taught, we are not to be judged by our color, ethnicity or status; we are judged by the purity of our hearts.

CHAPTER 17

A Passage to India

God has put us on earth to love our neighbors and to show it. And, he is omnipresent, even in India, to see how we are succeeding.

E.M. Forster, *A Passage to India*

Some of us call you as Ishwar (Lord Vishnu)
And some others as Allah
But we beg you Lord
To bless us all.

A song popularized by Bollywood singer Muhammad Rafi

Shahina and I broke with Indian tradition when we married. I was Muslim; she grew up Hindu. I spoke Urdu; she spoke Konkani, an Indian language I first learned about only when I met her. (India has 14 official languages and innumerable dialects.) Although we came from different backgrounds, we had a common cultural bond. As Indians, we shared an enjoyment of Bollywood movies. Our common language, other than love, was Hinglish—British English with an Indian accent. Shahina wore a sari at the time, like my mom did. A little difference in our skin color didn't matter, nor did the little dot on her forehead that existed before she accepted Islam. In marriage, we blended our colorful heritage.

Shahina describes the traditional tensions we had to overcome in the book *Friendship & Faith*:

> *I was born into a Brahmin-class family in Hinduism. Of course, the caste system is not as important as it once was, but our culture and our Hindu traditions were important to my family. I grew up in Bombay, now Mumbai, which is a very cosmopolitan city; I had friends of different faiths as I was growing up. Dad was the assistant commissioner of police for Bombay and Mom was a homemaker.*

Dad was very open-minded when he heard the news from America that I was planning to marry Victor. At first—as many Indian families do—he wanted to check on Victor's family in Hyderabad. He met Victor's family and he said to me, "Victor has a very good family. Now, I'm going to give you my blessing for your marriage."

The one piece of advice Dad gave me was this: "Don't think of moving back and settling in India again. The society still is not ready to let you live happily here. Make your life in America after this."

Shahina and I were not worried about that. We had come to America to build a better life, and we knew that our newly adopted homeland was the ideal place for us to make our own choices, succeed in our careers and raise a family. When we arrived in the U.S., we knew that we were not simply visiting. Like millions of immigrant families before us, we were a family with global connections—but America became our home.

In that same book, our daughter, Sofi, describes our diverse family as she was growing up.

Often during school breaks, my family would travel to visit my mother's relatives. My Hindu cousins sometimes spent entire summers at our home and, during weddings and other big celebrations, both sides of my family would come together. During these times, my parents fostered a welcoming environment where the tensions often associated with differing cultures and traditions could not be felt. Sometimes my father and my mother's uncle would talk and even debate about religious teachings—the way that I imagine other families debate about politics—but then they would sit down and have dinner together. Both my father and mother's uncle were devout followers of their separate faiths, but they did not allow the differences in their religious beliefs to interfere with family relationships.

My parents prioritized the values of hospitality, of respect to elders and of family. My brothers and I were not taught to see the lines that religion often places between people, but rather, we were shown how to love and admire the humanity that unifies them.

Shahina and I both were raised in this tradition of hospitality. During India's struggle for independence against colonial rule, Jawaharlal Nehru visited my grandfather's home. British officials were not happy that the chief justice of Hyderabad was hosting a freedom fighter, and they told him to evict Nehru—but my grandfather stood firm. He said that he would resign his position before disrespecting a guest in that way. My grandfather was a principled man, and hospitality was a principle he regarded as carved in stone.

The uncle Sofi mentions in her story, a retired NASA scientist, liked to describe the American family reunions we hosted in our home as "not just the union between two individuals, but between two families and two faiths." During one visit, I gave him a copy of the Quran. On the next visit, he gave me a Bhagavad Gita. Only in America! We would have never experienced this cordial give-and-take in India.

I am heartbroken to see the rise of Hindu nationalism and sectarian violence in India today. If these feuding partisans could step back and claim the full religious heritage of this ancient region, India could become one of the world's greatest spiritual destinations. This land is where many of the world's faiths were born: Hinduism, Buddhism, Sikhism and Jainism. Zoroastrians have lived in what is India today since ancient times. Christians believe that one of Jesus's original Twelve Apostles, St. Thomas, carried the faith to India not long after Jesus's crucifixion. Muslims have lived in India since the early years of Islam. Vibrant Sufi traditions are associated with India.

Despite today's tensions, many symbols and stories of unity remain—all across India. In the 17th century, the Taj Mahal couldn't have been built without the combined labor of Muslims and Hindus. A century before that, Muslim Emperor Akbar the Great built a house of worship, *Ibadat Khana*, where people of all faiths could gather for interfaith dialogue. Historians say that Christians, Muslims, Hindus, Jains, Zoroastrians and atheists took part in these conversations. The spirited discussions were described as a place where "wisdom and deeds were tested—and those who were founded on truth entered the hall of acceptance."

Over the centuries in India, some of the most inspiring appeals to religious cooperation have come through the arts—by means such as literature and, even, Bollywood movies.

The famous line from E.M. Forster's *A Passage to India*, about God being present everywhere, "even in India," actually is an example of entrenched bigotry during the British Raj. These words are spoken by one of Forster's most deeply flawed characters: the elderly British woman, Mrs. Moore. She seems kindhearted and is widely respected by the Indian characters in the novel, but when Mrs. Moore makes this profession of faith, she is referring exclusively to her Christian God. She is surrounded by racists and, in the end, she completely misses the larger vision of God that she could have glimpsed in India. The novel was published in 1924—long before India attained its independence. In the book, Forster's main focus is the harm people do to each other because of their ignorance and bias. Forster dearly loved India and left his readers with at least a few notes of hope about India's future. Today, some writers pass around Mrs. Moore's short quote about India, presenting it erroneously and without the irony that Forster intended in his novel. Today, many people mistakenly read Mrs. Moore's words as an affirmation of God's universal presence. Forster died in 1970, but I think he probably would smile at that transformation of this line—pleased that his novel continues to inspire cross-cultural understanding.

While these appeals to understanding came through in some of the best literature about India, they also were splashed across movie screens. One of my favorite Bollywood singers is Mohammed Rafi, who was born into a Muslim family in 1924. He earned the title "the Man with a Golden Voice"—one of India's legendary playback singers (the Bollywood term for voice-over artists who actually sing the songs in the movies). By the mid-1940s, he was India's top male singer. When Gandhi was assassinated, Rafi was part of a musical team that worked overnight to release a haunting musical tribute to the fallen hero. In the song, Rafi refers to Gandhi affectionately, as "bapu," which means "father." In English, the opening lines are:

> *Listen, people of this world, to Bapu's immortal story*
> *The bapu so divine, like the water of the Ganges*
> *Listen, people of this world, to Bapu's immortal story*

This was a Muslim singer giving the world an unforgettable tribute to a Hindu sage. Nehru loved this song, and had Rafi visit his home just to hear the song sung in person. In 1948, when India declared its independence, Nehru honored Rafi with a silver medal.

In India, such interfaith cooperation was stunning to the people who rarely saw such cordial collaboration in everyday life. Here in America, Shahina and I see that kind of interreligious cooperation emerging in nearly every community we visit. Throughout our own marriage, we have tried to approach everyone we meet with the hospitality that is one of the core values of our faith. We are Muslim, but we want our neighbors to feel free to practice their religious disciplines and observances throughout the year. In many cases, we are happy to join the crowd. I look forward to a hearty dinner of corned beef and cabbage on St. Patrick's Day, just as I enjoy lamb at our own Eid al-Adha.

In the small town of Vero Beach, I've formed a wonderful relationship with the local ashram. Swami Anjani and Swami Durga Dass already have welcomed a Sikh shrine and a Jewish shrine on their lovely property, with each shrine bearing an inscription from their respective scriptures. Now they have invited me to place a Muslim shrine nearby. I want the monument to bear this inscription:

> *O people, we created you from a single male and female,*
>
> *and rendered you distinct peoples and tribes,*
>
> *that you may know one another.*
>
> *The best among you in the sight of God is the most righteous of you.*
>
> *God is Omniscient, Cognizant.*
>
> **Quran 49:13**

America has been the focus of all my work through the years, so I never had a great desire to return to India. Finally, in 2008—28 years after my first trip back to India—Shahina and I decided to make a return visit to Hyderabad.

What I found was an alien landscape. As I searched for landmarks from my youth, I was disappointed again and again. My old neighborhood had declined, having lost its earlier warmth and charm. The house where I was born was no more. Our beautiful, old bungalow had been replaced with a housing complex. Most of the towering peepal, bamboo, banana and neem trees that once had shaded our home had all disappeared. Our garden, with flowering bougainvillea bushes and a fountain in the center—gone. I remember chasing colorful butterflies that landed on those flowers. One section of the garden was reserved for vegetables; it was no more.

I walked around the property, looking for childhood landmarks. I found the spot where we once kept water buffaloes and goats, to provide fresh milk every morning. We collected our eggs from nearby chicken pens. There once had been a pet white swan, which had always tried to chase me. If I was fast enough, I could grab its long neck before he could snap at me. All of these things were gone, of course.

One neem tree remained. How I loved to climb that tree, swinging through the limbs like a monkey! A vivid memory of my grandfather's open-top, horse-drawn buggy—like a snapshot from a Sherlock Holmes adventure—came flooding back. He used to park it right under that tree. I flew kites in this yard. So many fond images tumbled, one after another! I recalled delightful evenings on the veranda, when mango ice cream was prepared in the old-fashioned, hand-cranked churn in an ice-filled wooden bucket. Because we had no ice maker in the house, we had to go and get a slab of ice—then hope that it would not completely melt away by the time we got home again. And those mangoes! They were fresh from our tree and so tangy-sweet. We anxiously waited for those first scoops of ice cream under the starry, clear nights.

When it got hot, a fan was placed behind a dry-grass panel that was regularly sprayed with cool water—a natural air-conditioning system that is still used in parts of India. Drinking water was cooled in clay pots and then poured into silver cups. I remember one of those cups having Quranic verses inscribed inside of it, presumably to gulp down blessings with the liquid.

But as I walked further, I had trouble recalling the exact footprint of what had been our home. Memories surfaced, but memories also faded— or, rather, they were eclipsed by the squalor I found invading my old neighborhood. I wandered over to the creek where I used to fish. Dirt and debris was scattered along its banks—a sacrilegious act! I once played cricket in a nearby field, but that field was long gone, as well, so builders could pile in more homes. I now appreciate even more the need to protect our environment. Ragtag kids were begging on the poorly maintained streets. Poverty had exploded.

The dilapidated state of my old school, St. George's Grammar School, horrified me. Having served on my local school board in America, I expected to find my old school modernized and well kept. How could parents have let it crumble? India continues to produce brilliant minds, yet it is baffling how that is possible if children study in such poor conditions.

Friends and relatives have stayed in India, somehow coexisting with the yawning gap between wealth and poverty. They have accepted what they cannot change, they say. I would find it impossible to live with such disparity between the haves and have-nots. I kept thinking: The wealth gap is deepening in America, as well. I pray we take heed, as Americans, of what can happen if this disparity is allowed to grow; if our schools also crumble. The poverty that is obvious on many Indian streets reminded me of how disregard for inequalities can cripple an entire country.

As Shahina and I headed back to America, I was depressed. Sometimes I had dreamed of those scenes from my childhood, but now I realized that that's all they were—only dreams. India was no longer my home.

Forster struggled with the same disconnect during his two lengthy visits to India. He traveled across India for half of a year, in 1912-13, and then he returned to India in 1921 and served as private secretary to the Maharajah of Dewas. Between those two visits—in 1919—British officers had carried out the horrific massacre in Amritsar. At least 1,000 unarmed Sikhs were gunned down during a peaceful gathering because the British had declared that public meetings were forbidden. Rule was enforced with bullets, and with no regard for human life. Like so many others in that era, Forster regarded that massacre as a turning point that made him a committed anti-imperialist. He had started a novel about India after his first visit, but he never brought himself to finish it. When he returned to India in 1921, he seems to have been as frustrated with what he found, as I was in my own return trip. Over and over again in *A Passage to India*, Forster describes his frustration with the injustices and disparities all around him—and the complacency of so many in the upper classes. At one point in the novel, he describes a driver who, when asked by his passenger about local historical and religious sites, simply mumbled, "Old buildings are buildings; ruins are ruins."

As we flew home, I had similar thoughts. We can't return to places we lived long ago and expect to recapture our fondest memories. As Forster wrote: Old buildings are buildings; ruins are ruins.

I am proud of my heritage and, throughout my life, I have tried to contribute to strengthening communities both in America and around the world. Yet I know that we must not dwell in the distant past. That road leads to conflict over things that, in many cases, no longer exist.

Wherever we live around the world, we should hold dear and celebrate the best of our heritage. I certainly do in my family and my faith. These are the values that define us and that shape the talents that let us give back to our communities. But my trip to India made it clear to me: My story could never end in my reclaiming India as my home. That childhood home is gone. I am a citizen of a new land.

Even more important than telling stories of the past is telling stories, every day, of the new lives we are making in the communities where we live. That's how we welcome others to come together and glimpse the possibilities that can unite us. I pray that this memoir is one of those life-giving stories.

CHAPTER 18

Heralds of the Future

Worship God and associate nothing with Him, and to parents do good, and to
relatives, orphans, the needy, the near neighbor, the neighbor farther away, the
companion at your side, the traveler, and those whom your right hands possess.

Quran 4:36

I want to smooth over every ache
I want to grant every prayer on the lips
of everyone longing for solace.

Mona Haydar

Mementoes of my Indian family have always graced our home. In our
Florida condo hang portraits of my grandparents from both sides of the
family. Our children grew up surrounded by these photos, which illustrate
their ancestors dressed in robes and *dastar*, the judicial headgear of the
time. At the same time, I know that our three kids feel only a peripheral
attachment to those artifacts; only one of them has visited India as an
adult.

This does not worry me. The real value of family is the loving circle
that surrounds children and shows them, by daily example, how we hope
they will approach the world. In that way, Shahina and I have succeeded
as parents.

I became fully aware of the power of a family's loving embrace when I
left it behind, in 1970, to live alone in America. I discovered how difficult
it was to stay on a religious path as a loner, far away from those who loved
me. Looking back, I am thankful to a small circle of deeply observant
friends in Detroit who welcomed me as a kind of surrogate family and
made sure that I did not completely lose touch with Islam.

Shahina and I were not as observant when we first met as we are
today, but we committed ourselves to raising children in a religious home.
Through all of our labors in the community—helping to build a mosque

and establish Muslim programs—we always envisioned the safe harbor we were creating in order to support the educational, spiritual and emotional lives of the next generation. As our children were growing up, Shahina and I found ourselves becoming even more observant: If we were going to lead by example, the challenge was keeping ahead of the kids!

I still remember our surprise when our daughter, Sofi, decided that she would begin wearing hijab. She describes this in *Friendship & Faith:*

> *When I joined the sixth grade at a public middle school, I decided to begin wearing the traditional Muslim headscarf, knowing that I would be the only one to do so. It was a difficult transition, but even at such a young age, I was firm in my faith and confident that when others began to know me, they would accept me for who I was. My parents' example, in so many subtle and obvious ways, had given me proof that people who ultimately shared the same values would find friendship and amity. My best friends throughout my middle and high school years were Shannon Fink, a Jew, and Alka Tandon, a Hindu.*

One day, we got a call from Bloomfield Hills Schools Superintendent Gary Doyle about our son. "Victor, Yusuf says he wants to pray. What do we do?"

"Well, how do you usually handle requests like this?" I asked. I was both a parent and a member of the school board.

"We've never had such a request from one of our middle school students."

All I knew about this was my own experience in Hyderabad, where a small area of the school was designated for prayers. However, we had been part of a large Muslim population. As I thought back to my own school days, I started to feel a little guilty! I had not been as observant as Yusuf at his age.

"Could the principal find a corner somewhere, so he can pray?" I asked. "I mean, as long as this doesn't interfere with his classes or school policies. I don't want him to be disruptive."

"We can do that," Gary said. "We'll find something." Soon, a quiet spot was found not far from the principal's office where Yusuf could make the midday *salat.*

Once again, I realized that I was learning from my children. They were a different breed than the kids I knew when I was growing up. They were inspiring me with their devotion.

Our kids fasted during Ramadan throughout their school years. They attended classes and participated in sports programs—even when Ramadan fell in seasons with long, hot days. Teachers knew about their needs and accommodated them to the best of their abilities. Not all American Muslim children are as fortunate as ours were while attending public schools. Being a Muslim kid is not easy, which is why I cringe any morning that President Trump launches another anti-Muslim tweet into the world. I feel sorry for all the Muslim kids who are likely to face more bullying that day.

Then I think about our kids and how they made their way, as Americans. They never looked longingly at India—or any other country, for that matter—as a better place to live. From an early age, they were seizing every opportunity to make this country a better place for their classmates. Sofi describes this in *Friendship & Faith*:

> *My passion for working toward creating pluralistic societies with religious and cultural understanding is a direct result of my upbringing. During my senior year in high school, when I heard about The Children of Abraham Project, I was truly excited to get involved. This was an opportunity to work with young adults from over a dozen different racial, cultural, socioeconomic and religious backgrounds to tell a common story—the story of how Abraham's two sons, Isaac and Ishmael, patriarchs of two great religions, came together upon their father's death to bury him. The goal was to use this story as an example for how our communities today can overcome the hate and fear that divides us. As I worked with this diverse group on developing the storyline for the play, I once again found myself searching for the values that connected us and brought us together. It was only after we, as a group, were able to overcome the tensions of diversity that we could co-create what has now become an award-winning production and documentary that has traveled across the U.S. and even to Jerusalem.*

The reason I have always displayed my grandfather's memorabilia in our home is that he was my role model. He was a pious, Oxford-educated, sophisticated man who always spoke softly and, even though he was very busy, always made time for me. One day, I overheard him telling my grandma, "Ghalib is a *honehaar* young man," which meant "admirable" in Urdu. My grandfather financially supported my university education. Our older son, Sami, is named after him. To this day, I admire his moral courage as Chief Justice. Among other things, my grandfather taught my father and his brothers and sister to avoid intoxicants and smoking. He modeled good manners and hospitality. He knew Gandhi and shared the Mahtma's courage in speaking truth to power. I try to follow his example, although I often find myself falling short.

All religions teach respect for parents. "Honor your father and your mother" is one of the Ten Commandments for Jews and Christians. Hinduism also teaches us to revere our parents. The Quran sends the same message. One of my favorite passages from the Quran is in 17:23-24: "Your Lord has decreed that you worship none but Him, and that you be kind to parents. Whether one or more attain old age in your life, say not to them a word of contempt, nor repel them, but address them in terms of honor. And out of kindness, lower them the wing of humility, and say, 'My Lord! Bestow on them Your Mercy, even as they cherished me in the childhood.'" There are multiple hadiths from Prophet Muhammad on this theme. "He who wishes to enter Paradise through its best door must please his parents," he once said. And: "It is a pity that some people may not attain Paradise, on account of not serving their old parents."

This lifelong responsibility runs both ways. Children are called to respect their parents, but parents must play a proper role. Many centuries ago, Prophet Muhammad's cousin, Ali ibn Talib, described his approach to parenting. "Play with them for seven years of their life; then teach them for the next seven; then remain their friend and an advisor for the next seven."

When I told Sofi recently that, "In this next chapter, I'm going to write about the generational divide," she warmed my heart with her response!

"There is no divide," she said. "I don't feel one in our family."

In spite of what I have accomplished in my life, my greatest source of pride lies in the young American Muslim men and women I see stepping into leadership nationwide. As a generation, they are incredibly sophisticated and technologically savvy. They are concerned about living healthy lives, confronting injustice and helping to improve the lives of our less fortunate neighbors.

One piece of wisdom I always pass along to young people is this: "Hanging on to your faith takes strong arms in today's world!" I admire men and women who cling to their faith, whether they are Muslims or are adherents of the world's other great traditions. Promiscuity, booze and the glitter of luxury goods are mesmerizing. Today, all of these alluring temptations are as close as the colorful messages flashing across the phones most of us carry with us throughout the day.

Every Muslim parent I know is concerned about protecting their children from Islamophobia and other forms of bullying. Hateful attacks are hard to avoid. Today, bullies can hound our kids through social media. It is everywhere they turn, until there seems to be no safe corner left. What inspires me most is the wave of Muslim young adults who are creating new, supportive networks—online, and in the form of tangible nonprofits, as well. Many young Muslims continue to participate in the institutions their parents built, but they also are such an enterprising and diverse bunch that they are pushing in new directions. Their ideas and strategies are far more fluid and dynamic than anything we could have dreamed of in the 1970s.

I was recently invited by a group of Jewish and Muslim medical students to participate in a Jewish-Muslim panel at the University of Chicago campus. When the appropriate time came that day, the Muslim students lined up for prayer and welcomed their colleagues of other faiths—or of no faith—to observe prayers. The other students responded in a reverent way, pleased to be invited to stay and watch. It was a beautiful expression of solidarity among young people.

Back in the dawn of the interfaith era, we had to plan elaborate dialogues so that our various faith communities could meet—often, for the first time. Today, young adults feel more comfortable with diversity. They live, study and work in mixed communities. If a particular cause interests them, most are happy to join with people of other faiths and cultures. They stand up for each other. As I see all of this unfolding, I applaud. We all can learn from these young people's best examples.

After white supremacist Dylann Roof murdered nine people at the Emanuel African Methodist Episcopal Church in Charleston, South Carolina, in 2015, the tragic pattern of church burnings flared in the South. During Ramadan of 2017, young Muslims joined in a fundraising campaign with the goal of raising $10,000 for churches struggling to rebuild. Supporters surprised themselves by meeting their goal on the first day—so they kept going. By the end of Ramadan, they had reached an astonishing $100,000.

That same year, young Muslims went online to help restore a Jewish cemetery near St. Louis, where vandals had toppled 180 gravestones. In 24 hours, they raised more than $100,000. In the aftermath of the Tree of Life synagogue killings in Pittsburgh, they raised $150,000 for the victims' families, surpassing their original goal of $25,000.

One of my son Yusuf's friends, Abdul El-Sayed, is nationally known as a pioneer in combating many of southeast Michigan's most serious public health problems. At age 30, he was named the director of the Detroit Health Department and became the youngest health director in a major U.S. city. After the Flint, Michigan, water crisis, he led a campaign to test the plumbing in Detroit schools. More lead-tainted water was found. He championed an effort to give free eyeglasses to schoolchildren whose families could not afford them. He also wrote and published more than 100 peer-reviewed articles in journals for his colleagues—while also writing articles for the general public about how ordinary citizens can help improve public health. He appeared on CNN and in the pages of *The New York Times*. In 2017, he left his Detroit office to run for governor, largely because of his frustration with the policies of Michigan's Republican-controlled legislature. He lost, but in the autumn of 2018, he set up a political action committee to support a new wave of progressive candidates.

This kind of leadership by a Muslim was unimaginable when I first came to America.

El-Sayed wasn't alone in his concern for public health. Muslim young people responded in droves to an appeal to help Flint residents, collecting more than 1 million bottles of water. They also helped to raise more than $300,000 to help Flint families, in an effort coordinated by the Michigan Muslim Community Council (MMCC). In addition, MMCC worked with United Way for Southeastern Michigan and Islamic Relief to raise one-fourth of a million dollars to help Detroit families who could not pay their water bills and were facing cutoff.

That's just in Michigan. From Miami to Los Angeles, I could list pages of such projects.

What also impresses me about our young leaders today is their commitment to oppose extremism whenever it raises its ugly face. In 2004, my son-in-law, Farhan Latif, got wind of some extremist sermons by an imam who occasionally preached at Friday prayers at the University of Michigan-Dearborn campus. At the time, Farhan was president of both the student government and the Muslim students' organization. He worked with other campus leaders to have this imam officially banned from speaking on campus.

As a result, Farhan was returning to his apartment one evening when three men jumped on him, severely beat him and then tried to run him over with a car. He managed to get away but ended up in the hospital with a swollen face, head injuries, cracked ribs and a broken arm. He paid a personal price to stand up against extremism. University leaders stood firmly with Farhan, and the preacher was never again allowed to spread hate on campus. Eventually, he was imprisoned on unrelated charges.

Europeans are noticing the success of America's example as young Muslims continue to emerge in mainstream professions, nonprofits and government. In too many parts of Europe, Muslim immigrants have been systematically marginalized. Pushing unemployed young people— whatever their faith may be—into poor, hopeless ghettos will only breed extremism.

In 2009, a representative of the Dutch government called me with a question. "Mr. Begg, would you help in hosting Cabinet Minister Frans Timmermans?" he asked. "He wants to discuss how young Muslims in the U.S. promote tolerance and peaceful co-existence, while facing Islamophobia and hate speech."

We hosted the Dutch at ACCESS, the huge Arab-American-sponsored service center in Dearborn, Michigan. The nonprofit, which Sofi worked with at the time, serves thousands of families of all faiths and races through dozens of programs that range from education to health services. The Dutch delegation was impressed with what they learned about the good work and interfaith participation by Detroit-area Muslims.

One of the most sophisticated—and potentially the most powerful—campaigns to combat bigotry involves efforts to lift up Muslim cultural icons. Knowing a Muslim is the most telling factor in forming positive attitudes among non-Muslims. Back in 1970, there weren't many Muslim celebrities whom everyone agreed were model citizens. I considered Muhammad Ali and Malcolm X heroes, but not everyone shared my viewpoint. In Hollywood, we could point to Omar Sharif. Cat Stevens was a huge star, but a lot of his fans were not impressed when he converted to Islam in 1977 and fell silent.

Today, young Muslims can point to lots of stars who share their faith. Household names include Muslim actor-comedians such as Dave Chappelle, Aziz Ansari and Ahmed Ahmed. Mehmet Oz, aka "Dr. Oz," is considered as American as apple pie as he shares tips for healthy living and makes media appearances. There are dozens of American Muslim musicians now, including a host of rap and hip-hop artists. British singer Zayn Malik has topped both U.K. and American charts with his music and won an American Music Award. Muslim athletes are everywhere these days, too, including a growing number of Muslim women. In 2016, fencer Ibtihaj Muhammad became the first American to compete in the Olympics while wearing a hijab. The toy company Mattel even made a Barbie doll of her in her fencing attire—wearing a hijab. At that same Olympics, Dalilah Muhammad became the first American woman to win a gold medal in the 400-meter hurdles. Fans of National Public Radio regularly hear from Muslim newscasters, including Razia Iqbal. In 2017, Mahershala Ali became the first Muslim actor to win an Oscar for his performance in the highly acclaimed drama, *Moonlight*.

Up-and-coming Muslim authors are publishing critically acclaimed books with thought-provoking themes. For instance, *Throne of the Crescent Moon*, by Saladin Ahmed, portrays a fantasy world based on old Arab-Islamic tradition, replete with mythical creatures, heroes and villains. Jennifer Zobair's *Painted Hands* follows a group of young women as they attempt to reconcile their professional lives and ambitions with their family's expectations. Haroon Moghul's *How to be a Muslim: An American Story* and Wajahat Ali's *The Domestic Crusaders* delve into the changing dynamics of Muslim households within American society. A recent memoir, *An American Family: A Memoir of Hope and Sacrifice*, by Khizr Khan, highlights the story of the author's son's ultimate sacrifice for America. The Muslim Protagonist, a nonprofit founded in 2012, holds annual conferences that highlight Muslim writers and encourage new books in all of the popular genres, from science fiction and fantasy to young adult fiction and movie scripts.

Young activists are springing from the grassroots, as well. Sana Shareef was a high school student in Vero Beach when she organized the Breaking Barriers Club. She's the enterprising daughter of Babar Shareef, a cardiologist and co-founder of a mosque. Her club brought films and noted speakers to the school to highlight Islamic history and culture. Sana's brother, 16-year-old Omar Shareef, was moved by seeing blind children in an Indian orphanage. He created prototypes for a glove and eyeglasses that can assist the blind by using cameras that translate surrounding objects, faces and text into voice descriptions. He called his nonprofit *2nd Sight*. Florida media covered these events and spread the news about these cooperative programs.

In 2008, when she was 17, Samantha Elauf was denied a sales job at an Abercrombie & Fitch store in Tulsa, Oklahoma, because she wore a hijab. She filed a U.S. Equal Employment Opportunity Commission (EEOC) complaint. The federal commission sued the company on her behalf. The case went all the way to the U.S. Supreme Court, which ruled 8-1 in Samantha's favor. She had to wait seven years to receive justice, but she was patient and persistent enough to withstand those years of controversy. Her battle has become a case study, showing how young Muslims can step into the forefront of defending civil liberties.

On December 2, 2015, a Pakistani-American couple in California attacked a San Bernardino County Department of Public Health event, which was attended by about 80 employees and took place in a rented banquet room. They killed 14 people and injured 22 others. They had secretly amassed a stock of weapons and, after fleeing the scene, were killed in a firefight with police. In the aftermath, no one could recall any signs that this couple had been drawn toward extremism. They apparently had fallen into dangerous connections through the internet.

In the wake of that tragedy, Islamophobic responses spiked once more. Bomb threats closed down a number of school systems, primarily on the West Coast. Musician Mona Haydar—a hijab-wearing mother of a small child—along her husband, Sebastian (a convert to Islam), lived on the East Coast but barely left their home in the weeks following the incident. They feared verbal abuse from strangers that might traumatize their son. Eventually, they dreamed up their own quirky response, inspired by the image of Lucy in the *Peanuts* comic strip setting up her sidewalk psychiatric booth.

"I had this idea of Lucy and her sidewalk stand in my mind—this very homemade-looking thing," Sebastian said, while appearing in a short documentary about their project. "We took our son with us, my Mom's dog with us and three big boxes of coffee and three dozen donuts."

"People told us not to do it," Mona says. "They told us: You're putting a bull's eye on yourself."

Nevertheless, they made hand-lettered signs that said: "Talk to a Muslim" and "Free coffee & donuts. Take a flower."

"Our plan was to bribe them with the donuts," Mona laughs.

On a snowy winter's day, they unpacked their little booth. The first person who walked up said, "I just want you to know I'm Muslim and I think what you're doing is really cool."

The next visitor was a woman who, with tears in her eyes, said, "I'm so sorry for what your community is having to suffer through right now."

The story went global as a sign of hope in the midst of so much despair. Today, Mona continues to reach out through her music. *Billboard* magazine named her 2017 song, *Wrap My Hijab*, one of the top 25 feminist anthems of all time. Mona grew up in Flint, Michigan, in a Syrian-American family, so on the 10th anniversary of 9/11 I was able to introduce Mona at an interfaith memorial service in Royal Oak, just north of Detroit. I asked Mona to recite a poem for the occasion. Her moving words expressed the deep compassion young Muslims feel for the thousands of people affected by those despicable attacks.

She keeps the complete poem on her website. The poem is called *The Graces of Remembrance*. Here are the opening lines:

> I wait silently each year,
> praying that someone

will have the words to explain how
to explain why.
But everyone is silent like me.
We have moments of silence,
becoming years of silence,
that today became a decade of silence.

Today I speak because silence
hasn't healed the hurt.
It hasn't soothed the wound.
It hasn't caught this sinking falling feeling
without even a whisper singing
"I'll catch you if you fall—if you call—if you cry."
So today I speak in the song
in the grace
in the shade
in the love
in the hope of remembrance
for all those who fell
for all those who passed
for all those who lost
for all those who hurt.

I want to smooth over every ache
I want to untie every knot in every throat
I want to kiss every tear on every cheek
I want to grant every prayer on the lips
of everyone longing for solace.

CHAPTER 19

Walking Along the Shore

We shall show them the signs in the horizons and within
themselves until it becomes clear to them that it is the truth.

Quran 41:53

Take into one's heart the essential truth of God's
reality and God's expression in all things.

The poet Ghalib, in a letter, 1862

Come walk along the shore with me. The Creator's signs are everywhere in nature.

This is the kind of invitation that most Americans would accept. While a growing number of men and women feel alienated from organized religion, millions of us discover God's signs when we walk in the natural world. Recent Pew Research confirms this: "Americans have become less religious in recent years by standard measures such as how important they say religion is to them and their frequency of religious service attendance and prayer. But, at the same time, the share of people across a wide variety of religious identities who say they often feel a deep sense of spiritual peace and well-being—as well as a deep sense of wonder about the universe—has risen."

While walking along the Atlantic shore, that conclusion from Pew is easy to understand. A few steps along the sand, and I feel God is close at hand. I can relate to the Creator without confining that awareness to a single word or image. Nature's language speaks to me like a second Quran.

I especially love my evening walks along the ocean. Waves rush toward me, and then recede into the vastness of the sea—just as the Creator reaches out endlessly, throughout our lives. How can I believe in something I cannot see? When I peer into the eastern horizon I cannot see Africa, and yet I know that the vast continent lies just over the horizon.

Human sight is limited. I glimpse the hazy line where the heavens and the ocean meet and I wonder: What lies beyond? What lies beneath? What lies above?

God encourages us to reflect on the world's great waters. The Quran 21:30 states, "We made from water every living thing. Will they not then believe?"

In 45:3, the Quran states, "In the heavens and the earth there is evidence for the believers."

Come walk along the shore with me. If you are unfamiliar with the Quran, then you may recall these passages from the Bible:

"In the beginning, when God created the heavens and the earth, the earth was a formless void and darkness covered the face of the deep, while a wind from God swept over the face of the waters." Those are the opening words of Genesis.

Psalms sings of the power of nature to remind us of God. Psalm 90 begins, "Lord, you have been our dwelling-place in all generations. Before the mountains were brought forth, or ever you had formed the earth and the world, from everlasting to everlasting, you are God."

These are words that Muslims can join Jews and Christians in affirming. So, come walk along the shore with me.

I am closing my memoir with these words because my faith speaks of a God of the "worlds" with a universal presence. I am turning to poetic lines here, because my Indian roots continually call me back to poetry. My ancestor, Ghalib, the poet born Mirza Asadullah Baig Khan, eloquently called his readers to the deepest spiritual embrace of God. To this day, the Sufi poets continue to stir my heart. They wrote ghazals, or odes, that contemplated human love and loss; they sought comfort in the immense beauty of God's mercy, love and creation. I hold especially dear my copy of Ghalib's poems in the original Urdu. Sufi Qawwali, a form of sublimely chanted devotional poetry, stretches back more than 700 years—and still moves me to tears today.

Every day, millions of American say, "I'm spiritual, not religious." They are seeking deeper truths. The centuries-old Sufi tradition sings hauntingly of that yearning, describing a profound longing for the divine.

That's why I am surprised when people tell me, "Victor, you're a moderate Muslim."

I say, "No, I'm not. I'm a Muslim. I'm an observant Muslim, like most American Muslims. At the moment, our approach to the faith may seem 'moderate' to you because of the crazy acts of extremists who have misused the name of our faith." I go on to explain that I have been inspired by the great Sufi teachers and that I see no barriers that should prevent us from seeing Shia and Sunni Muslims as brothers and sisters.

"Extremism has no place in Islam," I say. "The Quran says so in 2:143: 'We made you to be a community of the middle way, so that (with the example of your lives) you might bear witness to the truth before all mankind.' The Prophet Muhammad specifically warned his followers about the dangers of extremism: 'Never be extreme regarding religion. Many nations have been destroyed before you only because of extremism in religion.'"

So, come walk along the shore with me. Watch the footprints we are making in the sand, just beyond the reach of the waves. Occasionally, a stronger wave touches our feet. Look back! The waves have wiped away all the footprints we just thought we left behind us.

The Quran reminds us of the fleeting nature of this world: "You will think that you lived (in this world) but a short while!" (Quran 17:52)

These words may sound familiar to Jews and Christians. Psalm 90 puts it this way: "For a thousand years in your sight are like yesterday when it is past."

As we walk, pay attention to the sounds, the smells and the salty taste of the breeze off the ocean. Let's rest a moment and watch the birds darting high and low above the waves. My knees need rest, so I prefer to sit for a time on the sand and play my Native American flute. As if answering my music, a flock of small sandpipers dance back and forth on their thin legs. An especially strong wave sends them scurrying for higher ground, then immediately reversing course: they are now chasing the ebbing water, in search of whatever goodies the sea has served up for them.

That's the truth of life on a coastline. Waves and winds are life-giving, yet they also can be deadly. Shahina and I moved to Florida to get away from Michigan's cold and snow. Now we face the storms each year, including the devastating threats of hurricanes. Our homes here are of newer construction that complies with more stringent safety codes, and we have hurricane shutters that are supposed to minimize damage even in the face of 150-mile-per-hour winds. We have dodged a couple of major hurricanes, but the future is uncertain.

I feel a bond with the Prophet Muhammad's companions who were Bedouin, moving across the ever-shifting waves of sand. They found deep comfort in a faith that accepts the all-too-brief nature of this world and meets that challenge with compassion and moderation.

A traditional story describes a Bedouin who rode in from the desert to see the Prophet Muhammad. He asked, "Besides the first requirement—'There is no god but God, and Muhammad is His messenger,' the *Shahada*—what else is required to be a Muslim?"

The Prophet Muhammad explained the next three requirements: Offer prayers five times each day; fast during the daylight hours of Ramadan; and give to the poor, in an act known as zakat.

The Bedouin wanted to be absolutely certain about this. "Is there any more?" he asked.

The Prophet Muhammad replied, "No, but if you want, you can do more."

Then, the man swore, "I'll do neither more nor less."

The Prophet Muhammad said, "If he is true to his word, then he will be successful."

That man who swept in off the desert to pose this question is my hero. Islam has always been a simple faith. To call someone a moderate Muslim is redundant. The five pillars are common sense: Our daily prayers keep us fully aware of God; fasting teaches us discipline, renews our faith and deepens our awareness of God and of the needs of the world; by helping the needy, we are humbled and we promote economic and social justice. In these pillars of faith, we build healthier communities.

There is, also, the fifth pillar: the pilgrimage. I made the hajj again later in my life, when I had a much deeper appreciation of my faith. I wrote about my experiences in a column that has been published on various websites and has been distributed to Christian congregations as well. That column illustrates how Islam really is all about the way we should move around this world—and the pilgrimage is the ultimate expression of people moving together, in all of their diversity.

Here is what I wrote:

One Pilgrim's Story of a Journey for Millions

Hajj is one of the five pillars of Islam, required to be performed once in a lifetime by able-bodied Muslims who are also financially able. Preparation for hajj includes asking for forgiveness from friends, relatives and acquaintances for any unresolved offenses we may have caused. Muslims often bid farewell by asking for everyone's goodwill and taking care of their obligations before they leave for hajj.

During hajj, men are mandated to dress in two pieces of un-sewn white cloth, one around their waist and one over their upper body, called "ihram" (similar to what Muslims are buried in upon their passing from this world). Dressed alike, divisions among people disappear as all pilgrims recite the same words in one language. We are praying together in Arabic. In English, it means: "I am here O Lord, the One and Only, Glory to You ..."

One of the important aspects of the pilgrimage is the tawaf, making seven circles around the house of worship (Kaaba) rebuilt by Prophet Abraham. It is said that the Kaaba originally was built by Adam—the common ancestor of all. It is also said: Angels worship God by circling His throne. Thus, the circling of Kaaba represents the "primordial form of worship," even before we were created—like the electrons revolving in an atom or the planets revolving around the sun.

The Kaaba has a black stone encased in a white silver case as one of the corner stones—at the point we initiate circling the Kaaba. It is said that the black stone is a remnant of white stones Angel Gabriel brought from heaven when Prophet Adam first built this House of Worship of One God, rebuilt by Prophet Abraham.

Malcolm X's views on race were transformed upon witnessing the sea of humanity echoing the same words, clothed alike. These are the words on our lips from the time we don the ihram, as we must do that when we get within 40 miles of Mecca, which could mean that we take on the state of ihram often in the plane before it lands.

After the tawaf we drink from the well of Zamzam, which was created instantly by the will of God, according to our teachings, by Archangel Gabriel to quench the thirst of Abraham's firstborn, left in the desert by father Abraham with his mother, Hajjara (Hagar). Water provided sustenance for Ishmael in answer to Hajjara's prayers.

In my pilgrimage, I was among millions of pilgrims who drank from the well. We wash faces, hands and feet in ablution. I was amazed how this water flows freely for all.

We then pray at the spot where footsteps of Abraham are preserved. Next we retrace the steps of Hajjara, running between the two hills called Safa and Marwa, looking for water or some caravan to help her newborn baby, Ishmael.

In the next few days, there are other rites we must perform. Millions of people move after the morning prayers on the eighth day of the lunar month Zul–Hijjah toward the plains of Arafa and spend the night in the tent city of Mina along the way, just as the Prophet did more than 1,400 years ago.

Next day, in Arafa, we gather where the Prophet gave his final sermon from a hilltop. Muslims believe that the gathering in Arafa, clothed in white shrouds, represents the assembly of the resurrected humanity on the Day of Judgment. We pray for forgiveness and for God's blessings. I prayed to God to grant me forgiveness and for my family, friends and our communities— and for peace in the world.

Then the millions move again from the plains of Arafa to an area called Muzdalfa, for night prayers, and where Prophet Muhammad spent the night. We pick up pebbles from the desert to demolish the Satan who tried to mislead Ishmael and Abraham on three different occasions. So, the next day, armed with these pebbles, we return to Mina to perform the rite of throwing the little stones. Then we live in the tent city, spending the next two nights praying and meditating and distancing ourselves from the evil Satan.

We return to Mecca for a farewell tawaf. Men shave their heads. Yes, that included me, because we are supposed to be newly born free of all sins upon proper completion of the pilgrimage. At the end of the pilgrimage, we sacrifice a lamb in commemoration of the sacrifice made by our great-grandpa Abraham, in quest for submitting unconditionally to God's will.

Prophet Abraham also prayed to God to bless this area with a city and the fruits to eat. We witnessed the bustling humanity, abundance of the fruits and goods from all over the world in the city of Mecca. God answered his prayers and continues to bless the desert city to this day. We pray, we meditate, we shop and we taste the international cuisine.

In our pilgrimage, we had a large American contingent plus Canadian, European, Asian and African brothers and sisters who traveled with us. During hajj, millions of people move from site to site over a period of days, which also makes one a very patient person.

In spite of occasional mishaps, during this enormous gathering of pilgrims, hajj is God's miracle in itself.

Life is a journey. We can go it alone, but our journey is so much richer if we follow the prophetic path. The Prophet Muhammad once said, "Take one step toward God; God will take 10 steps toward you. Walk toward God; God will run toward you."

"When we take one step toward God, he takes seven steps toward us." (Indian proverb)

This truth is taught by all of the faiths. One of the best-selling Christian writers in America is C.S. Lewis, and even though the Oxford professor has been dead for more than half a century, his books have sold more than 100 million copies. Every year, more than 100,000 copies of his simple book, *Mere Christianity*, fly off bookstore shelves. One reason why Lewis continues to be so popular is that he started his life as a rebellious young man: he even dared to declare himself an atheist in his 20s. What brought about his conversion? Walks in the English countryside with his friends. Lewis told his readers that it was while they were looking at the sights, sounds and smells of nature—and looking up into a starry night sky—that he finally dared to believe that God was real. To this day, Lewis's fans around the world retell his stories about these walks. They finally allowed him to see the reality of God as something so obvious in the natural world that he simply had to believe.

That story makes perfect sense to Muslims. I know many Muslims who fell away from the observances of their families for a variety of reasons. Some were uncomfortable with cultural customs that were passed along to them as an essential part of Islam; others have turned away because of personal differences among members of a mosque; still others have felt peer pressure to turn away. But the truth is that most are still seeking. That's the reality in all religious groups today. Pew Research confirms this, but we all can see this process unfolding among family, friends and neighbors.

My faith came alive to me during an especially difficult period in my life. I was trying to find the strength to bear varying pressures. I was instinctively drawn toward a higher power and opened the Quran after a long time away. The words of 13:28 leapt out at me: "Those who believe, and whose hearts find satisfaction in the remembrance of God; assuredly in the remembrance of God hearts will find rest!"

These words calmed my soul. I wanted to read more. The Quran's first chapter, *Surah al-Fatiha* or *The Opener*, is an appeal for guidance:

> *In the Name of Merciful Redeemer of Mercy;*
>
> *Praise be to God, the Lord of the worlds;*
>
> *Most Gracious, Most Merciful; Master of the Day of Judgment;*
>
> *You alone we worship,*

Your aid alone we seek;

Show us the right way; the path of those You favor;

Not of those who earn your displeasure and have gone astray.

That traditional English translation of the Arabic may not sound familiar to Christian readers, so I invite you to ponder a few of the words: "Your aid alone we seek." Christians pray: "Give us this day our daily bread."

We pray: "Show us the right way; the path of those you favor, not of those who earn your displeasure and have gone astray." Christians pray: "Lead us not into temptation, but deliver us from evil."

As Muslims, we do not think of Islam as a new religion. We are following God's timeless calling, as the Quran's 41:53 states: "We shall show them the signs in the horizons and within themselves until it becomes clear to them that it is the truth."

So, I say again: Come walk along the shore with me.

Look! A fishing boat appears along the horizon. How many stories in the Bible use fishing as a metaphor for learning about God? Too many to list. The Quran's 16:14 states, "It is God who has made the sea subservient, that you may eat thereof meat that is fresh and tender, and that you may extract therefrom ornaments to wear; you see the ships plowing through it, that you may seek His bounty, and that you happily give thanks."

"Ornaments to wear"? Look down at the seashells that visitors love to collect from these sands. A large, blue crab slowly moves toward us. He's heading toward a dune where the sand meets sprouting sea oats. The protruding black eyes of pale ghost crabs emerge from their tiny holes in the sand. We feel the pleasant evening breeze off the Atlantic. "And of God's signs is the creation of the heavens and earth and the creatures God has dispersed throughout them," says 42:29 of the Quran.

As the sun sets, we know it is time to return. We wash the sand off our feet under a faucet near the pathway to our home. Day is merging into evening. The horizon is a lovely reddish hue. "Behold!" states the Quran's 3:190. "In the creation of the heavens and the earth, and the alternation of night and day, are signs for those of understanding."

Ghalib would understand what I am writing here. He wanted us to truly embrace the wonders and grandeur of God's creation. In one of his longer poems, Ghalib described a debate with an angry zealot who

complained about all of the injustices and evils that exist in the world. This
zealot was so fed up that he prayed that God would destroy this world and
everyone in it. It was a terrorist's prayer.

Ghalib answered with a resounding negation: No! That idea is sacrilege! God loves the world. God hopes that we, as the residents of this
wondrous planet, will love and care for God's creation—not call for its
destruction.

Ghalib writes:

> *The Architect is fond of this edifice*
>
> *Because of which there is color in life;*
>
> *The Architect would not like it to perish and fall.*

Ghalib understood what I describe as our two Qurans: The scriptures
we read and the natural world God has given us, where we can see God
so clearly if only we take the time to walk, see, listen and taste this wonderfully beautiful world.

I wish I had taken the advice of my grandfather, when I spent time
with him years ago. He kept telling me, "Reading of the Quran, without
understanding its meaning, is like reading it in a state of drunkenness."
Had I heeded his advice, I might have found the spirit of my faith sooner.

Thank you for walking along these shores with me.

I pray that I have sought understanding in the paths I have walked in
this life.

I pray that my story has opened your eyes a little wider as you move
along your own pathway.

And, as my grandfather would tell me: I pray that, as this story comes
to an end, you depart with greater understanding.

Acknowledgments

I am in profound debt to my neighbors:

Betty Brinamen, for not only her encouragement, but also for patiently reading the entire initial 450-page manuscript, proofreading as an English teacher, and giving invaluable feedback. And to her husband, Charlie, for being the courier between our condos with proofed chapters.

Dave McDonough for his regular feedback. Tony and Bill Van Cleave, Jacqueline Coleman and Helene Stormer for reviewing the advance-release copy and telling me how much they loved it. I'm hoping all those who care to read my story would agree with them.

Barbara and George Viksne readily offer us a ride to the airport when we need one—a 90-minute drive to the nearest one, one way. Wow! I especially want to thank George for also giving me fishing lessons and taking our grandson with us to catch his first fish. Our neighbors are always ready to help with whatever our needs maybe.

Lynn and Bill Sprecher, Sis and Paul Hamilton for looking after our condo when we aren't around. Lynn's little granddaughter, Zoey, and ours, Dalia, have become friends, looking forward to meeting when they visit. And, Hector Rodriguez for always being ready with the heaviest tool box I ever lifted to help with any project in our condo.

Al Hess for bringing up our Sunday paper dumped in the lobby by the delivery person.

Marypi and Harry Goldman, Bernie and Rick Radman, and Chuck Schwartz for being just fun neighbors. Every one of our neighbors are wonderfully pleasant people. They're mainly Republican, mostly conservative, but some are also liberal Democrats. Just a few independent are included in the mix, as well.

I cannot possibly list everyone who greet me in the elevator, around our condo building, some walking their dog, and everyone who plays mahjong with Shahina. It'll be impossible to list them all, but I'm hoping everyone would buy a copy. Markedly for you, our neighbors, I wrote this memoir so you get to know your Muslim neighbors better. You're some of the most caring people I've met in my global travels. The ones I spent most of my life with in Michigan were equally good neighbors, although our residences weren't as close as we are now.

America is great because of who you are—as people, as neighbors. So, I acknowledge my deep gratitude to the living community of Americans who made my life story possible.

God bless America.

Next, I want to first thank my editor, David Crumm, for believing in my story and recognizing that sharing this book can make this world a little better. I am grateful to the Front Edge Publishing team for their enthusiastic support, especially Dmitri Barvinok and Susan Stitt, who guided me through this book's production. I also want to thank my publicist Kelly Hughes.

Michael Wolfe, a tireless voice for understanding Islam through his own books and films, encouraged me along the way. So did S.E. Smith, a best-selling author who helped me better understand the publishing world and enthusiastically responded with a warm heart and a critical eye in reviewing the advance-release copy.

Throughout the process of writing, Shahina, daughter Sofi, son-in-law Farhan, sons Sami and Yusuf provided constant support, love and encouragement. Nazira, our daughter-in-law, would constantly ask me, "How's the book doing babajan?" Yusuf, her husband, gave me valuable feedback. Sami, our eldest, not only helped me with initial proofreading, he set up my website and blog for me. I couldn't have done this without Sofi's input, edits, feedback and alerting me sometimes, "You sound preachy, baba"—and for occasionally telling me, "I don't agree with that."

Dr. John Esposito took time from his busy schedule to read my material and give advice, and for that I am deeply grateful. Thanks to Dr. Iltefat Hamzavi, Cofounder of the D.C. think tank Institute for Social Policy & Understanding, who grew up in our mosque, for his insightful feedback, "You lay out why there is mosque conflict but don't judge or personalize it. Much for us to ponder, contextualize and then apply the lessons." There were many others who offered valuable input and, in some cases, key details that shored up the accuracy of my own memories. That list is long, but it certainly includes Imam Steve Elturk, Saeed Khan, the Rev. Dan Buttry, the Rev. Dan Appleyard, Sharona Shapiro and two of my most tireless interfaith partners: Brenda Rosenberg and Bob Bruttell. I also want to thank Rabbi Bruce Benson, the Rev. Bob Baggott, Rob Volsky, Assistant Director of Public Affairs for the Church of Jesus Christ of Latter-day Saints in Vero Beach, and Sara Martz for taking their valuable time reading the advance-release copy—and I much appreciate their supportive feedback.

About the Author

Victor Begg is a retired entrepreneur, an immigrant from India who became famous for his Michigan chain of stores, called Naked Furniture, which sold quality, unfinished or custom-finished furniture. He also became one of the country's leading Muslim spokesmen.

Arriving in 1970 to complete an MBA at the University of Detroit, Victor was so determined to achieve the American Dream of family and financial security that he even pumped gas and sold vacuum cleaners door to door.

As a Muslim layman, Victor served as an interreligious leader in metro-Detroit, often speaking for the Michigan Muslim community in the wake of major news events. He is a co-founder of the Muslim Unity Center Mosque in Bloomfield Hills, an Emeritus Board Member of the Michigan Roundtable for Diversity & Inclusion and a founding member of the Interfaith Leadership Council of Metro-Detroit.

He was recognized by *The Detroit News* staff and readers as a Michiganian of the Year in 2009, and has been honored with many other awards, including Community Peacemaker of the Year by the Peace & Conflict Resolutions Studies Center at Wayne State University.

He has appeared in many media outlets, including *ABC, CBS, FOX, NPR, The Los Angeles Times, Voice of America* and *USA Today*. His ongoing columns on Muslim issues frequently appear in Michigan and Florida newspapers.

Originally from a prominent family in Hyderabad in India, Victor became a proud American citizen and believes that America's promise remains as true as it has been for centuries. He and his wife Shahina are the parents of three children; they also have four grandchildren. Shahina is a co-founder of WISDOM, the Women's Interfaith Solutions for Dialogue and Outreach in metro-Detroit.